TIME
LIFE ®
BOOKS

Other Publications:

This volume is one of a series that explains and demonstrates how to prepare various types of food, and that offers in each book an international anthology of great recipes.

Fruits

BY
THE EDITORS OF TIME-LIFE BOOKS

TIME-LIFE BOOKS/ALEXANDRIA, VIRGINIA

Cover: Just before serving, whole peeled pears are coated in a glistening sauce derived from their own cooking liquid. The pears were tenderized by gentle poaching in a cinnamon-spiced sugar syrup. Red wine, added for the last few minutes of cooking, contributes color and flavor to the sauce (pages 40-41).

Time-Life Books Inc.
is a wholly owned subsidiary of
TIME INCORPORATED

Founder: Henry R. Luce 1898-1967

Editor-in-Chief: Henry Anatole Grunwald
President: J. Richard Munro
Chairman of the Board: Ralph P. Davidson
Executive Vice President: Clifford J. Grum
Editorial Director: Ralph Graves
Group Vice President, Books: Joan D. Manley

TIME-LIFE BOOKS INC.

Editor: George Constable *Executive Editor:* George Daniels
Director of Design: Louis Klein *Board of Editors:* Dale M.
Brown, Thomas A. Lewis, Martin Mann, Robert G. Mason,
Ellen Phillips, Gerry Schremp, Gerald Simons, Rosalind
Stubenberg, Kit van Tulleken *Director of Administration:*
David L. Harrison *Director of Research:* Carolyn L. Sackett
Director of Photography: John Conrad Weiser
Design: Arnold C. Holeywell (assistant director), Anne B.
Landry (art coordinator), James J. Cox (quality control)
Research: Jane Edwin (assistant director), Louise D. Forstall
Copy Room: Diane Ullius (director), Celia Beattie
Production: Feliciano Madrid (director), Gordon E. Buck,
Peter Inchauteguiz

President: Reginald K. Brack Jr. *Executive Vice President:*
John Steven Maxwell *Vice Presidents:* George Artandi,
Stephen L. Bair, Peter G. Barnes, Nicholas Benton, John L.
Canova, Beatrice T. Dobie, Christopher T. Linen, James L.
Mercer, Paul R. Stewart

THE GOOD COOK
The original version of this book was created in London
for Time-Life Books B.V.
European Editor: Kit van Tulleken *Design Director:* Ed
Skyner *Photography Director:* Pamela Marke *Chief of
Research:* Vanessa Kramer *Chief Sub-Editor:* Ilse Gray
Chief of Editorial Production: Ellen Brush *Quality Control:*
Douglas Whitworth

Staff for Fruits: Editor: Ellen Galford *Series Coordinator:*
Debbie Litton *Text Editors:* Louise Earwaker (principal),
Nicoletta Flessati *Anthology Editor:* Tokunbo Williams
Staff Writers: Alexandra Carlier, Sally Crawford, Eluned
James *Researchers:* Caroline Baum (principal), Debra Raad
Designer: Mary Staples *Sub-Editors:* Kate Cann, Charles
Boyle, Frances Dixon, Sally Rowland *Editorial Department:*
Judith Heaton, Lesley Kinahan, Stephanie Lee, Debra
Lelliott, Jane Lillicrap, Linda Mallett, Janet Matthew, Sylvia
Osborne, Ros Smith, Molly Sutherland

U.S. Staff for Fruits: Editor: Gerry Schremp *Designer:* Ellen
Robling *Chief Researchers:* Barbara Fleming, Barbara Levitt
Associate Editor: Christine Schuyler (pictures) *Writers:*
Lynn R. Addison, Deborah Berger-Turnbull, Rachel Cox,
Rita Mullin *Researchers:* Tina Ujlaki (techniques),
Jane Hanna (anthology), Ann Ready *Assistant Designer:*
Peg Schreiber *Copy Coordinators:* Allan Fallow, Tonna
Gibert, Nancy Lendved *Picture Coordinator:* Betty H.
Weatherley *Editorial Assistants:* Andrea Reynolds, Patricia
Whiteford *Special Contributors:* Leslie M. Marshall,
Lydia Preston

CHIEF SERIES CONSULTANT

Richard Olney, an American, has lived and worked for some three decades in France, where he is highly regarded as an authority on food and wine. Author of *The French Menu Cookbook* and of the award-winning *Simple French Food,* he has also contributed to numerous gastronomic magazines in France and in the United States, including the influential journals *Cuisine et Vins de France* and *La Revue du Vin de France.* He has directed cooking courses in France and the United States and is a member of several distinguished gastronomic and oenological societies, including La Confrérie des Chevaliers du Tastevin, L'Académie Internationale du Vin, and La Commanderie du Bontemps de Médoc et des Graves. Working in London with the series editorial staff, he has been basically responsible for the planning of this volume, and has supervised the final selection of recipes submitted by other consultants. The United States edition of The Good Cook has been revised by the Editors of Time-Life Books to bring it into accord with American customs and usage.

CHIEF AMERICAN CONSULTANT
Carol Cutler is the author of a number of cookbooks, including the award-winning *Six-Minute Soufflé and Other Culinary Delights* (republished as *Cuisine Rapide*). During the 12 years that she lived in France, she studied at the Cordon Bleu and the École des Trois Gourmandes, as well as with private chefs. She is a member of the Cercle des Gourmettes, a long-established French food society limited to 50 members, and is a charter member of Les Dames d'Escoffier, Washington Chapter.

SPECIAL CONSULTANTS
Jolene Worthington received degrees from the Culinary Institute of America in Hyde Park, New York, and worked as a restaurant chef for many years. Formerly the Test Kitchen Chef in recipe development at *Cuisine* magazine, she contributes articles to food magazines and conducts cooking classes in Chicago. She has been responsible for demonstrating most of the step-by-step photographic sequences in this volume.
Pat Alburey is a member of the Association of Home Economists of Great Britain. Her wide experience includes preparing foods for photography, teaching cookery and creating recipes. She was responsible for many of the step-by-step demonstrations in this volume.
David Schwartz has run restaurants in Boston and London, and is the author of a book about chocolate. He prepared some of the dishes for the photographs in this volume.

PHOTOGRAPHERS
Aldo Tutino has worked in Milan, New York City and Washington, D.C. He has received a number of awards for his photographs from the New York Advertising Club.
Bob Komar is a Londoner who trained at both the Hornsey and Manchester Schools of Art. He specializes in food photography and in portraiture.

INTERNATIONAL CONSULTANTS
GREAT BRITAIN: *Jane Grigson* has written a number of books about food and has been a cookery correspondent for the London *Observer* since 1968. *Alan Davidson* is the author of several cookbooks and the founder of Prospect Books, which specializes in scholarly publications about food and cookery. FRANCE: *Michel Lemonnier,* the cofounder and vice president of Les Amitiés Gastronomiques Internationales, is a frequent lecturer on wine and vineyards. GERMANY: *Jochen Kuchenbecker* trained as a chef, but worked for 10 years as a food photographer in several European countries before opening his own restaurant in Hamburg. *Anne Brakemeier* is the co-author of a number of cookbooks. ITALY: *Massimo Alberini* is a well-known food writer and journalist with a special interest in culinary history. His many books include *La Tavola all'Italiana, 4000 Anni a Tavola* and *100 Ricette Storiche.* THE NETHERLANDS: *Hugh Jans* has published cookbooks and his recipes appear in several Dutch magazines.

Correspondents: Elisabeth Kraemer (Bonn); Margot
Hapgood, Dorothy Bacon (London); Miriam Hsia, Lucy T.
Voulgaris (New York); Maria Vincenza Aloisi, Josephine du
Brusle (Paris); Ann Natanson (Rome).
Valuable assistance was also provided by: Janny Hovinga
(Amsterdam); Berta Julia (Barcelona); Bona Schmid
(Milan); Mimi Murphy (Rome).

CONTENTS

Nature's Sweet Bounty

Fruit, in all its richly hued and succulent variations, is perhaps the purest expression of the earth's largesse. The most accessible of foods, it is infinitely satisfying in its pristine form: What confectioner, after all, could concoct a treat more luscious than a freshly picked raspberry? At the same time, fruit readily lends itself to transmutation by the culinary arts.

The pages that follow feature fruit as the primary ingredient in all manner of dishes, from simple compotes to a splendid fruit-based baked Alaska. First, a series of illustrated guides provides basic information on the entire spectrum of fruits— the everyday apple and peach as well as the exotic cherimoya and papaya. These guides explain how to distinguish a ripe fruit from an immature one, how to store the fruit you purchase, and how to peel, core and otherwise prepare it for eating or cooking. The section concludes with demonstrations of techniques to be used for puréeing fruit and juicing it, and for producing custards as enhancements.

The book's first chapter addresses ways of presenting fruit raw—shaping pineapple into boats, sculpting a watermelon basket for summer fruit, assembling an old-fashioned strawberry shortcake. The second chapter is devoted to cooking fruits gently with moist heat: pears poached in wine; plum dumplings; steamed fig pudding. The third deals with sautéing and deep frying. The fourth introduces techniques for baking and broiling, with special attention given to methods of protecting delicate fruit from the dry heat of the oven. The last chapter features a wide variety of fruits presented in molded and frozen forms.

Finally, the second half of the book offers the reader an anthology of more than 200 fruit recipes, garnered from countries throughout the world and representing the culinary literature and traditions of the past as well as the finest available contemporary sources.

Most of the fruits we eat today can be traced through several millennia of cultivated ancestors. Apples are an outstanding example of what horticulturists can achieve. The Roman historian Pliny knew of a dozen varieties; the Europeans of the Middle Ages, a few score; and each century of cultivation added its own improvements at an increasing rate until, by 1911, *The Encyclopaedia Britannica* could confidently claim that 2,000 named varieties were in existence. Today the number is far greater, and growing at such a pace that an accurate count would be impossible.

Needless to say, no supermarket can stock—or even acquire—so many varieties of the same fruit, but at least six kinds of apples, and four kinds of pears, are relatively easy to obtain regardless of the time of year they are harvested. This is because both fruits respond well to controlled-atmosphere storage, which provides a refrigerated environment abnormally low in oxygen and high in carbon dioxide and nitrogen. The altered atmosphere slows the picked fruit's final ripening stage, thus lengthening the fruit's life cycle.

The effective use of refrigeration in shipping has increased the availability of almost every kind of fruit, including many that could be enjoyed only in the tropics just a few decades ago. For example, chilled cherimoyas, mangoes and guavas from Latin America and the West Indies now regularly arrive in the United States and Canada by airplane and by refrigerated truck to supplement the supplies from North American farmers. Similarly, kiwi fruit is flown from New Zealand and the Granny Smith apple from South Africa, where an exceptionally long apple-growing season produces the best-tasting specimens of this variety.

Fruit in the menu

Within the structure of a meal, fruit traditionally appears in the guise of a sweet dessert. But it can perform delightfully in other roles as well. Unadorned grapefruits, melons or figs are delectable as hors d'oeuvre. A fresh-fruit macedoine, or salad, can make up the centerpiece—or the entirety—of a light lunch. And raw fruit served with cheese may be preferable to a sweet fruit concoction at the end of either a simple repast or a more formal menu.

When fresh fruit is presented as a first course, the best wine to accompany it is a crisp, young white one, still full of its own fruit—a Sancerre from the Loire Valley, for example, or perhaps a Chenin Blanc. For a final course of assertive cheese and firm-fleshed fruit such as apples or pears, the selection might be a full-bodied Italian Bardolino or a California Zinfandel; for mild cheese with grapes, choose an Alsatian or American Riesling.

The best partner for a lush fruit dessert is a "noble rot" wine such as a French Sauternes or a Hungarian Tokay Aszu; these are made from grapes whose sugar content has been concentrated by evaporation—the result of fungus piercing their skins in an advanced stage of ripeness. Remember, though, that desserts served with these opulent wines should be less sweet than the wine itself and, preferably, less cold; serving wine with a fruit water ice, for example, will do justice neither to the wine nor to the dessert.

Favorites from the Orchard

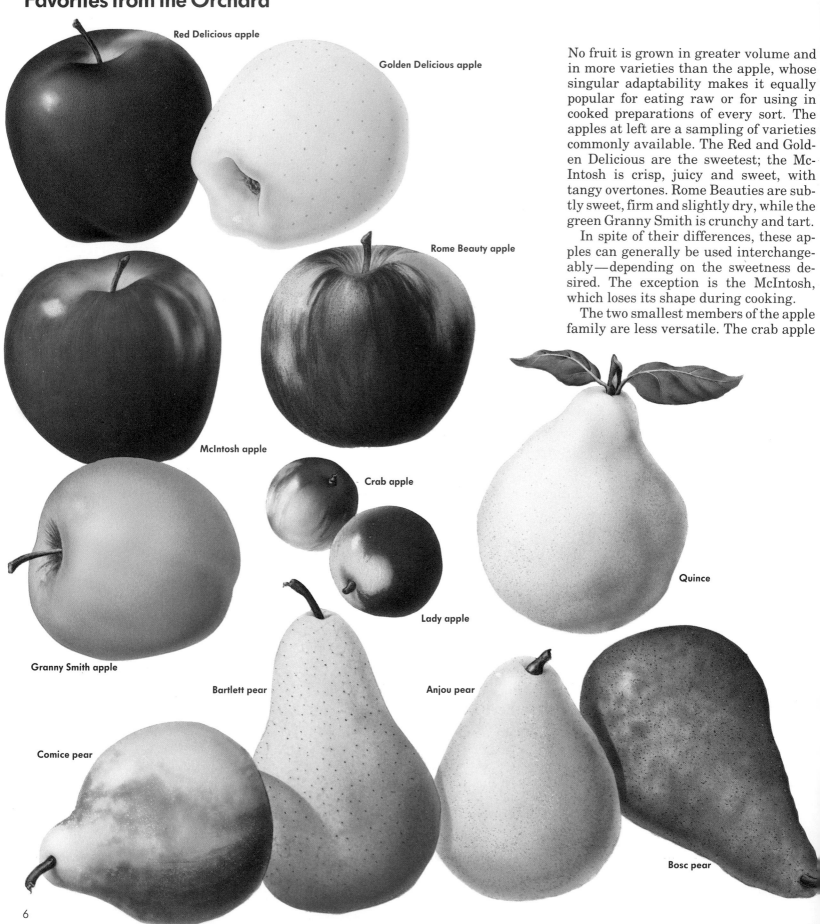

Red Delicious apple

Golden Delicious apple

Rome Beauty apple

McIntosh apple

Crab apple

Quince

Granny Smith apple

Lady apple

Bartlett pear

Anjou pear

Comice pear

Bosc pear

No fruit is grown in greater volume and in more varieties than the apple, whose singular adaptability makes it equally popular for eating raw or for using in cooked preparations of every sort. The apples at left are a sampling of varieties commonly available. The Red and Golden Delicious are the sweetest; the McIntosh is crisp, juicy and sweet, with tangy overtones. Rome Beauties are subtly sweet, firm and slightly dry, while the green Granny Smith is crunchy and tart.

In spite of their differences, these apples can generally be used interchangeably—depending on the sweetness desired. The exception is the McIntosh, which loses its shape during cooking.

The two smallest members of the apple family are less versatile. The crab apple is too tart to be eaten raw, but it makes delicious jellies or pickles and can add tang to a sweet apple cobbler or pudding. The diminutive lady apple—crisp, sweet and dry—ornaments a fruit bowl, but is costly to use for cooking. Compared with most apples, which can be stored for months and are available all year, crab and lady apples are marketed only when harvested in late fall and early winter.

Like apples, pears are firm-fleshed, with a central seedy core. The varieties at left can be served raw or cooked. However, the spicily sweet Comice, with its fine-grained, juicy flesh, and the musky, smooth-textured Bartlett are considered best for eating raw. The spicy Anjou and mildly sweet Bosc have the firmest flesh, making them ideal for baking.

Pears are available for most of the year—the Bartlett from midsummer to December and the Anjou, Bosc and Comice from autumn through spring. Less common varieties are available mainly in autumn, when they are harvested.

The quince is tough and dry compared with its juicier cousins. Available only during late autumn and early winter, the bitter quince is used mainly for jellies, and for lending tartness to puddings and compotes based on sweeter fruits.

□ *How to shop:* Choose mature and fully ripe apples and quinces; they should be firm, free of bruises and have good color. Buy firm, slightly underripe pears if they will be used for cooking; for eating raw, select pears with good color that have begun to soften at the stem end.

□ *Storing:* Store underripe pears away from direct sunlight in perforated paper bags. Refrigerate ripe fruits: Pears will keep for three to five days, apples for at least a week, quinces for several weeks.

□ *Preparation:* Rinse firm-fleshed fruits before serving them with their skins intact. If the fruits are peeled, drop them in acidulated water—5 or 6 tablespoons [75 or 90 ml.] of lemon juice per quart [liter] of water—to prevent discoloration.

Pears and most apples can be cored whole with an apple corer, or they can be cut in half and cored with a melon baller. Both crab apples and quinces should be quartered and cored with a knife.

Extracting an Apple Core

Using a corer. Peel the apple—in this case, a McIntosh—with a vegetable peeler or a small, sharp knife. Stand the apple, stem end up, and plunge an apple corer down through its center. Then lift the apple in one hand and twist the corer, gently pulling out both the corer and the core. Immediately put the apple in acidulated water.

A Routine for Handling Pears

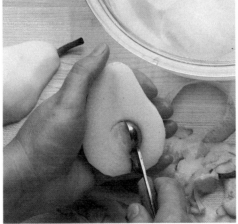

1 **Peeling.** With a vegetable peeler or a small, sharp knife, peel strips in a circle around the wide end of the pear— here, a Bartlett. Then, starting at the center, peel straight toward the stem end. Using this two-part technique removes the skin without ruining the pear's graceful contours.

2 **Coring.** Cut the pear in half lengthwise and scoop out the core from each half with a melon baller. Then grasp one end of the fibrous stem and pull it away from the pear. If portions of stem remain, slice a shallow, V-shaped groove along the length of the fruit to cut them out. Place the pear sections in acidulated water.

Preparing a Quince

Coring and peeling. Cut the quince lengthwise into quarters. Working from the stem end to the base, carve the core out of each section. Then, starting at the base and working back to the stem end, peel the skin from the outside of the section. Drop the quarters into acidulated water.

A Panoply of Pitted Fruits

Among the most fragile and succulent of fruits are the soft-fleshed, pitted ones. Because their skins are thin and their flesh tender, all of these fruits are difficult to ship or store—and thus they are in their prime only during the summer months, when they are harvested locally.

Peaches and nectarines are the most versatile of these summer treats for presentations raw and cooked. Both come in varieties with maroon-splashed ivory skin enclosing creamy white flesh and crimson-highlighted golden skin protecting yellow flesh; the white varieties are sharper in flavor, the yellow sweeter.

Both fruits also come in clingstone and freestone varieties, classified, as the names suggest, according to how tightly the flesh clings to the pit. In cooking, peaches and nectarines can be used interchangeably, although peaches have a slightly higher water content and soften more in poaching, frying or baking.

The orange-gold flesh of the easily pit-ted apricot is sweet but more musky than that of the peach or nectarine. Its skin is also slightly tougher and its flesh drier, so the apricot holds its shape especially well in cooked dishes.

Plum skins are even tougher than apricot skins, so this fruit, too, is good for poaching or baking as well as for eating raw. Of the three common varieties shown below, the Santa Rosa has juicy, pleasantly tart amber flesh; the Italian

White peach

Yellow peach

Nectarine

Bing cherries

Apricot

Royal Anne cherries

Montmorency cherries

Santa Rosa plum

Kelsey plum

Italian Prune plum

Date

Mango

Prune plum's tart purple skin encases sweet greenish-amber flesh that is dry and meaty. The yellow-skinned, yellow-fleshed Kelsey is the juiciest but also the blandest tasting.

Sweet cherries are rarely cooked and sour varieties seldom eaten raw. The Montmorency is the favorite sour cherry for puddings, cobblers and dumplings. Of the sweet varieties, the most popular are the Royal Anne and the Bing cherry.

The sweet, sticky-fleshed date is so rich it is generally treated as a confection in both its fresh and dried forms. The smooth, juicy, pink-orange flesh of the mango is most often enjoyed raw; its flavor evokes pineapples and peaches.

□ *How to shop:* As a rule, peaches, apricots, plums and mangoes are fully mature when they have good color and yield slightly to gentle pressure. Nectarines, however, may develop their characteristic red blush while still hard and immature; choose specimens that have softened slightly. Another exception is the Kelsey plum, which will ripen and turn yellow if bought in the green stage.

Cherries should be plump and brightly colored; dates should be plump, smooth and shiny. Avoid dates covered with sugar crystals—a sign that the skin of the fruit has been bruised or broken.

□ *Storing:* If ripe, all these fruits should be stored in the refrigerator. Most will stay fresh for up to a week; dates will keep indefinitely. To ripen peaches, nectarines, apricots, plums and mangoes, store them at room temperature away from direct sunlight.

□ *Preparation:* Wash all fruits with pits thoroughly in cold running water before serving them with their skins on. To pit nectarines, apricots and plums, use the technique for peaches *(Step 2, right)*. You can pit cherries the same way, or pop out their pits with a cherry pitter. Mango flesh clings tightly to the pit; it must be scraped off with a knife.

Some peach and apricot preparations call for peeling by the method shown in Step 1, right; plums and nectarines are generally prepared with their skins on, but may be peeled in the same manner. Peeling a mango is simpler when the skin is scored first, as described in the box at far right.

Peeling and Pitting a Peach

1 **Blanching the fruit.** Blanch each peach by immersing it in boiling water for 10 seconds; transfer it to ice water to stop the cooking. With a small knife, nick the skin near the stem end, hold the skin against the blade with your thumb and pull it from the flesh in narrow strips. Rub the fruit with lemon juice.

2 **Removing the pit.** Cut lengthwise into the fruit until the blade touches the pit, then rotate the fruit to cut all around the pit; pull the halves of the fruit apart. For freestone varieties, use your fingers to dislodge the pit from the flesh; for clingstone varieties, cut the pit out with a knife.

Pitting a Cherry

Using a pitter. Rinse and drain cherries, then pull out their stems. Cradle one cherry, stem end up, in the opening at the base of a cherry pitter. Grasping the pitter firmly, press the plunger down so that it pushes the pit out of the fruit and through the hole in the base of the pitter.

Cutting Mango Slices

Freeing the flesh. With a sharp knife, score the skin lengthwise, dividing it into quarters. Peel half of the fruit as you would a peach *(Step 1, above)*, then rest the unpeeled half in your palm and slice the peeled flesh; scrape each slice from the pit with the knife. Peel and slice the other half of the fruit.

Sweetness on a Small Scale

Blueberries

Strawberries

Blackberries

Wild strawberries

Gooseberries

Raspberries

Nuggets of juicy flesh encased in thin skins, berries, currants and grapes are the most compact of fruits. Whatever they lack in size, they make up in flavor: A ripe blueberry or raspberry is one of summer's most tantalizing treats.

Like most of their kin, blueberries are available both wild and cultivated. The cultivated blueberries are larger, sweeter and more widely marketed; the silvery sheen on their dark blue skin is actually a natural waxy coating.

The glossy plumpness of the cultivated strawberry is a token of its familiar juiciness. The largest of the cultivated berries, however, often taste bland and have a cottony texture. By contrast, the small wild strawberry is tender, if not moist, and intensely fragrant.

Blackberries and raspberries resemble each other somewhat; both are made up of clusters of tiny, fleshy sacs. However, both wild and cultivated blackberries are bland with slightly acid overtones, and have more eye appeal than flavor.

Raspberries, on the other hand, are so sweet and highly perfumed that even a few will make their presence known in a big bowl of mixed fruit. Raspberries can be yellow, purple, black or white, as well as the familiar red variety shown here.

Tartness is the distinguishing trait of gooseberries, currants and cranberries. The most common varieties are the light green gooseberries and the red currants and cranberries seen here. All are edible raw, but cooking with sugar reduces their acid tang to a pleasant piquancy.

Although most grapes are produced for wine making, about 16 table varieties are cultivated for eating. Of the three varieties shown here, the Thompson Seedless is the sweetest and most suitable for eating out of hand. The purplish black Ribier is more subtly sweet and highly perfumed; the dark red Emperor has a faintly cherry-like flavor.

□ *How to shop:* Cranberries are available only in the fall, and currants only in the summer, but other berries and table grapes are shipped worldwide and are obtainable year round. They should be evenly colored: Red tinges on blueberries and blackberries, and bleached areas on strawberries and grapes, indicate underripeness. The fruits should feel plump and firm, except for blackberries, which are not ripe until they are quite soft.

When buying grapes, pick out well-formed bunches, but do not reject those with one or two bare stems. Often, the sweetest grapes are found in bunches with a tendency to shed a few grapes.

□ *Storing:* Buy cranberries fresh and store them in the freezer—they will keep for months. Grapes wrapped in perforated plastic bags will stay fresh for two to three weeks in the refrigerator. Currants and most berries are perishable and can be kept in the refrigerator for no more than two days. Before storing them, pick over the fruits and discard any that are moldy—mold spreads rapidly.

□ *Preparation:* Rinse all berries gently under cold running water before using them. Rinse strawberries before hulling them, lest the fruit absorb too much water. Use the technique shown opposite, center, to remove currants from their stems. Grapes are the only berries that need to be seeded. The best tool to use is a straightened paper clip *(opposite, right).*

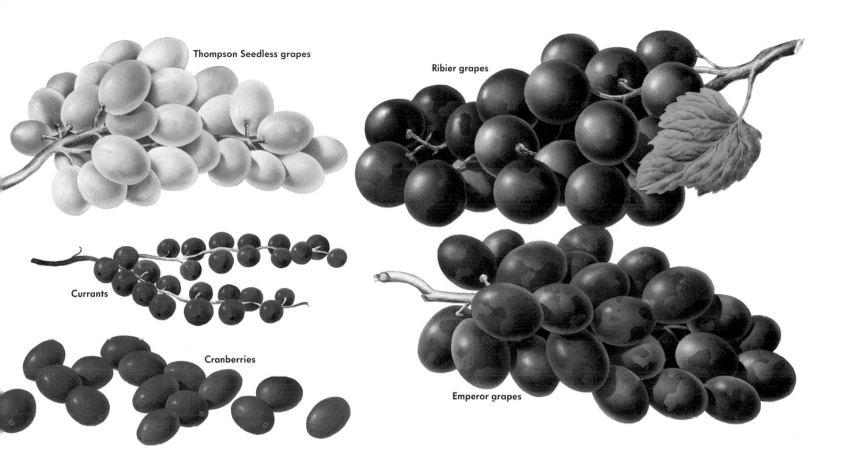

Thompson Seedless grapes

Ribier grapes

Currants

Cranberries

Emperor grapes

Hulling Strawberries

Hulling strawberries. Rinse the strawberries quickly—too much water will make them soggy—and then drain them. Gather up the leaves of each stem cap and, with the tip of a small, nonreactive knife, cut a shallow circle around the base of the cap. Pull the leaves; the white strawberry core will pull away with them.

Stemming Currants

Separating currants. Hold a bunch of currants over a plate. Slip the stem between two tines of a fork and push the fork toward the plate to strip the currants from the stem.

Seeding Grapes

Using a makeshift tool. Straighten a paper clip, leaving only the innermost loop bent; push the loop into the center of the grape from the stem end. Jiggle the paper clip to catch a seed in the loop, then pull the clip and the seed carefully out of the grape. Remove the remaining seeds in the same way.

Melons: Cool and Refreshing

On a hot day, a slice of chilled melon is as refreshing as a cool drink—and with good reason: Melon's sweet flesh is more than 90 per cent water. Although this high water content usually limits the flesh to raw presentations, no part of a melon need be wasted. The shell makes a container for medleys of all kinds of fruits *(pages 30-31);* the seeds can be toasted and served as snacks; and the thick inner rind of watermelons and of smooth-skinned muskmelons can be candied or pickled.

Watermelons—"the food that angels eat," according to Mark Twain—are traditionally huge and oblong; the widely grown Charleston Gray averages 30 pounds [15 kg.]. Modern varieties, however, are small and round: The Sugar Baby weighs only 6 to 10 pounds [3 to 5 kg.]—no more than some muskmelons.

Whatever its size, a watermelon has a hard green outer skin—plain, striped or mottled; its juicy, seeded flesh is usually red or pink. All melons belong to the botanical family of cucurbits. Whereas watermelons are akin to summer squashes and have solid flesh, muskmelons are hollow centered like winter squashes.

Muskmelons are classified according to whether their skin is smooth or covered with netting. Cantaloupes and Persian melons both have netted skin and sweet orange flesh. The flesh of smooth-skinned melons varies from white in the casaba to green in the honeydew and salmon colored in the Cranshaw.

□ *How to shop:* Watermelons are available from March to October, peaking in midsummer. Netted muskmelons are most plentiful from June to August, and smooth muskmelons—sometimes called winter melons because they ripen late—are best from August through October.

Whatever the variety, choose a melon that is symmetrical, evenly colored and heavy for its size. Avoid melons marked with dark, sunken, water-soaked spots.

A watermelon should have a yellow bottom; white or pale green signals immaturity. The flesh of watermelon pieces should be crisp and shiny, not cracked or streaked with white. Avoid pieces with soft seeds, another sign of immaturity.

Any ripe muskmelon will give slightly when pressed at the blossom end and, if not chilled, will have a flowery aroma. A ripe cantaloupe has yellow-green to creamy yellow skin, a Persian grayish green, both beneath beige netting.

The skin of a ripe honeydew has a creamy color and a velvety, almost sticky texture. If the skin is white, smooth and waxy, the honeydew will ripen in a few days at room temperature; if the skin is greenish, the melon has been picked too early and will never ripen. The skin of a casaba turns golden when the melon is ripe; a Cranshaw turns gold and green.

□ *Storing:* Whole melons will keep for several days in the refrigerator. With the exception of honeydews, melons will not ripen after harvest, but will soften and become juicier if kept at room temperature for a day or two. Tightly covered with plastic wrap, cut melons can be kept refrigerated for up to two days.

□ *Preparation:* Watermelons need only be sliced or cut into wedges or chunks for serving. Muskmelons should be halved as shown below. The seeds and soft fibers can then be scooped out, and the cleaned flesh either sliced in wedges to serve plain or peeled, or shaped into balls.

Seeding, Slicing and Peeling Muskmelon

1 **Spooning out seeds.** Use a long, sharp knife to halve the melon—in this case, a cantaloupe. Cut from stem to blossom end, as shown here, if you plan to make wedges or balls, but crosswise if you plan to serve the halves intact. Hold a melon half in one hand and spoon out the seeds and fibers from the cavity.

2 **Cutting off rind.** Slice each melon half into wedges. Steadying a wedge with one hand, slip a sharp knife between the flesh and the rind at the tip of the melon piece and gently guide the knife back and forth along the base of the flesh to free it.

Shaping Melon Balls

Using a melon baller. For each ball, insert the scoop of a melon baller into the flesh of the melon—here, honeydew. Pressing down on the scoop, rotate it to cut out a ball-shaped piece of flesh. Transfer the ball to a bowl. As you proceed, sprinkle the balls with lemon juice or sugar syrup to keep them moist.

Charleston Gray watermelon

Sugar Baby watermelon

Cantaloupe

Persian melon

Cranshaw melon

Honeydew melon

Casaba melon

13

The Citrus Family: Tart and Sweet

Depending on their type, citrus fruits may be prized for their flesh or their juice or both. In some, the colorful peel has enough aromatic oils to make a valuable flavoring or garnish; and orange or grapefruit shells can serve as baskets for fruit desserts *(pages 28-29, 69, 82-83)*.

Oranges are the most versatile citrus fruits; the two most common oranges are the Valencia and Navel. The Valencia is classed as a juice orange: Though its skin is too thin for easy peeling or grating and its flesh is hard to segment for eating, the Valencia has abundant, sweet juice. By contrast, the Navel orange, identified by the knobby navel at one end, has a thick skin, and its somewhat dry, almost seedless flesh is readily sectioned.

The exotic blood orange takes its name from the ruby marks that streak its skin and flesh, which is easily segmented, juicy and sweet. Another uncommon citrus is the kumquat. Its flesh is slightly tart, but its skin is sweet and so thin that, unlike other citrus peel, it is eaten along with the rest of this diminutive fruit.

The largest citrus is the grapefruit; its skin ranges from pale yellow to pink to bronze, and its flesh from white to deep red. The skin is thick enough to grate; the flesh is easy to segment or cut free with a knife *(Step 1, page 28)* and is rich in juice. Florida grapefruits tend to be sweeter and juicier than those from California.

The tangerine is a cousin of the orange, but with sweeter and slightly drier flesh. Its outstanding traits are its loose, peelable skin and neatly defined segments.

Crossing tangerines with grapefruits has produced two popular offspring, the ugli fruit and the tangelo. Ugli fruit is about the size of grapefruit and as juicy, but tastes sweeter; its skin is lumpy and mottled. The tangelo resembles the tangerine but is juicier and harder to peel.

The tangiest of the citruses are lemons and Persian limes, which resemble each other in shape. The sweeter and juicier Key lime has a more rounded form and a decidedly yellowish tint. All are valuable sources of juice and aromatic peel.

□ *How to shop:* Oranges, grapefruits, lemons and Persian limes are plentiful year round; kumquats, ugli fruits, tangerines, tangelos and Key limes are sold only in late fall and early winter.

All citrus fruits must meet federally set standards for ripeness before they can be marketed. However, citrus fruits tend to fade in color once they are picked and refrigerated. To counter this, some are dyed; if you plan to blanch the peel, avoid fruits from boxes marked "color added."

The skins of oranges, grapefruits, lemons and limes should feel firm and be free of bruises. Tangerines, tangelos and ugli fruits may seem slightly puffy because of their loose-fitting skins. Fruits that seem heavy for their size have the most juice.

□ *Storing:* Refrigerate citruses uncovered. Most will keep for up to two weeks.

□ *Preparation:* Kumquats should be rinsed under cold running water before being presented intact. Oranges, grapefruits, tangerines, ugli fruits and tangelos can be peeled and segmented by hand; grapefruits also can be halved and the flesh scooped out with a sharp, pointed spoon. However, for slices and segments completely free of membrane, the fruits should be peeled and cut apart *(right)*.

Valencia orange

Navel orange

Grapefruit

Kumquats

Blood orange

14

Segmenting an Orange

1 **Peeling.** With a sharp, stainless-steel knife, cut off a disk of skin from one end of the fruit—here, a Navel orange—slicing through the colored peel and white pith to expose the flesh. Then insert the knife blade at an angle beneath the pith on one side of the fruit and slowly rotate the fruit to cut away the skin in a long, spiral strip.

2 **Segmenting.** To separate the segments from the internal membranes, hold the fruit over a bowl that will catch juices. Slice down to the core on either side of each segment. Let the segment fall into the bowl.

Paring Off Peel

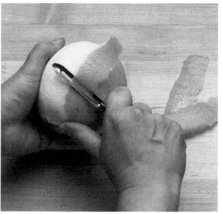

Using a peeler. With a vegetable peeler, pare off strips of the thin colored layer of the skin, leaving the bitter white pith attached to the flesh. The peel can then be cut into julienne. For grated peel, use the small rough-edged holes of a box grater to scrape off the colored peel and a nylon brush to remove it from the holes.

Ugli fruit

Persian lime

Key lime

Tangelo

Tangerine

Lemon

Soft Fruits: A Multiplicity of Tastes and Textures

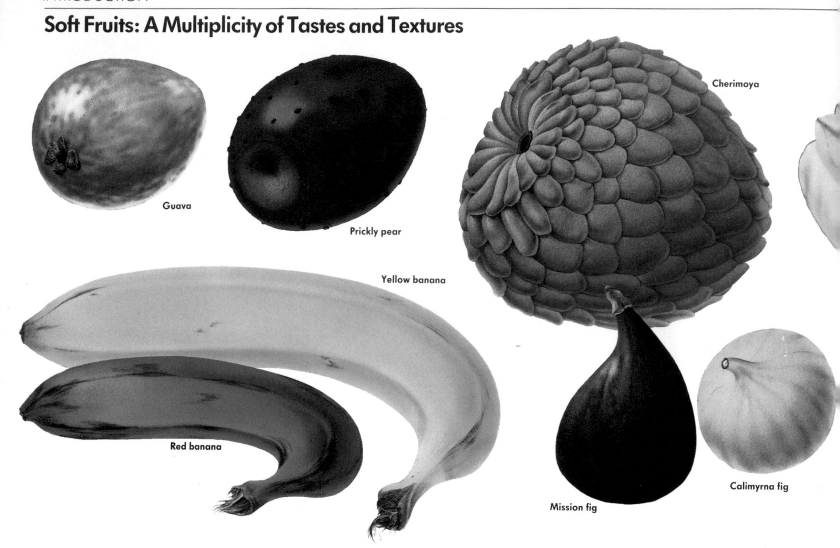

Guava

Prickly pear

Cherimoya

Yellow banana

Red banana

Mission fig

Calimyrna fig

The flesh of soft, heavily seeded fruits—a diverse group ranging from exotic guavas to common bananas—enriches everything from compotes and macedoines to fritters, mousses and ice creams. In some of these fruits, such as the guava or prickly pear, the seeds are tough and hard; in others, such as figs, they are soft; and banana seeds—although visible—cannot be distinguished in texture from the rest of the flesh.

Each of these fruits boasts a unique flavor and texture. The white-to-salmon-colored flesh of the guava, for example, has the taste of strawberry or pineapple, but the texture of peach. The small, tough seeds peppering its flesh can be eliminated by cutting them out or by puréeing the fruit *(page 20)*.

The prickly pear is the fruit of a cactus; the spines on its skin are trimmed when the pear is harvested. The red or yellowish flesh is mildly sweet and meaty, but only sieving will remove its tough seeds.

The thick olive-colored armor of the cherimoya, or custard apple, envelops custard-soft white flesh that tastes like a blend of banana, pineapple and strawberry. The large black seeds distributed through the fruit can be removed one by one, or the flesh can be sieved.

The brown seeds of the acid-sweet and waxy-skinned carambola are as soft as those of a cucumber and as edible. When sliced crosswise, the fruit produces decorative five-pointed stars.

The fuzzy brown skin of the kiwi fruit resembles nothing so much as the plumage of the New Zealand bird after which the fruit is named. Inside, the juicy and somewhat slippery flesh is electric green, with a ring of tiny black seeds at the center. The seeds are edible: They give the flesh, which has a tart, melon-like flavor, a slightly crunchy texture.

In figs, by contrast, seeds fill nearly the entire fruit and are as tender as its flesh. Two of the most common varieties of fig

are the yellowish green Calimyrna and the purplish black Mission. The flesh of both is white with a pink center, dry, slightly sticky, and sweet but nutty.

The familiar yellow banana and its smaller, lesser-known red cousin have soft, yellow-white flesh that grows sweeter as the skin becomes speckled. When fully ripe, the red banana's flesh is slightly drier and—some say—even sweeter than that of the yellow banana.

☐ *How to shop:* Prickly pears and guavas are available from midsummer to midwinter, cherimoyas from midwinter to spring, carambolas during the early fall and winter, and fresh figs from late summer to early fall. Bananas and kiwi fruits are plentiful year round.

With the exception of bananas—one of the few fruits that ripen after picking and can sensibly be bought green—soft and seeded fruits should be fully mature when purchased. Cherimoyas should be olive colored, carambolas bright yellow.

Carambola

Kiwi fruit

Peeling a Guava

Pulling strips of skin. With a sharp paring knife, slice off enough skin at both ends of the guava to expose the flesh. Then, rotating the fruit in the palm of your hand as you proceed, pull off the remaining skin in lengthwise strips.

Peeling a Prickly Pear

Rolling the fruit. Slice off both ends of the prickly pear, then slit the skin from end to end. Insert the tines of a fork parallel to the slit and slip the blunt edge of a knife under the skin at the slit. Then simultaneously roll the fruit in one direction with the fork and pull the skin away from the flesh in the opposite direction with the knife.

In guavas, prickly pears, kiwi fruits and figs, softness is a sign of maturity: Guavas should be firm for cooking; for eating raw they should yield slightly to gentle pressure, as should kiwi fruits. Prickly pears should be firm, not hard; figs should be soft, not mushy.

□ *Storing:* All these fruits should be refrigerated when fully ripe. Cherimoyas and fresh figs should be used within a day or so; the others will keep for a few days. Refrigeration turns the skin of a banana brown, but does not affect the flesh.

□ *Preparing:* Carambolas are eaten skin and all, and need only be washed and sliced for serving. Figs can be eaten with their skins on or peeled. All other seeded fruits need peeling. Kiwi fruits and guavas should be topped, tailed, then peeled lengthwise. To avoid touching the spines, steady a prickly pear with a fork when preparing it. Soft cherimoya flesh should be spooned from the skin rather than the skin being peeled off the flesh.

Preparing a Cherimoya

Scooping out the flesh. Halve the cherimoya lengthwise. Cradle each half in your palm and slip the edge of a spoon down between the flesh and the skin. Keeping the back of the spoon against the skin, work around the fruit to free the flesh. Gently lift the flesh out of its skin in one piece.

Peeling a Fig

Stripping off skin. With a sharp paring knife, cut off the stem of the fig. Then nick the skin at the stem end, grasp a corner of skin between your thumb and the knife and pull a strip of skin away from the flesh. Peel the rest of the fruit in the same way.

A Potpourri of Singular Varieties

Pineapple

Papaya

Persimmon

Passion fruit

Pomegranate

Lychees

Hothouse rhubarb

Field-grown rhubarb

Although most fruits can be grouped by shared traits, a few defy labels. The most familiar of these is the pineapple, which is not one fruit but many, formed by the fusion of about 100 separate flowers that are discernible as "eyes" on its thorny skin and on its yellow flesh. The pineapple is juicy and sharply sweet—a perfect dessert because it contains the enzyme bromelin, which aids digestion.

The papaya, too, doubles as a digestive aid; its protein-splitting enzyme is stored in its smooth, orange-yellow flesh. The juicy papaya is really a berry, although it reaches the size of a small melon—up to 2 pounds [1 kg.]—and has a similar seed-filled central cavity.

Whereas papaya seeds are discarded, pomegranate and passion-fruit seeds—each enclosed in a pulp sac—form the edible part of both fruits. The black seeds of passion fruit are encased in a sweet-and-sour pulp, the white seeds of pomegranates in a sharply sweet, jelly-like pulp.

The orange flesh of persimmons is also gelatinous. This outsize berry resembles a heart-shaped tomato; it is sweet, spicy and enjoyable raw or cooked. The slick, sweet white flesh of the lychee, however, is eaten raw. It clings to a central pit, and is sheathed in a papery shell.

Rhubarb has neither seeds nor skin and, in fact, is not a fruit but a leaf stem. Of the two varieties shown here, the red hothouse rhubarb is milder than the red or green field-grown variety, but both are much too tart unless cooked with sugar.

□ *How to shop:* Pineapples and papayas are plentiful all year. Passion fruits are available only in summer, and pomegranates in autumn. Rhubarb is easiest to obtain from midwinter to midsummer, lychees in midsummer and persimmons from late fall to early winter.

Each fruit has its own way of signaling ripeness. A pineapple grows powerfully fragrant and yields slightly to gentle pressure at the base. A ripe papaya has smooth, unshriveled skin, at least half of which will have turned yellow; the fruit feels heavy for its size, and soft.

The skin of a ripe passion fruit is leathery and wrinkled; the flesh yields to gentle pressure. Look for a pomegranate with smooth, unbroken skin.

A ripe persimmon is glossy, deeply colored and translucent; its stem cap is attached. If it feels soft when squeezed, it is ready to eat. Ripe lychees have firm, unshriveled, brownish red shells.

Fresh rhubarb stalks will be firm and crisp; choose fairly thick stalks. If leaves are attached, they should not be wilted.

□ *Storing:* Pineapples, papayas and persimmons will soften to ripeness if stored for a day or two at room temperature, away from direct sun. Once soft, persimmons must be used right away; pineapples and papayas will keep refrigerated for a few days. Wrap pineapple in plastic so its odor will not permeate other foods.

Lychees will keep in the refrigerator for up to three weeks. Passion fruits and pomegranates will keep for about a week either in or out of the refrigerator. Rhubarb wilts fast at room temperature, but if refrigerated it lasts four or five days.

□ *Preparation:* Persimmon skins are edible; the fruit may be washed and served whole. Rhubarb should be washed well and the tips and leaves cut off; rhubarb leaves are poisonous and no shred should be left on when the stalks are sliced.

The rest of the fruits shown should be skinned, and some seeded, using the techniques at right.

Peeling and Coring a Pineapple

1 **Cutting away the skin.** Slice off about 1 inch [2½ cm.] at the top and base of the fruit. Stand the pineapple up and slice off strips of skin, cutting down along the contours of the fruit.

2 **Cutting out the core.** Cut out any remaining eyes with the knife. Quarter the pineapple lengthwise, then stand each quarter on end and slice down to cut away the fibrous core.

Freeing Pomegranate Seeds

Removing the skin. Cut off the knob by the base of the fruit, then slit the skin lengthwise into strips. Pull the skin away from the membranes enclosing the seed clusters; scoop the clusters into a bowl.

Emptying a Passion Fruit

Scooping out the pulp. Cut the fruit in half crosswise. Hold one half at a time over a bowl and use a spoon to scoop out the pulp and seeds.

Preparing a Papaya

Removing the seeds. Peel the papaya as you would a pear *(page 7)*. Then halve the papaya lengthwise and, with the tip of a spoon, scrape the seeds out of the cavity in each half.

Opening a Lychee

Removing the pit. Nick the loose-fitting shell with a small, sharp knife, then pull it off with your fingers. Split the lychee with the knife and use the tip of the blade to pry out the pit.

Simple Steps to Smooth Purées

The flesh of any fruit, crushed to a purée, makes not only a versatile sauce but also a basic ingredient for concoctions as wide-ranging as soufflés and custards, ices and ice creams.

Fruits can be puréed raw or cooked, with a sieve, a food mill or a processor. The best method depends on the character of the fruit and the texture desired for the purée. No matter what the technique, it will work best if you first prepare the fruit as you would for eating: Peel and core the flesh; remove hulls, stems and as many seeds as possible. Finally, cut the flesh into manageable pieces.

Use only nonreactive equipment—nylon or other plastic; ceramic, glass or wood; tin-lined copper, enameled cast iron or stainless steel. Aluminum or iron will interact with the acids in the fruits, causing discoloration or a metallic taste.

Berries, currants and other small, soft fruits can be puréed whole and raw simply by pressing them through a sieve that will hold back their thin skins and any small seeds. Larger soft fruits such as bananas also pass readily through the sieve, although they must, of course, be peeled. Both flat drum sieves and hemispherical strainers, with meshes ranging from coarse to fine, are suitable.

A food mill that boasts interchangeable fine, medium and coarse disks is the most convenient tool for puréeing tougher or more fibrous fruits—guavas, peaches, kiwis and prickly pears, among them. The turning of the food mill's handle rotates a blade that does the work of the spoon, pestle or scraper required with sieves and strainers.

A food processor will purée any fruit, but it works best on tough and fibrous flesh: pineapple, for example. The more delicate flesh of softer fruits will pulverize in seconds and turn into an aerated liquid rather than a purée of substance.

Some fruits can be successfully puréed only after light poaching or sautéing. The firm-fleshed fruits—apples, pears and quinces—and tough, stringy rhubarb fall into this category. They can, of course, be crushed raw in a processor, but the result will be coarse and grainy. Tenderized by cooking, these fruits will pass easily through a sieve, strainer or food mill to yield smooth sauces.

Sieving Soft Fruits

Using a drum sieve. Prepare the fruit—raspberries are shown—and set it in a drum sieve atop a large plate. With a plastic scraper, crush the fruit, pushing it through the mesh with repeated firm strokes. From time to time discard the seeds from the sieve and turn it over to scrape off the purée clinging to the underside.

Straining Out Seeds

Using a strainer. Prepare the fruit—in this case, cherimoya—and put several pieces at a time in a nonreactive strainer set over a bowl. With the back of a stainless-steel or wooden spoon, press the flesh of the fruit through the mesh. After each batch, discard the seeds and scrape the purée from underneath the mesh.

Crushing Firm Fruits

Using a food mill. Prepare the fruit—here, guava—and put a handful of pieces at a time into a food mill set securely over a bowl. Rotate the handle of the mill to purée the fruit. Periodically remove and discard the seeds from the mill.

Pulping Fibrous Fruits

Using a food processor. Prepare the fruit; for this demonstration, a pineapple has been peeled, quartered, cored (page 19) and the flesh cut into even-sized pieces. Put the pieces in the bowl of a processor, one small batch at a time. Run the processor in short bursts until the fruit is puréed.

Creating Clear Juices

Fruit juices, like purées, serve many culinary purposes. Fresh lemon or orange juice is a standard and indispensable ingredient in any cook's repertoire. But the juice from almost any fruit can form the base for syrups, sauces and flavorings.

With naturally juicy fruits such as citruses and melons, select the heaviest specimens for juicing; these contain the most liquid. Certain varieties within a group are juicier than others; McIntosh apples are juicier than Rome Beauties, for example, and Santa Rosa plums are juicier than Italian Prune plums. Some fruits, on the other hand, will produce negligible amounts of juice under any circumstances; bananas and figs, for example, have dry, meaty flesh that contains very little liquid.

Fruit juices may be obtained by various combinations of cooking, squeezing, crushing and straining; the regimen is tailored to the characteristics of the fruit.

Citrus fruits need only be squeezed to render their copius juice; a reamer provides an anchor for the fruit as you press and squeeze. Softer fruits—grapes, berries and melons, for example—can be crushed with a wooden pestle and then strained through cheesecloth *(right, top)* or, for a thinner, clearer juice, through a jelly bag *(right, bottom)*. More fibrous fruits like peaches or pineapple may be difficult to crush by hand; these can be puréed first in a food mill or a processor *(opposite, bottom)* and then strained.

Some fruits—firm-fleshed apples and quinces, tough cranberries or stringy, fibrous rhubarb—will yield ample juice only after they are cooked and infused in water *(Step 1, right, bottom);* this process breaks down their tissues, allowing them to release moisture.

Squeezing Fruit through Cheesecloth

1 **Crushing the fruit.** Prepare fruit—Ribier grapes are shown. Place it in a bowl and, with a pestle or the back of a stainless-steel or wooden spoon, crush the fruit until it releases its juice. In the case of dark-colored grapes, let the mixture stand for 15 minutes to allow it to take on the color of the skins.

2 **Squeezing juice from the fruit.** Wet a section of cheesecloth under running water, squeeze out excess moisture and lay the cloth, doubled, over a bowl. Ladle the crushed-fruit mixture into the center of the cheesecloth. Gather the corners of the cloth and twist them together tightly until no more juice drips through the cloth.

Using a Jelly Bag

1 **Cooking the fruit.** Prepare the fruit—in this case, cranberries. Put it in a pot and cover it with water. Bring the water to a boil, then turn down the heat and simmer the fruit until it yields its juice. Cranberry skins will burst as the juice is released. Turn off the heat and cool the mixture; the fruit will break down and release more juice as it steeps.

2 **Straining out the juice.** With a wooden pestle, crush the cooked fruit in the pot a little bit more. Then moisten and wring out a jelly bag and suspend it in its frame over a bowl. Ladle the fruit mixture from the pot into the bag and let the juice drip through the cloth into the bowl.

Mellow Companions Founded on Egg Yolks

The custards that lend elegance and flavor to so many fruit preparations are all based on a smooth amalgam of egg yolks, sugar and liquid—usually milk—thickened over gentle heat.

The version known as pouring custard (*crème anglaise* is its French name, signaling its English origin) is a traditional sauce for fruit dumplings and puddings and for poached and baked fruits as well. It is made by adding scalded milk to blended egg yolks and sugar, then cooking the mixture slowly until it becomes a stable emulsion thick enough to coat the back of a spoon (*right; recipe, page 163*). Scalding—a process in which the milk is heated until bubbles form around the edge of the pan—reduces the custard's cooking time and improves its flavor.

With a few simple additions, a pouring custard can be transformed from a sauce into a delectable confection. Incorporating whipped cream and gelatin will enrich the custard and firm it into a Bavarian cream (*recipe, page 164*); adding a fruit purée as well will create a mousse such as the one on pages 78-79. Mixing cream and chopped or puréed fruit with the custard and freezing them in a churn (*pages 86-87*) yields lush ice cream.

When wine rather than milk is the basic ingredient, and the proportion of egg yolks to liquid is doubled, the custard becomes a foamy emulsion called sabayon (*recipe, page 163*)—a perfect hot or cold accompaniment to raw or cooked fruit. Spooned over fresh fruit and broiled, it forms a light gratin (*pages 70-71*). Marsala is the classic choice, but other fortified wines such as sherry or Madeira can be used, as can almost any white wine.

Since sabayon has so many more egg yolks than a simple pouring custard, it must be heated gently to keep the eggs from curdling—usually in a bowl above simmering water. Whisked over steam in this way, the yolks triple in volume.

Pastry cream (*opposite, bottom; recipe, page 163*) begins as a pouring custard, but is balanced with flour so that it can be boiled and thickened until firm. Whether used plain, enriched with cream or flavored with fruit, candied peel, nuts or liqueur, pastry cream is a luxurious filling for fruit tarts, trifles and layered desserts such as the *rosace* on pages 80-81.

Pouring Custard: A Sauce Made with Milk

1 **Mixing yolks and sugar.** Separate the eggs and reserve the whites for another use. In a mixing bowl, whisk the yolks with the sugar until the mixture is creamy white—about 10 minutes. At this point the mixture will have reached the ribbon stage and a small amount dribbled from the whisk will form a trail across the surface.

2 **Adding the milk.** Over medium heat, scald milk in a pan—with a vanilla bean, if you like. Remove the pan from the heat, cover it and let the milk infuse for 15 minutes before removing the bean. Return the milk almost to the scalding point, then slowly pour it into the yolk-and-sugar mixture, whisking constantly but gently.

Sabayon: A Winy Blend

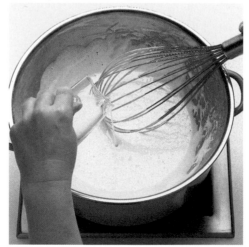

1 **Adding the wine.** Set a large heatproof and nonreactive bowl over a pot of simmering water. Add the egg yolks and the sugar, and whisk them together until the mixture is pale, thick and foamy—about five minutes. Whisking continuously, pour in the wine.

2 **Cooking the sabayon.** Whisk the mixture for about 10 minutes—until the sabayon is quite frothy and three times its original volume. Serve the sabayon immediately or, for a cold sauce, set the bowl in ice to stop the cooking, and continue to whisk the mixture until it has chilled sufficiently.

3 **Heating the custard.** Transfer the mixture to a heavy saucepan and set it over low heat. Using a wooden spoon, stir the custard continuously in a figure-8 motion to distribute the heat evenly throughout the mixture. Bring the custard to just below the simmering point; the consistency is correct when the custard coats the back of the spoon.

4 **Cooling the custard.** When the custard coats the spoon evenly, stop stirring and remove the pan from the heat. Immediately place the pan in a bowl of ice to keep the custard from cooking any further. Stir the custard for another minute or so to cool it slightly.

5 **Straining the custard.** To remove any lumps, strain the custard through a sieve into a bowl. Serve at once, or keep the custard warm by placing the bowl over hot water. If you wish to serve the custard cold, stir it over ice until chilled; or stir it until cool, press plastic wrap against its surface and refrigerate it.

Classic Pastry Cream

1 **Beating egg yolks.** In a large bowl, whisk sugar into egg yolks and beat until the mixture is thick and cream colored—about 10 minutes. Gradually sift in flour to which a tiny pinch of salt has been added. Stir to blend the mixture well.

2 **Cooking the cream.** Infuse milk with a vanilla bean (*Step 2, above*). Remove the bean and, stirring with a wooden spoon, pour the hot milk into the egg mixture in a thin stream. Strain the mixture into a heavy pan. Stirring vigorously, bring the mixture to a boil (*above, left*). Reduce the heat and stir for two minutes until the mixture is thick (*right*). Cool the pastry cream, stirring occasionally to keep a skin from forming on the surface. Transfer the cream to a bowl, press plastic wrap lightly against the surface of the cream and chill it for at least an hour before serving.

1
Raw-Fruit Presentations
Capturing Freshness and Flavor

Maceration for added taste
Shaping natural containers
Cream and cheese complements
Molding coeurs à la crème
Old-fashioned shortcake

Pleasing in shape, vivid in color and bursting with flavor, fruits come ready to eat from the tree, vine and bush—delectable treats that require little or no preparation. For the simplest of desserts, you need only select the finest, ripest, freshest specimens and present them in a way that will display them to best advantage—alone or in tandem.

Even a single fruit, or kind of fruit, can make a splendid show. The filmy skin of a persimmon, for example, can be scored and pulled down from the fruit to surround its gleaming flesh with a vibrant orange star *(page 27)*. Grapes can be frosted with a bit of egg white and granulated sugar; pineapple can assume the form of scalloped rings. Like all raw fruits, these will taste richest if removed from the refrigerator about an hour before serving time and allowed to warm to room temperature. Chilling keeps fruits fresh, but it also diminishes their flavor.

Macedoines, or salads, offer assemblies of different fruits, and great scope for imaginative composition and presentation. Almost any assortment of fruits—large ones cut up, small ones left whole—can be used, but the best results usually reflect restraint: a collection of many closely related fruits—citruses or berries, perhaps—or a sampling of only two or three contrasting varieties. The juiciness of the fruits brings natural moistening to the macedoine, but for a sweeter or more piquant sauce the juices may be supplemented either with sugar syrup or with spirits ranging from wine and hard cider to rum and liqueur. Whether simple or elaborate, macedoines of all sorts can be given a final flourish by serving them in natural containers made from the hollowed shells of citruses, pineapples and melons *(pages 28-31)*.

Besides harmonizing well with each other, fresh fruits show fundamental affinities to cream and cheese. The lushness of a fig, for example, merges smoothly into a coating of heavy cream; a purée of berries blended with whipped cream creates a sublime concoction with the odd name "fool"—from *fouler*, the French word for "crush." A crisp apple is delightfully enhanced by a wedge of Cheddar, a cluster of grapes by a slice of Camembert. For more elaborate delectations, strawberries can be juxtaposed with molded, sweetened farmer cheese in the French dish called *coeur à la crème (pages 34-35)* or combined with biscuits and whipped cream for the American classic, strawberry shortcake *(pages 36-37)*.

A sauce of puréed raspberries completes a fresh-fruit macedoine cupped in the shell of a pineapple. For the macedoine, whole strawberries and sliced kiwi fruit have been combined with chunks of pineapple flesh. Ice packed around the shell adds an inviting sparkle to the dessert's presentation and keeps the shell upright.

Artful Handling for Single Fruits

A presentation that focuses on a single kind of raw fruit can be as eye-catching and delicious as the most complex of assemblies. The challenge is to exploit the special characteristics of that fruit to the fullest, dramatizing its distinctive color, texture and shape while enhancing its natural flavor.

A persimmon, for example, has a thin, papery skin that need only be scored at equal intervals, then pulled downward segment by segment to create a sunburst around the globe of flesh *(opposite, top)*.

Strawberries acquire a tangy taste if they are doused with wine, then sprinkled with vinegar before confectioners' sugar is sifted over them *(below)*. The wine rinses the fruit as it adds flavor. The vinegar, unlikely though it seems, heightens the sweetness of the strawberries. For a milder flavor and frostier coating, any of a wide array of small whole fruits—from berries and cherries to currants and grapes—can be brushed with raw egg white before being sprinkled with granulated sugar *(opposite, center)*.

Pineapple lends itself to diverse and dramatic shaping. One effective but simple tactic is to quarter the fruit, core it and separate the flesh from the rind of each piece in one unit *(bottom)*. The flesh is then sliced and drawn apart into a serrated pattern. Muskmelons of any kind could be treated similarly.

The scalloped edges of the slices shown at bottom right are a decorative bonus of the pineapple's unique anatomy. But any sort of large or medium-sized fruit—from peaches and oranges to mangoes and papayas—makes a beautiful display when cut into uniform slices and garnished with fresh berries or cherries.

Strawberries with Wine and Vinegar

1 **Steeping the berries.** Hull strawberries *(page 11)* but do not rinse them. Place the berries in a bowl and pour in enough red wine to cover them.

2 **Draining.** After five minutes, use a slotted spoon to transfer the berries to serving dishes. Discard the wine. Drizzle a little vinegar over each serving.

3 **Serving.** Sift a light dusting of confectioners' sugar over the strawberries. If you like, garnish the berries with fresh mint before serving.

Pineapple Pieces in a Pattern

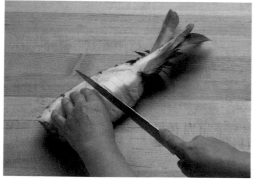  

1 **Cutting the pineapple.** Cut a pineapple lengthwise into quarters. Core each quarter, then cut from leaf end to base to free the flesh from the rind in one piece. Slice each quarter crosswise.

2 **Arranging the slices.** Leave the slice adjacent to the leaves in place. With your forefingers, slide the remaining slices alternately left and right to create a zigzag pattern.

3 **Garnishing.** Finely chop fresh mint leaves. Supporting a quarter in one hand, gently dab the overhanging tips of the slices with mint. Garnish the remaining quarters in the same way.

A Persimmon Sunburst

1 Peeling. Make a conical cut around the core of each persimmon; remove the core. Score the skin from the tip almost to the base at eight equal intervals. Peel back the segments of skin.

2 Garnishing. Arrange each persimmon on a plate with the peeled skin segments radiating outward. Cut off the tip of the fruit and remove a thin slice to garnish the plate.

3 Serving. Moisten the persimmon with a few spoonfuls of fruit juice or brandy—here, kirsch is used. Serve the persimmon immediately.

A Sugary Glaze for Grapes

1 Applying egg white. Trim washed grapes into bunches. Beat egg white lightly, then use a brush to paint one bunch of grapes with egg white.

2 Sugaring. Hold the coated grapes above a wire rack set on a baking pan and sift sugar over the grapes. Paint and sugar the remaining grapes.

3 Serving. Let the sugared grapes sit on the rack until the coating hardens— about two hours. Then arrange the clusters attractively on a serving dish.

Scalloped Pineapple Slices

1 Removing "eyes." Trim and peel a pineapple *(page 19)*. Following the spiral line of the eyes, make a series of two parallel diagonal cuts to remove all the eyes from the fruit.

2 Coring. Slice the pineapple in half crosswise. Following the technique on page 7, top right, use an apple corer to remove the fibrous center of the fruit.

3 Serving. Cut the cored pineapple halves into 1/4-inch [6-mm.] slices. Arrange the slices on a plate and garnish them, if you like, with berries— in this case, blackberries.

Fresh-Fruit Mixtures in Natural Shells

Fresh fruits combine so well with one another that any selection can succeed as a macedoine—a fruit salad. A macedoine can be lavish or spare, with many or only a few fruits of the season. For harmony, the macedoine might be based on similar fruits such as an assortment of berries, melon balls or—as in the demonstration at top right—citruses. For contrasts of texture as well as flavor and color, the components can be unrelated types; pineapple, strawberries and grapes compose the macedoine at bottom right.

Before a macedoine is assembled, the fruits should be washed, peeled, hulled, stemmed or cored, depending on their type. The elements of a macedoine should be similar in size—although not necessarily in shape—so large fruits will need to be sliced, cubed, segmented or cut into balls or wedges.

The process of preparing the flesh may also yield containers for the macedoine; grapefruits, oranges, melons and pineapples are all suitable for this sort of double service. If natural shells are lacking, macedoines can of course be presented in plain or stemmed bowls, in fruit cups or on dessert plates.

For maximum flavor and color, prepare the fruit at the last moment, and protect any specimens that may discolor by brushing them with citrus juice or dropping them in acidulated water *(page 7)*. Macedoines need no dressing other than their intermingled juices, accented perhaps with a little lemon or lime juice. However, for a richer effect, the fruits can be macerated, or steeped, for up to an hour or so in sugar syrup *(recipe, page 162)*, rum, wine or brandy. Or the macedoine can be moistened at the last moment with a fresh purée of fruit.

Citruses Assembled in Grapefruit Shells

1 **Preparing citruses.** Peel and segment oranges and a grapefruit *(page 15)* over a large bowl to conserve juices. Halve two grapefruits and run a paring or grapefruit knife along the inner contours of the rind to free the flesh from each half. Gently pull out the freed fruit; remove the membrane and add the flesh to the bowl.

2 **Cleaning the shells.** Starting along the rim of one emptied shell, grasp the fibrous lining between a spoon and your thumb, then pull down on the lining to remove it. Work your way around the rim until the entire lining is removed. Repeat the process to clean each of the remaining grapefruit shells.

A Colorful Filling for Hollowed Pineapple

1 **Opening the pineapple.** Trim the base so that the fruit will stand upright. Cut a conical plug from the top of the fruit to remove its crown of leaves. Then cut straight down around the inner edge of the rind, to a depth about halfway down the fruit. Make a similar cut around the fibrous core.

2 **Cutting wedges.** To divide the flesh in the upper half of the fruit into neat pieces that can be easily removed, make spokelike cuts radiating from the inner to the outer circular cut.

3 **Opening a coconut.** With a skewer or screwdriver, pierce the dark indentations called eyes that appear at the top of a coconut. Then turn the coconut upside down to drain its milky liquid. With a hammer or the back of a cleaver, as here, rap the coconut sharply along its equator until the shell cracks open.

4 **Grating the coconut.** Break the halves of the coconut into smaller pieces. Using a small, sharp knife, pry a chunk of coconut flesh away from its shell and pare the barklike skin from the white flesh. Grate the coconut flesh, add it to the citrus segments and toss gently.

5 **Serving.** Place the emptied grapefruit shells on individual plates and fill each one with the citrus mixture. For decorative effect, garnish each plate with a few citrus leaves and sprinkle pomegranate seeds *(page 19)* over the fruits. Serve at once.

3 **Removing the wedges.** Using a spoon, lift out the freed chunks of pineapple and transfer them to a large bowl. Make circular cuts around the rind and core in the lower half of the fruit, divide the fruit into wedges and add the wedges to the bowl. Cut out the core and discard it.

4 **Serving.** Scrape the inside of the pineapple shell clean. Cut large pineapple wedges into bite-sized pieces and mix them with hulled strawberries and stemmed seedless grapes. Set the pineapple in a bowl of ice, crushed to hold the shell upright. Spoon the fruits into the shell and sauce them with kiwi purée.

Melon Containers for Fruit Medleys

The pleasing shapes and sturdy rinds of melons make them ideal fruits for sculpturing into natural containers. In the top demonstration here, a Cranshaw melon is hollowed to create an asymmetrical showcase for a melange of melon balls. In the bottom demonstration, a watermelon becomes a huge basket for a trompe-l'oeil still life of fruits that appear whole but are, in fact, sliced and ready to eat.

The flesh removed from a melon shell provides the primary ingredient for its filling. A muskmelon yields only about half as much flesh as is needed to fill it. A watermelon, on the other hand, provides more than enough flesh.

Almost any fruit will complement melon flesh: Berries, grapes, mangoes, papayas, pineapple and plums are among them. However, for melon shells that will double as centerpieces, avoid fruits that tend to discolor—apples, bananas, pears and peaches—or brush them with citrus juice before adding them to the shells.

An Elegant Muskmelon Bowl

1 Cutting an opening. Trim a slice from the base of a muskmelon—here, a Cranshaw—to make it stand upright. Cut a slice off the top of the melon. With a pencil, draw a loop that starts on one side at the back of the cut surface and ends on the other side. Cut through the line with a sharp knife.

2 Cleaning the melon. Lift off the cut section of melon and reserve it. Scoop out the seeds and fibers from the melon. Use a melon baller to shape balls from the flesh inside the melon and the cut section *(page 12)*. With a spoon, scrape the remaining flesh to a thickness of about ¼ inch [6 mm.].

A Watermelon Basket Brimming with Fruit

1 Taping. Wrap 1½-inch [4-cm.] paper tape horizontally around the melon about a third of the way from the base. Outline a diagonal handle with tape. Make a V-shaped incision in each of the four corners where the tapes meet. With a long, sharp knife, cut down along each side of the handle to the top of the horizontal tape.

2 Removing the top. Starting from one end of the melon, cut along the top edge of the horizontal tape to free one side of the upper portion of the fruit. Work slowly near the handle to avoid cutting through it. Lift off the freed section of melon. Then carefully remove the upper portion on the other side of the handle in the same way.

3 Hollowing the basket. Cut around the inner rim of the melon basket at a 45-degree angle; leave about ¼ inch [6 mm.] of red flesh on the rind. Slice down through the flesh in the basket and remove the flesh in large chunks. Then carefully cut the flesh from the underside of the handle and ease it out. Gently remove the two pieces of tape.

3 **Trimming the shell.** Using the knife, bevel the edge of the opening in the melon by cutting away the flesh at an angle. Cover the melon with plastic wrap to keep the inner surfaces moist and—if the melon must wait for more than an hour—refrigerate it.

4 **Macerating the balls.** Combine equal amounts of rum and sugar syrup *(recipe, page 162)* with lime juice to taste. Cut additional balls—here, from honeydew, casaba and cantaloupe—and mix them with the Cranshaw balls. Add the rum mixture and let the balls macerate for 30 minutes.

5 **Serving.** Use a slotted spoon to transfer the melon balls to the hollowed melon. Garnish the finished salad, if you like, with fresh herb sprigs—mint, lemon thyme, rose geranium or the lemon verbena used here.

4 **Preparing large fruits.** Scrape the interior of the watermelon basket clean with a spoon. Remove the seeds from the watermelon chunks and line the basket with some of the watermelon. Peel, core, slice and reassemble an assortment of large fruits—in this case, oranges, pineapples and a papaya.

5 **Adding smaller fruits.** Arrange the large fruits in the basket attractively. Prepare a variety of smaller fruits for the top—here, Ribier and Thompson Seedless grapes, a sliced carambola and Kelsey plums that have been halved, pitted, sliced and reassembled.

6 **Serving.** Distribute the smaller fruits atop the basket. If you do not plan to serve the fruit immediately, cover the whole basket loosely with plastic wrap and refrigerate it. To give the surfaces of the fruits an appealing, moist look, brush them lightly with citrus or pineapple juice just before serving.

The Pleasing Partnership of Fruit and Cream

Fruit and fresh cream combine with remarkable felicity. The underlying sharpness of the one perfectly counterbalances the bland richness of the other. Even when the cream is cultured—tart cream (recipe, page 162) or sour cream—its consistency is lush, and its taste is mild compared with that of fruit.

The simplest version of this combination consists of whole or sliced fruit doused with heavy cream—berries and cream are the classic. With a little extra effort, the cream can be whipped and perhaps sweetened or flavored with liqueur, and the fruit presented more formally. In the demonstration at right, for example, ripe figs are decoratively cut, crowned with dollops of whipped cream and drizzled with raspberry purée.

Fruit purée provides the starting point rather than the topping for the mellow blends of fruit and cream that are known as fools. Berries make particularly attractive fools because of their abundant

juice and jewel-bright colors. But any fruit, puréed fresh or cooked, and sweetened to taste, is suitable.

Whatever type of fruit is used, the purée should be well chilled before being blended with the cream. Proportions can be varied to taste, but traditionally a fool is made with 1 cup [¼ liter] of heavy cream—which doubles in volume when whipped—to 1 cup of purée. Before being served, the fool itself should be chilled for about an hour to allow the mixture to firm slightly; if chilled for more than two hours, it will begin to separate.

Fruit fools can be garnished with more whipped cream, topped with berries or fruit slices, or layered in different flavors. In the demonstration below, blackberries are topped by a blackberry fool.

Fools usually are served in glass containers. Here, the fool is assembled in goblets, but it could also be prepared in a large bowl and spooned into individual ones for serving.

Figs with a Ruby Sauce

1 **Preparing figs.** Peel fresh figs with a small, sharp knife (page 17). Then cut a cross in the top of each fig, slicing down almost to the base of the fruit. Place your thumbs and forefingers at the base of the four segments of the fig. Press simultaneously into the fig at the base to force the segments apart to resemble a flower with its petals open.

A Luxurious Blackberry Fool

1 **Incorporating sugar.** Purée fresh, ripe blackberries through a sieve over a mixing bowl. Sweeten the purée to taste with granulated or superfine sugar and stir well to dissolve the sugar. Chill the purée for at least two hours.

2 **Blending in cream.** Beat chilled heavy cream until it forms soft peaks. Using a spoon, gently stir the blackberry purée into the cream a little at a time. Stir the mixture until it is an even color throughout.

3 **Assembling the fool.** Toss fresh, whole blackberries in a little sugar to sweeten them. Spoon the berries into glass goblets. Spoon the fool over the berries to fill each goblet.

2 **Whipping heavy cream.** Purée chilled raspberries *(page 20)*; set the purée aside. Pour chilled cream into a large bowl and, with a wire whisk, beat it until it forms soft peaks.

3 **Serving the figs.** Transfer the raspberry purée to a small pitcher. Arrange the figs on individual plates; then spoon a dollop of whipped cream onto the center of each fig and pour the raspberry sauce over it. Alternatively, fold the cream into the purée and spoon the blended mixture over the figs.

4 **Serving the fool.** Finish each serving of blackberry fool by making a decorative whirl on top. Chill the fool for about one hour to firm it. If you like, garnish the fool with a little grated orange or lemon peel or more whole blackberries before serving it.

Cheese: The Perfect Counterpoint

Fruits and cheeses, like fruits and cream, have a natural affinity. Their contrasting flavors and textures provide a fitting end to any meal, whether they are served simply with crusty bread or assembled in a rich dessert *(right)*.

The choice of which fruit to partner with which cheese depends ultimately on personal taste. However, a useful rule of thumb is that firm-fleshed fruits complement hard, assertive cheeses while soft fruits go well with soft or mild-flavored cheeses. Apples, pears and pineapple are all excellent with Cheshire, Gouda or Gruyère, or with blue cheeses—Gorgonzola, Roquefort and Stilton, for example. Melons, peaches, plums and grapes of any color may be served with soft cheeses such as ricotta, Petit-Suisse, *explorateur* and Camembert, or the semisoft types—Taleggio, Saint-Nectaire, reblochon and Port-Salut among them.

Whole berries or currants or chunks of peaches, dates or papayas can be folded into an amalgam of cottage, farmer or cream cheese, whipped cream and sugar to create a delicious, impromptu dessert. Alternatively, a fruit purée may be blended with the cheese-and-cream mixture to make a kind of cheese fool.

Cheese and cream also provide a rich basis for dessert molds. The *coeurs à la crème* shown here start with a mixture of farmer cheese, whipped cream, sugar and stiffly beaten egg whites that is spooned into small, cloth-lined, heart-shaped perforated molds and left to drain overnight *(recipe, page 119)*. The hearts are unmolded, then surrounded by whole wild or cultivated berries or slathered with a berry purée.

Shapes other than hearts are suitable, and one large mold can replace many individual ones. However, it is essential that the molds have drainage holes so that all excess liquid will gradually drain out of the cheese; otherwise the mixture will not become compact enough to unmold. For an even firmer mold, beaten egg yolks can be mixed with the cheese, and the cream can be thickened with gelatin before the cheese and cream are blended and combined with egg whites *(recipe, page 120)*.

1 **Preparing molds.** Line perforated molds—heart-shaped molds are used here—with muslin or cheesecloth to facilitate unmolding later. Press the cloth well into the edges of the molds with the fingers of one hand and pull the material smooth with your other hand, so that each unmolded shape will have a fairly distinct outline.

2 **Sieving cheese.** Whip heavy cream until it forms soft peaks. With a wooden spoon, press soft cheese—in this case, farmer cheese—through a fine sieve to eliminate any lumps.

Serving Fruit with Cheese

Assembling the presentation. An hour or two before serving, place wedges, rounds or large chunks of cheese on a cutting board and let them warm to room temperature. In this case, Stilton *(top left, above)*, Cheshire *(top right)* and *explorateur* are arranged on fresh grapevine leaves. At the same time, heap a basket or bowl with fruit—here, Bosc pears, McIntosh and Golden Delicious apples and Emperor and Ribier grapes.

3 **Stirring in the cream.** Beat egg whites until they hold stiff peaks. Gradually mix the whipped cream into the sieved cheese. Add superfine sugar to taste, then gradually fold the beaten egg whites into the cheese-and-cream mixture.

4 **Filling the molds.** When the mixture is well blended, spoon it into the lined molds, making sure all corners are filled. Smooth the top surfaces with the back of the spoon. Place the molds on a tray and refrigerate them for at least six hours, or until they feel firm and compact.

5 **Unmolding the hearts.** Invert the molds onto a serving plate; position them in a ring, with the points of the hearts facing inward. Gently lift off the molds. Carefully peel the cloth away from the hearts, which will be slightly marked with the pattern of the draining holes.

6 **Serving coeurs à la crème.** Just before serving, pile fresh wild strawberries in the center of the ring of hearts and scatter more berries around the rim of the plate *(left)*. Serve individual hearts surrounded by berries and pour cream over them *(below)*.

Strawberries and Shortcake: Traditional Companions

Writing in 1642, Roger Williams, the founder of the colony of Rhode Island, praised the plump American strawberry as "the wonder of all the Fruits growing naturally in those parts." He also noted, "The Indians bruise them in a Morter, and mix them with meale and make strawberry bread"—a concoction colonists refined as strawberry shortcake.

Over the years, endless variations of this tiered assembly of cake, strawberries and cream have evolved. Although the base is sometimes sponge- or pound-cake, or even angel food, the classic cake is a baking-powder biscuit—short in the sense that it contains a high proportion of shortening. In this demonstration the shortening is butter, and the dough is further enriched with eggs and cream to yield fine-textured biscuits that can absorb fruit juices without becoming soggy.

Modern baking powder helps guarantee the lightness of the biscuits because it is double-acting—that is, it releases carbon dioxide at two stages: when the dry ingredients are moistened and when the dough is baked. Even so, the elements should be mixed quickly and gently to forestall the development of the gluten that is present in flour and likely to make dough tough if handled very much.

By contrast, the strawberries themselves need little attention, but must be prepared well ahead of time. After being rinsed and hulled, the berries should be halved, mixed with sugar and allowed to stand for at least an hour. The sugar draws out the fruit's liquid—cooks call the process sweating—to create a rich, juicy syrup. When strawberries are not available, other fruits can be substituted, and these too need sweating. Among the best candidates are raspberries or blueberries, crushed slightly to render their juices, and cut-up apricots or nectarines.

Whatever fruit you choose, the cream for strawberry shortcake must be the heaviest, richest sort available. Some cooks insist on keeping it liquid and pouring it over the berries and biscuits; others whip it to fluffy peaks for the most spectacular-looking dessert possible.

1 **Sweating the berries.** About an hour before serving time, hull and halve fresh strawberries and place them in a large bowl. Add sugar—about 2 tablespoons [30 ml.] for each cup [¼ liter] of berries—and toss the sugar and berries together gently. Set the berries aside at room temperature.

4 **Cutting out the biscuits.** Line a jelly-roll pan with parchment paper. Using a large, sharp biscuit cutter, press straight down through the dough repeatedly to cut as many biscuits as possible from the flattened sheet. Draw the leftover bits gently together, flatten them and cut a last biscuit. Bake the biscuits in a preheated 425° F. [220° C.] oven until lightly browned—about 10 minutes.

5 **Opening the biscuits.** Place the pan of biscuits on a wire rack to cool for a few minutes. Then use a fork—not a knife—to pry the layers apart and split each biscuit in half. Return the halved biscuits to the pan and set them aside until you are ready to serve them.

2 **Mixing the dough.** Beat egg yolks and cream together in a small bowl. Sift flour, baking powder, salt and sugar together into a large bowl. Add chunks of chilled butter to the dry ingredients; with your finger tips, quickly work the butter into the ingredients *(above, left)* until the mixture has the consistency of coarse meal. Add the egg-and-cream mixture *(right)* and blend gently with a fork until the dry ingredients are just moistened. With your fingers, gather this dough together into a loose mass.

3 **Kneading the dough.** Use your fingers and the heel of your hand to fold the dough over in the bowl, kneading it lightly seven or eight times. Lay the dough on a floured board and use your hands to pat it into a sheet about 1 inch [2½ cm.] thick.

6 **Assembling and serving.** Beat heavy cream with a little sugar until it forms soft peaks. For each shortcake, place the bottom half of a biscuit on a serving plate and spoon over a generous portion of berries. Spoon a dollop of whipped cream onto the berries *(left)* and add the biscuit top. Finally, spoon on more berries *(inset)* and dribble berry syrup over the dessert. Serve the shortcake immediately.

2
Poaching, Stewing and Steaming

Moist Heat for Succulent Fruit Creations

Pouring custard spreads a golden pool around a pair of plum dumplings. For the dumplings, pitted plums were filled with cinnamon sugar, sandwiched between rounds of dough and poached until tender. Before serving, the warm dumplings were sprinkled with nuts and more cinnamon sugar.

As long as it is kept gentle, moist heat—whether supplied by steeping, poaching, stewing or steaming—can be turned to good advantage in coaxing out the flavor of fruits and making them sublimely tender. The ultimate in gentleness is achieved by steeping fruits in hot liquid briefly without ever putting them on the stove *(pages 40-41)*. However, the effects of such treatment may be too subtle to benefit any but juicy, delicate varieties—berries, grapes, citruses and the like.

Poaching and stewing can produce dramatic results with almost every kind of soft and firm, fresh and dried fruit. Both methods depend for success on liquid kept at a constant simmer. Poaching requires enough liquid to cover the fruit completely so that it cooks at an even rate with no stirring or other handling that might break its skin or mar its shape. By contrast, stewing calls for only enough liquid to keep the fruit from scorching while it cooks down into a thick sauce *(pages 46-47)*.

Steaming works only in special circumstances. Steam is too hot for the direct cooking of fruit; however, it can produce an ambient temperature appropriate for puddings insulated in a covered dish *(pages 48-49)*.

Plain water, of course, provides the liquid for steaming. With other moist-heat methods, though, sugar syrup is the liquid of choice, not only for its taste, but also for its ability to help keep fruit shapely. The ideal syrups for cooking fruit have a relatively low proportion of sugar—½ to ⅔ cup [125 to 150 ml.] of sugar to 1 cup [¼ liter] of water *(recipe, page 162)*—and need only a few minutes of boiling to ready them for use. Plain granulated sugar is the foundation of the classic crystal-clear syrup, but enticing variations can be improvised with almost any sweetening agent: Brown sugar, Demerara sugar, maple sugar or syrup, molasses, dark corn syrup and honey all will yield a more robust syrup and an amber tinge. The ratio of sweetener to water can be varied to taste.

For further flavor experiments, sugar syrup can be augmented with fruit peels, whole or ground spices and sweet herbs such as mint or lemon verbena. The water for the syrup can be replaced or supplemented with fruit juice, wine or cider. Efforts made to enhance sugar syrup bring an extra dividend for the cook. When the fruit has cooked, the syrup can be boiled over high heat to thicken its consistency and can then be used to drench the fruit with a glistening glaze.

39

Steeping and Poaching for Tender Results

The gentlest way to cook fresh fruit is with liquid. For delicate berries and for citruses such as oranges, tangelos and the tangerines shown at top right, mere steeping in hot liquid is sufficient to mellow their flavor and soften their flesh. Firmer fruits—pears, peaches, apples, pineapples and quinces among them—need to be poached in liquid kept at 195° F. [90° C.] to become tender. Higher temperatures will cause the fruit to break apart; at lower temperatures, the cooking will be prolonged and more of the fruit's juices will leech out.

The basic liquid for both methods is a simple sugar syrup, made in copious enough volume to cover the fruit: As the fruit cooks, it releases its juices while simultaneously absorbing the syrup and thus maintains its color and texture. The sugar in the syrup slows the cooking, but ensures that the fruit does not collapse as it would in plain water.

Depending on the variety of the fruit, the syrup may be of light or medium density (recipe, page 162). Its sweetness can be underscored or counterpointed by adding whole or ground spices, liqueurs, brandies or wines.

Wine can be used two ways: Fruit poached from the raw stage in a mixture made of one part syrup to one part wine—especially a full-bodied red variety—will fully absorb the wine's color and flavor. On the other hand, when wine is added near the end of the cooking period, as shown in the bottom demonstration, it imparts a more subtle color and taste. In this case, however, the wine must first be boiled briefly to evaporate its alcohol and smooth its flavor.

For steeping or poaching, it is imperative to use a bowl or pot that will not react chemically with the acid in the fruit. The container must be deep enough to hold the fruit fully immersed in liquid; a piece of parchment paper, cut to the diameter of the pot, is a convenient means of keeping the poaching fruit submerged. While the fruit is steeped or poached, the syrup takes on flavor, too. After the fruit is done, the syrup can be boiled down to provide a sauce for glazing the finished dish.

Tangerines Steeped in Syrup

1 **Preparing the fruit.** Peel tangerines with your fingers and use a sharp knife to cut the peel into long, thin julienne. Set the julienne aside. Then remove the bitter strings from the tangerines and put the fruit into a nonreactive, heatproof bowl.

2 **Poaching the peel.** Prepare a medium sugar syrup, flavoring it with freshly grated nutmeg. Drop the tangerine julienne into the boiling syrup. Reduce the heat and simmer the peel for about 15 minutes. Using a fine-meshed skimmer, transfer the peel to a small pan; set it aside. Then pour a little orange liqueur into the syrup.

Poached Pears in Wine

1 **Preparing the pears.** Peel pears—Bartletts are shown—leaving the stems intact. As you peel them, place the pears in acidulated water (page 7). In a nonreactive pot, make a light sugar syrup flavored with a split vanilla bean or a cinnamon stick. Immerse the pears in the syrup and cover them with a parchment-paper disk.

2 **Testing doneness.** Place the lid on the pot, leaving it slightly ajar, and poach the pears over medium heat. After about 20 minutes, remove the lid and the parchment paper and lift out a pear with a slotted spoon. Insert the tip of a small knife into the base of the pear: When it meets only slight resistance, the pear is almost done.

3 **Steeping the fruit.** Scatter a few leaves of a sweet herb—in this case, lemon balm—over the tangerines in the bowl. Pour all but 1 cup [¼ liter] of the liqueur-flavored syrup over the fruit. Cover the bowl tightly and allow the tangerines to steep for two hours.

4 **Candying the peel.** Pour the remaining sugar syrup over the reserved julienne. With the pan uncovered, cook the julienne over medium heat until all of the syrup has evaporated and the peel is slightly caramelized. With a fork, spread the julienne on a wire rack and separate the strips.

5 **Serving.** To serve the fruit, place each tangerine in a small bowl and ladle some of the syrup over it. Garnish the fruit with candied julienne and a few fresh leaves of lemon balm.

3 **Adding wine.** Pour a bottle of red wine into a nonreactive saucepan and bring it to a boil over high heat. Boil the wine for two or three minutes to reduce it slightly, then add it to the pears and cook them gently for five minutes.

4 **Reducing the syrup.** Transfer the pears to a heatproof bowl. Discard the vanilla bean or cinnamon stick. Pour half of the poaching liquid over the pears and let them cool. Cook the remaining poaching liquid over high heat until it has reduced to a thick syrup.

5 **Serving the pears.** Drain the pears and stand them upright in a large serving bowl. Ladle some of the wine syrup over the pears to glaze them and pour the rest into a sauceboat to be presented separately.

Composing Perfect Compotes

For a classic compote, fruit is poached and served in a sweet liquid. During poaching, the sweetness of the liquid mellows the acidity of the fruit; afterward, if the liquid is boiled, it evaporates to form a syrupy sauce. The liquid may be a light or medium sugar syrup *(recipe, page 162)* or fruit juice, sweetened with either honey or white or brown sugar. The fruit should be cooked just long enough to become soft; in a compote of mixed fruits, each piece of fruit should retain its own unique structure and distinctive flavor.

Almost any type of fresh fruit will make a successful compote: The only requirement is that the specimens be firm to prevent them from falling apart during cooking. Dried fruits—prunes, figs or apricots—are equally suitable. Before cooking, they should be soaked to swell and soften them. In the prune-and-kumquat compote shown at right *(recipe, page 131)*, the soaking liquid of the prunes is used to cook them, then it is combined with orange juice and honey to poach the kumquats.

For a mixed compote, choose fruits whose flavors, textures and appearance complement one another; for example, offset large, sweet apples with tart, diminutive cranberries.

In the boxed demonstration on the opposite page, pears, nectarines, plums, cherries, grapes and blueberries are combined for an ensemble of varying colors and shapes. Each of the fruits needs a different amount of poaching to achieve the ideal degree of tenderness. Pears will require from 10 to 40 minutes, depending on type and ripeness. Nectarines and plums should poach for five to 10 minutes; cherries and grapes for two to three minutes. The blueberries will require little more than a dip in the hot syrup. For this step, remove the pot containing the liquid from the heat, put the berries into a skimmer and immerse them in the syrup just long enough to darken their color. When all the fruits have been cooked, the syrup can be infused with fruit peels before the compote is served.

1 **Poaching prunes.** Soak the prunes overnight in enough water to cover them. Transfer the prunes and soaking liquid to a nonreactive pot; add water, if necessary, to submerge the prunes. Bring to a boil and simmer until the prunes are tender—about 10 minutes. Let the prunes cool in the liquid.

2 **Preparing kumquats.** Using a sharp knife, slice unpeeled kumquats crosswise into rounds that are about ¼ inch [6 mm.] thick. Pick out the seeds with the tip of the knife.

3 **Pitting the prunes.** Drain the prunes through a sieve set over a bowl. Set the poaching liquid aside. Cut lengthwise along each prune, peel back the flesh and remove the pit.

4 **Poaching the kumquats.** Pour equal amounts of the reserved poaching liquid and fresh orange juice into a nonreactive pot. Add honey and bring the mixture to a boil. Immediately reduce the heat to a simmer and drop in the sliced kumquats. Cook the kumquats for five minutes, or until tender.

Adjusting the Timing to Suit the Fruit

1 **Poaching.** Peel and core pears; peel and pit nectarines and plums; pit cherries; stem grapes and blueberries. Reserve the peels. Prepare medium sugar syrup. Poach large fruits one type at a time, cherries and grapes together and blueberries separately; assemble them in a bowl as you proceed.

2 **Flavoring the syrup.** Put the reserved peels into the syrup and bring it to a boil. Reduce the heat and simmer until the liquid reduces slightly and is imbued with the flavor of the peels— about 10 minutes. Then strain the flavored syrup through a sieve.

3 **Serving.** Pour the thickened syrup over the fruits assembled in the bowl. Serve the compote warm or chilled— decorated, if you like, with a few geranium leaves, as shown here.

5 **Adding the prunes.** Place the pot containing the poached kumquats on a trivet. Add the pitted prunes and stir gently to combine the fruits.

6 **Serving the compote.** Ladle the warm fruits and liquid into small bowls and serve the compote immediately. Or, if you prefer, cool the compote to room temperature, refrigerate it for a few hours and serve it chilled.

Fruit-filled Dumplings Gently Simmered

Fresh fruit and tender dough unite deliciously in sweet dumplings. At their simplest, dumplings may be mere lumps of biscuit dough *(recipe, page 164)* that are simmered—tightly covered—with stewing or poaching fruit for 10 minutes, or until the dough cooks through. With a little extra effort, chopped dried fruits and nuts can be bound into the dough to give it added texture and flavor. And for sweet dumplings with real panache, you can adopt the strategy demonstrated on these two pages. A special egg-rich dough is kneaded to silkiness, rolled thin and stamped into small rounds; fresh fruit is then sandwiched between pairs of rounds, and the edges of the dough are pinched together to hold the dumplings sealed while they poach.

Small pitted fruits—cherries, apricots or the plums used here—are especially appropriate for filled dumplings: The pit can be removed and the center of the fruit packed with a small whole nut such as an almond or macadamia, chopped nuts or raisins, or a blend of sugar and ground spices. Berries or chunks of large fruits, such as tangelos or mangoes, could also be used if rolled in a coating of sugar and ground spices or nuts before being wrapped in dough.

The dough for any stuffed dumplings should be soft but not sticky, and firm enough to hold together during cooking. Flour, eggs and milk form a successful combination, with butter beaten into the eggs to add extra fat *(recipe, page 164)*.

Do not become alarmed if the egg-and-butter mixture looks curdled at first: This occurs because the fat in the egg yolks and butter cannot absorb the water in the egg whites. The curdled appearance will vanish when the mixture is added to flour.

To give the dough strength and make it elastic enough to be shaped easily, the gluten in the flour must be activated by considerable kneading—up to 10 minutes. However, for tender dumplings, the kneaded dough must then be set aside for at least half an hour to give the gluten time to relax.

1 Mixing eggs and butter. Remove the eggs and butter from the refrigerator an hour or so in advance and let them warm to room temperature. Then sift flour and salt together into a mixing bowl, and measure out the milk. Put the softened butter into a second bowl. Using a wooden spoon, beat the eggs, one at a time, into the butter.

2 Combining with flour. Pour the egg mixture into the flour and stir the ingredients together. Stir in the milk a little at a time, adding only enough to make a firm but pliable dough.

6 Poaching the dumplings. Bring salted water to a boil in a large pot. Gently drop in the dumplings, in batches of eight to 10. Reduce the heat and simmer, uncovered, for 10 to 12 minutes, or until the dumplings float to the surface. Use a slotted spoon to place the dumplings side by side on a cloth-lined tray to drain.

7 Garnishing. Chop walnuts into small pieces and sauté them in butter for one to two minutes, or until they are hot and crisp. Sprinkle the sautéed nuts over the dumplings. Then strew the rest of the cinnamon sugar over them.

3 **Kneading the dough.** Gather the dough into a ball and transfer it to a smooth surface. To knead the dough, push it away from you with the heel of your hand, then fold it back toward you, twisting it slightly. Continue for five to 10 minutes, or until the dough is smooth and satiny. Cover it and let it rest for at least 30 minutes.

4 **Cutting dough rounds.** Halve and pit plums. Dip the cut surfaces in lemon juice to prevent them from discoloring, and set the halves on a tray. Mix sugar and cinnamon in a small bowl; set it aside. On a floured surface, roll the dough to a thickness of ⅛ inch [3 mm.]. Stamp out rounds with a 3-inch [8-cm.] cookie cutter.

5 **Filling the rounds.** For each dumpling, first place a plum half, cut side up, on a dough round. Fill the cavity of the plum half with a little of the cinnamon sugar, then place another plum half on top and cover with a second dough round. Pinch the edges of the dough between your thumb and forefinger to give the dumpling a decorative seal.

8 **Serving the dumplings.** While they are still hot, transfer the dumplings to a serving dish *(above)*. You can serve them as they are *(right)* or, if you wish, present them accompanied by pouring custard *(pages 22-23)* or sour cream.

Tender Blueberries in Cream-cheese Pancakes

Unlike poaching, where the aim is to keep fruit intact, stewing is designed to cook fresh fruit until it begins to lose its shape and breaks down into a chunky-textured sauce—delightful on its own and also ideal for filling dessert crepes, as in this demonstration. Stewed rhubarb and applesauce are the paradigms, but prosaic. More adventurous stews can be based on everything from papayas and guavas to figs and such berries as the blueberries used here.

Small fruits may be left whole for stewing, large ones cut into chunks or sliced. Before the fruits are cooked, they should be stemmed, cored, pitted or peeled, according to their kind.

The fruits should be cooked in just enough liquid to keep them from scorching before they begin to release their own juices. As a rule of thumb, a ¼-inch [6-mm.] layer is adequate. Sugar syrup, because it provides liquid in which the sweetener is already dispersed, is the ideal base. For a more intensely flavored stew, the syrup can be enriched with fruit juice or, as here, puréed fruit, and it can be spiced with nutmeg, allspice or cinnamon, or slivers of lemon peel.

How long the stew cooks depends on the fruit. Berries begin to burst their skins in a matter of minutes. Rhubarb, at the other extreme, may need to stew for 25 minutes. In either case, tenderness signals that the fruit is done; this is best established by sampling the stew.

The crepes that enclose the stew must also be tender. In this demonstration, the crepes are given extra smoothness and a special fluffy quality by using cream cheese as the base for the batter. Nonetheless, once the flour is added, the batter must be stirred gingerly lest overworking toughen the flour's gluten. The finished batter must then be allowed to rest for at least half an hour to give the gluten time to relax.

1 **Stewing.** Stem blueberries and purée a quarter of them *(page 20)*. Prepare a medium sugar syrup *(recipe, page 162)*. Stir in the purée, grated orange peel and cinnamon, and bring to a simmer over low heat. Add the berries and stew them until they begin to burst—about two minutes. Set the berries aside to steep in their syrup.

2 **Preparing crepe batter.** Beat softened cream cheese until it is fluffy; stir in salt and sugar. Add heavy cream and beat the mixture until it is soft. Stir in beaten eggs a little at a time. Add flour and flavoring—in this instance, brandy—and blend just until the batter is smooth. Then allow the batter to rest for about 30 minutes.

5 **Filling the crepes.** Gently reheat the stewed blueberries. Place a finished crepe, pale side up, on a serving plate, and spoon a generous measure of berries in a thick line across the center of the crepe *(above, left)*. Fold one edge of the crepe so that it covers some of the filling *(right)*, then bring up the opposite edge. The two edges should overlap slightly in the middle.

3 **Forming crepes.** Wipe a crepe pan with a cloth moistened with oil or butter. Set the pan over medium heat. When a light haze forms above the pan, ladle in a small amount of batter. If the pan is the correct temperature, the batter will sizzle as it touches the metal. At once, spread the batter as thin as possible by tilting and rolling the pan *(above)*. Cook the crepe until the upper surface looks dry: This should take about 30 seconds.

4 **Turning the crepe.** Free the edges of the crepe by sliding a narrow-bladed spatula around the sides of the pan. The edges will be cool enough to touch: Pick up one side with your fingers and flip the crepe over. The second side will cook in eight to 10 seconds and will be paler. Stack the finished crepes on a warmed plate.

6 **Serving the crepe.** Carefully turn the filled crepe over: The overlapped edges will now rest on the plate. Spoon some more blueberries and syrup over the top of the crepe and serve the crepe with a spoonful of whipped cream or, if you like, sour cream.

A Steamed Fig Pudding

Hearty steamed puddings of dried fruits incorporated into a thick, rich batter are favorite English fare. Christmas pudding—abounding in a variety of dried and candied fruits—is perhaps the best known; the dried-fig pudding shown at right is a simpler version *(recipe, page 151)*. Here, the pudding is based on golden Calimyrna figs, but black Mission figs could be used to give the pudding a deeper brown color. Other alternatives are dried dates, apricots, currants, raisins, apples or pears—alone or in combination with such tangy flavorings as candied lemon peel and ginger.

The batter for a steamed fruit pudding contains flour or bread crumbs for bulk, baking powder for leavening, eggs for binding, milk or spirits for moistening, sugar and fat—usually grated suet. Suet is the hard, white fat that surrounds beef kidneys; it is available fresh from the butcher. Pick the suet clean of membranes and fibers before grating it.

Classically, the pudding is molded and steamed in a glazed porcelain basin (or bowl) with a pronounced indentation under the rim to anchor the string used to tie down a protective cloth cover *(Step 6)*. A metal or ceramic mold or other heatproof bowl could be substituted. Butter the inside of the basin or other mold generously so that the pudding will unmold cleanly. To make doubly sure, line the bottom of the basin with parchment paper *(Step 4)* or, if you prefer, with a layer of jam or molasses.

For steaming, the basin is set on a trivet in a pot with the bottom two thirds of the basin submerged in steadily simmering water. Some steam will penetrate the cloth cover, plumping the dried fruit and helping the pudding to rise slightly. Although the pudding will be ready to eat after an hour or so, its flavors will blend more completely with longer cooking. During steaming, keep the water at the two-thirds level by pouring in more boiling water as necessary.

Pouring custard *(pages 22 and 23)* provides a contrast for the dense texture of a steamed fruit pudding; fresh heavy cream—either whipped or plain—or a tart cream *(recipe, page 162)* are good alternatives.

1 **Preparing the figs.** Wipe the dried fruit—here, golden Calimyrna figs—with dampened paper towels. Pinch the plump base of each fig to expose the woody stem at the top. Break off the stem and discard it.

2 **Chopping the figs.** Using a sharp knife, cut the figs into strips about ½ inch [1 cm.] wide. Gather the strips together with one hand and slice across them to produce roughly square pieces.

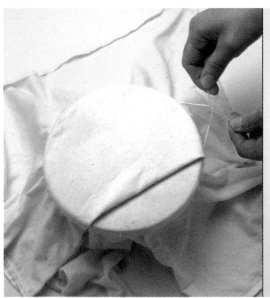

6 **Sealing the pudding.** Flour a dampened cloth and place it floured side down over the pudding mixture. Pleat the cloth to allow room for the pudding to expand, then secure the cloth by tying a string beneath the rim of the basin *(above, left)*. Bring two opposite corners of cloth over the basin and tie them together *(right)*. Tie the other two corners over the first knot, forming a convenient lifting handle for the basin.

3 **Assembling ingredients.** Place the figs in a large mixing bowl. Add sifted flour, baking powder, salt, superfine sugar, bread crumbs, a pinch of nutmeg and finely grated suet. Mix the ingredients well and add beaten egg diluted with milk. If the mixture is very stiff, gradually add more milk—a little at a time—to moisten it.

4 **Greasing the pudding basin.** Use your finger tips to rub the inside of a pudding basin liberally with softened butter. To make the pudding easier to unmold, cut a disk of parchment paper to fit the bottom of the basin, set the paper in place, and butter the paper.

5 **Filling the basin.** Use a spoon to transfer the pudding mixture to the basin. Since the fig pudding will rise only slightly during cooking, you can fill the basin to the rim. Smooth the surface so the bottom of the pudding will be flat.

7 **Steaming and serving.** Place the basin on a trivet in a pot of simmering water *(above)*. The water should submerge two thirds of the basin. Cover the pot and steam the pudding for two and one half hours. Lift out the basin and remove the cloth. Unmold the pudding onto a warmed plate. Serve it at once.

3
Frying
Sizzling Fruits to Enhance Delicate Flavors

Simple sautés and sauces
Sealing in natural sugars
Controlled deep frying
Two tactics for fruit fritters

Frying—whether sautéing in a shallow layer of oil or fat or deep frying in a 2- to 3-inch [5- to 8-cm.] layer—can intensify the sweetness of fruit while endowing even firm varieties with melting tenderness. However, frying depends for its effects on temperatures as high as 375° F. [190° C.], and fruits must be coddled protectively if they are to be cooked with success in such heat.

In a sauté, small fruits or pieces of fruit are fried briefly in just enough fat—butter is the usual choice—to film the fruit and prevent it from touching the pan directly and sticking to the metal. Depending on the delicacy of the fruit, it may be handled gently or with a certain vigor; the term "sauté" comes from the French word meaning "to jump"—and may be interpreted quite literally with firm-fleshed specimens such as the apples shown at left.

The whole sautéing process, in any case, is executed with speed so that the fruit tends to maintain not only its color, but even its texture and shape *(pages 52-53)*. As an additional boon, any juices or bits of fruit that do collect in the pan during sautéing can be retrieved and used as the starting point for a variety of complementary sauces based on fruit juices, table or fortified wines, spirits or—most lusciously—cream.

For deep frying, fruit requires a starchy coating to shield it from the searing heat of the cooking medium—generally peanut or corn oil, which are bland enough to be unobtrusive and can be heated to high temperatures without burning. When the coating is a batter of flour and eggs, it forms crisp crusts around sizable chunks of fruit—fritters. The Chinese, who spare no pains to make the most of every kind of foodstuff, substitute a water-chestnut flour for wheat flour and encase each fritter in a glittery sesame-seed-and-caramel shell *(pages 54-55)*.

The most elegant of deep-fried fruits, nonetheless, are souffléed fritters—a French concoction incorporating small pieces of fruit in chou paste, the kind of dough from which cream puffs are made. Like batter, chou paste is composed of the simplest kitchen staples: flour, water, butter and eggs. But the paste is cooked twice—once when its ingredients are being mixed and again when the paste is being deep fried. During the second cooking, the moisture in the paste turns to steam, expanding the fritter and puffing it up like an airy soufflé.

Tossed into the air to turn them, sugar-coated apple slices sauté in clarified butter until the sugar caramelizes to a golden brown. After the apples are done, the concentrated juices and caramel left in the pan will be deglazed with cream to make a sauce for the fruit.

Three Variations on the Sautéed Fruit Dessert

Sautéing is a simple way to cook fruit, and with little extra investment of effort, it will also provide the makings for a sauce. A sauté calls for a thin layer of sizzling oil or fat that will quickly fry the fruit to bring out its flavor. Butter, being mild tasting, is the choicest cooking medium. Because sautéing requires fairly high heat, the butter cooks best if clarified—that is, melted and decanted to produce a pure fat resistant to burning.

The frying process itself can be modified to accommodate the fruit at hand. For a subtle effect, delicate fruits may be merely warmed through without turning *(right, top)*. Firm fruits, however, can benefit from longer cooking and can be tossed about vigorously in the pan *(right, bottom)*.

Whatever the fruit, its sweetness can be intensified with white or brown sugar and accented with a few drops of lemon juice or a dash of ground spice: ginger, cinnamon, mace, nutmeg, cloves or allspice. When a sprinkling of sugar is melted in the butter before the fruit is added, the sugar will caramelize slightly as the fruit cooks. However, when sugar is used lavishly to coat the fruit pieces before sautéing begins, it forms a kind of caramel shell around each piece. Because sugar may require 10 minutes or so to caramelize, this technique is best suited to fruits that can be sautéed for long periods without collapsing.

A multiplicity of delectable sauces can be produced by deglazing the sauté pan with fruit juice, cream, wine, liqueur, rum or brandy. Here, passion-fruit pulp and Sauternes create a sweet sauce for papayas, mangoes and kiwi fruits. Brandy—ignited to burn off its harsh alcohol taste—perfumes peaches and sauces them; cream combines with caramel in a candy-like sauce for apples.

As varied as the list of sautéed fruit concoctions might be, one general rule applies to their creation: Always sauté fruit pieces in a single layer that covers the bottom of the pan. Overlapping fruit will steam, rather than fry, because of the moisture trapped between the pieces; in areas left bare, butter may burn.

A Mixed Sauté of Tropical Fruits

1 **Preparing the fruits.** Peel kiwi fruits and slice them. Peel and slice mangoes *(page 9)*. Cut strawberries into tulip shapes by slashing the tip of each unhulled berry into six segments. Peel, halve and seed papayas *(page 19)*, then cut the flesh into triangles. Finally, scoop passion-fruit pulp into a bowl *(page 19)* and set it aside.

2 **Sautéing the fruit.** Melt butter, preferably clarified butter, in a skillet over medium heat. Place a batch of the fruits in the pan in a single layer and heat them for one or two minutes, shaking the pan gently. When the fruits are heated through, transfer them to a warmed plate and cover them with foil while you sauté the remaining fruits.

Sweetened Peaches in Flaming Spirits

1 **Cooking the fruit.** Peel, pit and slice peaches. In a shallow pan, heat clarified butter over medium-high heat. Add sugar and stir until it melts. Then add a single layer of peach slices; shake the pan gently and turn the fruit with a wooden spatula until the peaches brown lightly on both sides— about five minutes.

2 **Flaming the fruit.** Warm several ounces of brandy and pour it over the peaches. Using a long match, ignite the brandy, then shake the pan to distribute the flaming liquid evenly over the fruit pieces. When the flames die down, spoon the fruit and sauce into individual serving dishes.

3 **Making the sauce.** When all the fruits have been sautéed, pour a generous splash of wine—here, Sauternes—into the pan. Stir the liquid briskly with a wooden spatula to dissolve any coagulated fruit juices in the wine. When the liquid reduces slightly, add the passion-fruit pulp; stir until the sauce is heated through.

4 **Serving.** Arrange the fruit pieces on individual serving plates, garnishing each arrangement with a strawberry. Spoon sauce over the fruits. If you like, garnish the dessert with sweet herb leaves or other edible leaves; here, strawberry leaves are added.

Caramelized Apples Cloaked in Cream

1 **Sautéing the fruit.** Peel, core and slice apples; put the fruit in a large bowl. Add sugar, and toss the apples with your hands until the slices are coated evenly. Heat clarified butter in a skillet over medium-high heat, then add the fruit slices to the pan.

2 **Making a sauce.** Sauté the apples for about 15 minutes, turning them occasionally until they soften and are caramelized. Transfer them to a plate. Pour heavy cream into the pan. Stirring briskly, dissolve the caramel.

3 **Reheating the fruit.** Stirring constantly, cook the cream sauce until it thickens—about 10 minutes. Then return the apples to the pan. Reduce the heat and stir the mixture until the fruit is warmed through and evenly coated— about two minutes. Serve at once.

Deep-fried Fritters in Crisp Caramel Jackets

Dunking fruits in batter and deep frying them quickly in oil yields fritters, golden and crispy on the outside, sweet and succulent on the inside. Because the batter coating affords ample protection against the searing heat of the cooking oil, all but the softest of fruits can be successfully fried by this method.

The formulas for batter are as diverse as the kinds of fruit they envelop, but most are based on flour or some other starch, bound with eggs. The starch used in this demonstration of Chinese-style fruit fritters *(recipe, page 90)* is water-chestnut powder, obtainable from Asian grocers. With its fine texture and mild taste, the water-chestnut powder yields a batter that is ready for use as soon as it is assembled. If the batter contains wheat flour, it must rest for at least 30 minutes so that the gluten in the flour can relax. Otherwise, the batter may be too elastic to adhere well to the fruit.

Although fritters are delectable served straight from the frying pan, the ones shown here are given an extra crunchiness by being enveloped in a thin layer of caramel flecked with sesame seeds.

Any oil that is relatively flavorless and will not, therefore, affect the taste of the fruit is suitable for the fritters: corn, safflower or the peanut oil used here. A wok, because of its sloped sides, spreads a minimum volume of oil over a maximum surface area. But any pot or pan can be substituted, providing it is deep enough to hold a 3-inch [8-cm.] layer of oil when no more than half-full.

To ensure that the fritters will be crisp, the temperature of the oil must remain at 375° F. [190° C.]—hot enough to make a drop of batter sizzle instantly when the temperature of the oil is tested. Keeping the oil at a constant temperature requires that the fritters be cooked in small batches that float freely. If the pan were to be overcrowded, the temperature of the oil would drop and the fritters would cook more slowly, thus absorbing oil and becoming soggy.

1 **Mixing the batter.** In a large bowl, whisk eggs until they begin to froth. Sift water-chestnut powder into a small bowl, then whisk it all at once into the eggs. When the batter is thoroughly blended, set it aside.

2 **Preparing the fruits.** Peel, halve and core pears *(page 7)*, then cut each half into six pieces. To prevent the fruit from discoloring, add the pieces to the batter as you cut them. Peel bananas and cut them into chunks that are roughly equal in size to the pear pieces. Then gently stir all of the fruit in the batter, coating each piece evenly.

4 **Making the caramel.** Combine sugar and oil in a heavy saucepan set over medium-high heat. With a wooden spoon, stir the mixture frequently, scooping the melting sugar from the pan bottom *(above, left)*. When the sugar has melted to become a light brown caramel *(right)*, stir in sesame seeds. Immediately remove the pan from the heat and set it in ice water for a few moments to arrest the cooking. Put the pan on a trivet.

3 **Deep frying.** Heat about 3 inches [8 cm.] of oil in a wok set over high heat until a drop of batter sizzles instantly on contact with the oil. Using tongs, add batter-coated fruit pieces one at a time; keep each batch small. Turn the fritters once or twice so that they fry evenly. When the fritters are golden brown, lift them from the oil with a wire skimmer. Drain them briefly on paper towels, then set them on the rack. When all the fritters are done, set the rack in a 250° F. [120° C.] oven.

5 **Coating the fritters.** Remove the rack of fritters from the oven and set it over a tray. Fill a bowl with ice cubes and a little water. Using chopsticks or tongs, transfer the fritters a few at a time to the caramel; turn them until they are coated evenly. Remove each fritter from the caramel and immediately drop it into the ice water; the caramel will harden instantly. Set the coated fritters back on the rack to drain.

6 **Serving the fritters.** When all of the fritters have been coated with caramel and have finished draining, transfer them from the rack to a platter. Serve the fritters immediately, while they are still warm inside.

Fried Puffs of Fruit-filled Chou Paste

The special fritters known in France as *beignets soufflés* are more substantial than batter-coated fritters *(pages 54-55),* yet even more puffed and crisp. Instead of being made with large fruit chunks, souffléed fritters start with morsels of chopped or diced fruit that can be amalgamated into chou paste—a thick, soft dough cohesive enough to be shaped into fritters with a pair of spoons *(recipe, page 165).* In the sizzling hot oil of deep frying, the bits of fruit cook through as the fritters brown and expand to nearly twice their original size.

Chou paste owes its remarkable puffing capacity both to the way its ingredients are combined and to the way they are finally cooked. In the mixing process, flour is stirred into boiling water and butter; after the blend is heated through, eggs are added to turn the mixture into a rich paste. When the paste is then deep fried, the water within turns to steam, and the paste itself—made resilient by the proteins of the eggs it contains—swells outward to form a crisp and golden globe.

Controlling these reactions requires care and attention. To begin with, the butter and water must be brought to a boil quickly, and the flour must be added immediately, before too much water can evaporate (the water is needed to produce steam for puffing). Once the butter, water and flour mixture has formed a paste, it must be cooled slightly before the eggs are added; otherwise the eggs may coagulate before they can be incorporated.

During the frying, the temperature of the cooking oil must be maintained at 375° F. [190° C.]. If the temperature falls too low, the fritters will take too long to cook and will absorb excess oil in the process; if the temperature rises too high, they will burn on the outside before they can cook through. A frying thermometer clipped to the side of the pan, as shown here, is the most reliable method for measuring oil temperature, but you can also test the oil by dropping in batter as described on page 55, Step 3.

Beyond these basic caveats, souffléed fritters encourage the cook to experiment with a wide range of ingredients. In this demonstration the fritters contain raw apricots, but almost any fruit, raw or dried, is well suited so long as it is not overripe or mushy. To add flavor, the diced fruit can be macerated ahead of time in spirits of some sort, providing it is drained scrupulously before it is added to the paste. Alternatively, the paste may be flavored with a splash of liqueur, rum, bourbon, brandy or vanilla extract. The raspberry purée illustrated on these two pages makes a sweet accompaniment for apricot *beignets;* a pouring custard or a sabayon *(pages 22-23)* offer richer alternatives.

1 **Preparing the fruit.** Peel, halve and pit apricots as shown for peaches on page 9. Slice each apricot half lengthwise into strips, then cut the strips crosswise into dice. Place the fruit in a bowl; sprinkle a light coating of sugar over each handful of dice.

2 **Starting the chou paste.** Sift flour and salt together onto a piece of parchment paper. Cut the butter into cubes, then combine it with water in a heavy saucepan set over high heat. When the butter melts and the mixture boils, add all of the dry ingredients and stir vigorously with a wooden spoon until the mixture forms a uniform mass that draws away from the pan sides. Remove the pan from the heat.

3 **Incorporating eggs.** Cool the flour mixture for a minute or two. Next, to prevent eggshell from falling into the paste, break the first egg into a small bowl and then add the egg to the saucepan. Beat the mixture vigorously until it becomes smooth. Add each egg in the same manner, beating until the paste is smooth and shiny.

4 **Frying.** Using a perforated spoon, add the fruit to the paste and stir until the fruit is evenly incorporated *(above)*. Fill a deep, heavy pan half-full with oil and heat it to 375° F. [190° C.]. Scoop up a spoonful of the paste mixture and, with a second spoon, push it into the oil *(right)*. When the fritters are crisp and golden—after about six minutes — transfer them to paper towels to drain.

5 **Serving.** When all the fritters have been fried and drained, mound them on a serving platter and dust them with confectioners' sugar. Serve the fritters immediately, accompanied by the sauce of your choice—here, a raspberry purée sweetened with a little sugar and flavored with a splash of kirsch.

4

Baking and Broiling
Traditional Methods
for Diverse Delights

The dry, all-enveloping heat of the oven draws out natural juices from food even as it tenderizes and browns. For this reason, achieving success with baked fruits depends first on safeguarding them from dehydration.

The simplest method of preserving the natural juices of fruits while they bake for prolonged periods is—logically enough—to coat them with liquid: sugar syrup, wine or spirits, or some combination of these elements *(pages 60-61)*. If the fruit has a compact texture, even a small amount of liquid will suffice to keep it succulent.

Pastry dough offers another kind of shield for use in baking and, as a bonus, it contributes a textural contrast to the finished dish. For firm whole fruits, such as apples or pears, the kind of rich short-crust dough familiar in pie crusts can be cut and molded into golden parcels that will help to keep the fruit in shape *(pages 62-63)*. Soft fruits, such as plums or blueberries, and cut-up firm fruits, including rhubarb and apples, can be layered in a baking dish and blanketed with a mixture of flour, rolled oats, sugar and butter that will blend and become crisp in the oven. Alternatively, the assembly can be covered by rounds of shortcake dough, producing a lid that looks remarkably like cobblestone paving—which may explain why the dessert is sometimes called a cobbler *(pages 64-65)*.

Instead of just topping the fruit, a delicate egg-rich batter *(pages 66-67)* can enclose it entirely to yield a moist pudding. Any soft fruit will do, with small ones usable whole and large ones chopped or sliced; dried fruits are as suitable as fresh ones, providing they have been macerated. Even more delicate and dramatic than a baked pudding is a soufflé that enfolds fruit in pastry cream lightened with egg whites *(pages 68-69)*.

Broiling, too, is applicable to fruit, although the heat of this cooking method is so intense that it can serve only in a finishing role. If the fruit is topped with cream or custard and broiled for a brief period, the dish will take on a tawny cast that adds an extra touch of temptation.

The broiler, too, can be an aid in the art of fruit cookery. The intensity of the broiler's heat will enhance the flavors of even the most delicate fruits, so long as they are protected by a moist, rich topping of cream or custard. Applied at the last possible moment before the fruit is served, the topping is broiled just long enough to color its surface without heating, much less cooking or drying, the fruit beneath *(pages 70-71)*.

An apple baked in a pastry wrapper is moistened with a generous splash of heavy cream. The apple has been cored and its cavity filled with sugar and spices; baking softens the fruit and crisps the outer covering.

Simple Baking for Sturdy Fruits

Many fruits fare well in the oven, baked whole or halved, with nothing more than a smattering of liquid to protect them from the oven's dry heat. A compact texture—soft or hard—is the only requisite. The starchy pulp of a banana, for example, withstands the heat without losing its shape *(top demonstration; recipe, page 143)*. So does the firm flesh of the pear *(bottom demonstration; recipe, page 99)*. Other sturdy fruits that can hold their own uncovered in the oven include apples, peaches, plums, papayas, mangoes and pineapples.

Preparing a fruit for baking generally involves peeling it and halving it to remove its core, pit or seeds; fruits that discolor rapidly should be rubbed with lemon juice. However, apples and pears may be cored without being halved and baked without peeling, providing the skins are scored to prevent them from splitting.

If the fruits have natural cavities for seeds or pits, the emptied cavities can be enlarged slightly, if necessary, and packed with any of a wide variety of fillings. The pears shown here contain a nut mixture, but many solid ingredients—dried fruit, cookies or macaroons, for example—crushed and bound with egg or butter into a soft paste will complement the flavor of the fruit.

The cooking liquid may also be chosen to suit the tastes of the cook. Wine makes a thin, flavorful juice to moisten pears; melted butter moistens well, too, and it enriches delicate fruit flavors. Sugar syrup flavored with fruit juice and liqueur makes a thicker, more elaborate sauce for bananas. No matter what the liquid, however, it is important to baste with it periodically to keep the cooking fruit from drying out.

For ease in basting and serving, always bake fruit in shallow containers. Avoid aluminum pans; the metal may react with the acids in the fruit or with the wine used for basting. Serve baked fruit hot or cold, accompanied by the liquid in which it has cooked, or topped with cream, pouring custard *(pages 22-23)* or tart cream *(recipe, page 162)*.

Bananas Baked with a Hint of Rum

1 **Peeling and slicing bananas.** Cut fresh dates in half, remove the pits and slice the flesh lengthwise into julienne. Peel bananas—in this case, red bananas—and halve them lengthwise. Arrange the halves, cut side down, in a single layer in a baking dish, and scatter the date julienne over the bananas.

2 **Moistening the fruit.** Melt butter in a small saucepan over medium heat, then stir in orange juice, brown sugar and rum. Cook the mixture until the sugar has dissolved completely. Pour this syrup over the bananas.

Nut-filled Pears Baked in Wine

1 **Preparing the fruit.** Peel, halve and core pears *(page 17)*. Enlarge each cavity enough to hold 2 to 3 tablespoons [30 to 45 ml.] of filling; reserve these trimmings. Rub the pears with lemon juice and set them, cavities upward, in a baking dish.

2 **Making the filling.** In a mortar, crush the pear trimmings with a pestle to form a coarse purée. Pound in sugar and chopped nuts, add an egg to bind the mixture and continue pounding until the ingredients blend thoroughly.

3 **Garnishing.** Drain and crack a coconut, remove the meat from the shell and peel away its brown skin *(page 29, top demonstration, Steps 3 and 4)*. Holding a piece of coconut over the bananas, use a vegetable peeler to shave the coconut meat into thin strips. Scatter pecans over the fruits.

4 **Baking and serving the fruits.** Bake the bananas in a preheated 375° F. [190° C.] oven for 20 minutes, basting them occasionally to keep them moist. Test the cooked bananas by piercing them with the tip of a knife—they should feel soft; the liquid in the baking dish should be syrupy. Serve the bananas warm with their syrup, or accompanied by sour, tart or whipped cream.

3 **Stuffing the pears.** Spoon filling into each pear cavity so that the nut mixture is level with the cut surface of the fruit; do not overstuff the pears lest the filling overflow during cooking. Sprinkle sugar over the pears, then drizzle wine onto them.

4 **Baking and serving.** Basting occasionally *(above)*, bake the pears in a preheated 400° F. [200° C.] oven until they feel tender when pierced with a knife tip—about 40 minutes. If the filling browns before the pears are done, cover them with foil. Serve the pears warm, accompanied by pouring custard *(inset)*.

Whole Fruits Wrapped in Pastry

The firm flesh of apples and pears makes them ideal for baking whole, and they are particularly delicious when stuffed with a sweet filling and enveloped in pastry. The pastry protects the fruit during cooking, and the sweetness of the filling complements the fruit's natural tartness.

To ensure crisp pastry and to prevent the fruit's flesh from becoming so soft it loses its shape, select the firmest and least juicy varieties—Comice or Bosc pears, for example, and Rome Beauty or Golden Delicious apples. In this demonstration, apples are filled with a mixture of softened butter, sugar and cinnamon *(recipe, page 92)*. A mixture of crumbled macaroons moistened with brandy or a combination of ground nuts with honey, plum or quince jam make equally good fillings for the fruit.

For the pastry, you can use any pie dough; here, rich short-crust dough *(recipe, page 164)* wraps the fruit in tender cookie-like crusts. Because the dough includes eggs and a high proportion of butter, it should be prepared in advance and refrigerated for at least two hours to make it easier to roll out.

While the dough is resting, prepare the filling and core the fruit with an apple corer. With pears, you may choose, for the sake of appearance, to core the fruit from the bottom and leave the top third of the core and all of the stem intact. Both pears and apples may be left unpeeled, if you prefer. When using unpeeled fruit, it is important to score the skin around the center to prevent it from splitting when the fruit is in the oven.

The shape of the fruit determines how you will slice the dough. Squares are more easily wrapped around pears; circles work best for apples. In either case, make sure that the pieces of dough are large enough to envelop the fruit completely. If in doubt, cut a larger piece than you think you need and trim off the excess dough after you have molded it around the fruit.

A light glaze of beaten egg, milk or cream will give the pastry case a shiny, golden crust. If you like, you can sprinkle a little cinnamon sugar over the wrapped fruit before baking, or sprinkle sugar over the pastry just before serving.

1 **Combining the ingredients.** Sift flour, sugar and salt into a mound on a cool work surface—marble is ideal. Make a well in the center and put softened butter and eggs into it. Use the fingers of one hand to pinch together the ingredients in the well *(above, left)*. When they are lightly blended, draw in the flour mixture from the edges of the mound and mix all the ingredients together *(right)*.

5 **Cutting circlets.** Sprinkle the circles of dough with flour to prevent them from sticking together, and put them to one side. Gather the scraps of dough together and roll them again. With a fluted cookie cutter, stamp out a circlet of dough to cap each apple.

6 **Filling the apples.** With the tip of a knife, score the skin around the middle of each apple. Place an apple in the center of a dough circle and spoon filling into the cored center. Use a finger to push the filling down into the apple. Turn the apples upside down on the dough.

2 **Smoothing the dough.** Gather the dough together, adding a few drops of cold water, if necessary, to make the dough cohere. Using both hands, knead the dough gently until it is smooth. Wrap the dough in a cloth or in plastic wrap, and chill it for two hours.

3 **Preparing the filling.** Place softened butter, sugar and cinnamon in a mixing bowl. Using a wooden spoon, beat the ingredients together until they are blended into a smooth paste.

4 **Cutting the dough.** Wash and core apples (page 7). Roll the dough to a thickness of about 1/8 inch [3 mm.]. Using an inverted plate as a guide, cut out a large circle of dough for each apple with a sharp knife.

7 **Wrapping the apples.** Gather the dough around each apple into pleats, gently drawing the pleats upward. Press the edges of the pleats together to enclose the apple completely. Trim off excess dough and turn the apple over. One at a time, brush the dough circlets with water and place them, moistened side down, on top of the apples.

8 **Brushing with egg.** Place the apples on a baking sheet and brush them with beaten egg. Using a thin skewer, pierce the top of each apple to allow steam to escape from the central cavity during baking. Bake the apples in a preheated 400° F. [200° C.] oven until the pastry is golden brown—30 to 40 minutes.

9 **Serving the apples.** Remove the apples from the oven and sprinkle them with superfine sugar. Serve them either hot or cold, topped, if you like, with heavy cream or pouring custard (recipe, page 163).

Crisps and Cobblers: Fruits Baked under Cover

Crisps and cobblers are variations on the same motif: Both consist simply of a layer of fruit baked beneath a crust. Since the fruit need not hold its shape and the crust is not required to wrap or enfold it, the cook can experiment with a wide array of ingredients for both elements.

The crisp in the top demonstration here *(recipe, page 92)* is made from a single fruit, tart rhubarb, sweetened with brown sugar and orange juice. The cobbler shown below contains peaches and blueberries, lightly sugared and spiked with lemon juice. But almost any fruit or fruits—firm or soft, sweet or tart, fresh or dried—can be baked in either dish.

For easy serving and eating, the fruit should be peeled, pitted, stemmed and cored, then cut into bite-sized portions. Very juicy fruits, such as berries, should be tossed with a little flour or cornstarch before cooking to prevent them from becoming soupy. Dried fruits—including raisins and dates as well as prunes and apricots—must be plumped by presoak-ing and then baked with fresh fruits that will provide ample moisture.

Toppings for crisps all are coarse mixtures based on a combination of starch and sweetener moistened with butter. For the rhubarb crisp here, rolled oats and flour provide the starch; alternatives include whole-wheat flour, bread or cookie crumbs, shredded coconut, grated pecans or almonds, and even wheat germ. The sweetener might be white or brown sugar, honey or molasses.

The crust for a crisp is simply sprinkled over the fruit. The topping for a cobbler, on the other hand, is made of a cohesive batter or dough, which may be either spread evenly like the top crust of an old-fashioned deep-dish pie or—as shown here—cut into shapes and laid in an open pattern over the fruit.

Since crisps and cobblers are generally served from the baking dish, the container should be deep enough to hold a generous volume of fruit and attractive enough to bring to the table.

A Crust for Rhubarb

1 **Preparing rhubarb.** Trim off and discard the ends and the leaves of rhubarb, then cut the stalks into 1-inch [2½-cm.] pieces. Put the rhubarb in a bowl and add a mixture of light brown sugar, orange juice, cinnamon and nutmeg; toss the ingredients well.

A Cobbler of Mixed Fruits

1 **Preparing fruits.** Peel and pit peaches *(page 9)* and cut them into slices ½ inch [1 cm.] thick. Stem, rinse and drain blueberries. In a large bowl, toss the peaches with sugar, cornstarch and lemon juice. Add the blueberries to the peaches.

2 **Preparing the dough.** Make shortcake biscuit dough *(recipe, page 164)*. On a lightly floured work surface, roll the dough into a rectangle ¼ inch [6 mm.] thick. Using a pastry cutter—a round one is shown—cut out dough shapes. Cut the shapes as close together as possible.

3 **Assembling the cobbler.** Drain the peach-and-blueberry mixture and transfer it to a lightly buttered baking dish. Using a spatula, lay the dough shapes atop the fruit in any pattern you desire. Brush the tops of the dough shapes with cream, which will leave a light glaze when the cobbler is baked.

2 **Mixing the topping.** As butter melts in a small saucepan, put rolled oats, flour, light brown sugar, salt, cinnamon, cloves and grated orange peel in a large bowl, and toss the mixture well. Pour the melted butter over the mixture and, with a wooden spoon, stir until all the dry ingredients are moistened by the butter.

3 **Assembling the crisp.** Drain the rhubarb pieces and transfer them to a lightly buttered baking dish deep enough to leave about ¾ inch [2 cm.] above the fruit. Then sprinkle the topping mixture in an even layer over the rhubarb, covering the fruit completely.

4 **Baking and serving.** Bake the crisp in a preheated 350° F. [180° C.] oven for about 30 minutes, or until the rhubarb feels tender when pierced with the tip of a knife. Remove the crisp from the oven and serve it directly from the baking dish with any topping you wish—here, lightly whipped cream.

4 **Baking and serving the cobbler.** Bake the cobbler in a preheated 425° F. [220° C.] oven for about 20 minutes, or until the dough is lightly browned and the fruits feel tender when pierced with the tip of a knife. Remove the cobbler from the oven and serve it directly from the baking dish with any desired topping—at right, heavy cream.

Prunes and Raisins Enveloped in Batter

Bits of fruit sheathed in the kind of batter used for crepes and baked in a shallow dish produce a hearty pudding liberally studded with juicy morsels. The method suits almost any fruit, fresh or dried.

In the demonstration at right *(recipe, page 156),* dried prunes and raisins are used. Dried apricots or peaches would work just as well. So, too, would such fresh fruits as pitted cherries; peeled, cored and chopped apples or pears; and pitted and chopped plums or nectarines.

Macerating the fruit ahead of time in rum, brandy or a fruit liqueur will add extra flavor. Fresh fruits should be first sprinkled with sugar, which will help to draw out their juices, then drenched with spirits. Macerate them at room temperature for an hour or so.

Dried fruits need no sugaring but take longer to absorb liquid; they should be left to steep all day. Drain the fruits well before adding them to the batter, and reserve any extra liquid to sprinkle over the mixture just before baking it.

The pudding should be baked in a dish made of porcelain, cast-iron or earthenware—materials that will absorb heat slowly but conduct it evenly, averting any danger that the batter might brown too fast. During baking, the pudding will rise markedly above the rim of the dish. Appealing as this effect may be visually, the pudding will taste best after it has had a chance to settle slightly and has cooled to lukewarm.

Delicious when served plain, as shown here, the pudding might also be topped with heavy cream, tart cream *(recipe, page 162),* pouring custard or sabayon *(pages 22-23).*

1 **Preparing the raisins.** To soften and plump the raisins, put them in a pan, cover them with cold water and set the pan over medium heat. Bring the water to a boil and immediately take the pan off the heat. Let the raisins soak in the water for 10 minutes, then drain them through a sieve set over a bowl.

2 **Macerating the fruits.** Halve dried prunes and remove the pits *(page 42, Step 3).* Place the prunes and raisins in a jar with a tight-fitting lid to prevent evaporation. Pour in brandy, close the jar securely and steep the fruit for at least six hours. From time to time, shake the jar and turn it over to make sure every fruit piece soaks up some liquid.

6 **Adding the fruits.** Drain the macerated prunes and raisins, and reserve any liquid remaining in the jar. Add the fruits to the pudding batter and stir the mixture with a wooden spoon to coat the fruit pieces evenly.

7 **Ladling in the batter.** Ladle the batter into a shallow, liberally buttered baking dish, making sure the fruits remain evenly distributed throughout the batter. Drizzle the reserved macerating liquid, if any, over the batter

3 **Beating the eggs.** Measure flour into a sieve set on a plate. Break eggs into a large mixing bowl; add sugar and a pinch of salt to the eggs. Beat the mixture with a whisk until the ingredients are thoroughly combined.

4 **Sifting in flour.** Still beating with the whisk, sift the flour, a little at a time, into the mixture in the bowl. Continue to beat the mixture until it is smooth and completely free of lumps.

5 **Stirring in milk.** Combine milk with vanilla extract. Stirring with the whisk, pour the milk mixture into the bowl. Continue stirring until the batter is smooth and has the consistency of cream.

8 **Serving.** Bake the pudding in a preheated 375° F. [190° C.] oven for 20 minutes, until the batter has risen uniformly and a thin skewer inserted in the center comes out clean. Let the pudding cool until it is tepid—about 15 minutes. Serve the pudding directly from the baking dish.

Soufflés: Puffed Fruit Concoctions

Delicate fruit flavors gain richness and allure when blended into airy-textured soufflés. A soufflé (the name is derived from the French word meaning "to puff up") is essentially a sauce lightened with beaten egg whites; in the oven, the egg whites inflate to give the soufflé its celebrated lightness.

At its simplest, the sauce base for the soufflé may be no more than a sweetened fruit purée. Blueberries provide such a base in the demonstration at right *(recipe, page 122)*. A more substantial dessert can be made by using pastry cream as the soufflé base and flavoring it with chopped fresh or candied fruit, fruit purée or grated citrus peel. In the classic soufflé shown below *(recipe, page 135)*, grated orange peel is an integral part of the pastry cream, and orange liqueur heightens the effect of the fruit.

Although soufflés have a reputation for being difficult to cook, they present few problems so long as the egg whites

are beaten properly and are incorporated correctly. Whatever the soufflé base, the whites are ready when they glisten and stand in stiff peaks.

For a soufflé based on a fruit purée, the process is simple: The purée is beaten directly into the egg whites. When the base is heavier—a pastry cream, for example—some of the whites are folded into the base to lighten it, then the lightened base is added to the remaining whites and the ingredients blended until only just incorporated. It is better to have a few patches of white in the mixture than to deflate the egg whites by overmixing.

The orange-soufflé mixture shown at right is baked and presented in scooped-out orange shells, but it could just as easily be baked in a large soufflé dish or individual ramekins. The blueberry mixture is baked in a soufflé dish, outfitted in this case with a paper collar that supports the mixture as it rises and ensures that it forms a relatively even crown.

A Sweet Purée Soufflé

1 **Cooking fruit purée.** Stem blueberries, reserving a handful for garnish. Purée the remaining berries *(page 20)* and pour the purée into a heavy, nonreactive pan. Add sugar and lemon juice, and cook the purée over medium heat, stirring with a wooden spoon until the sugar dissolves.

Miniature Soufflés in Citrus Shells

1 **Grating peel.** Halve oranges and remove the flesh and lining *(page 28, top demonstration, Steps 1 and 2)*. Set the shells aside; reserve the flesh for another use. Simmer a vanilla bean in milk for two minutes; let the milk cool. Sift flour into a bowl. Combine egg yolks and sugar; grate the peel of an orange over them.

2 **Assembling the base.** Whisk the egg yolks, sugar and peel until the mixture is thick and creamy—about two minutes. Stir in the flour. Remove the vanilla bean, and add the milk to the egg-yolk mixture. Whisk until this soufflé base is smooth, then pour it into the pan in which the milk was heated.

3 **Adding the liqueur.** Simmer the mixture—whisking it constantly—for two minutes, or until it is thick. Remove the pan from the heat and whisk in several spoonfuls of orange liqueur—here, Grand Marnier is used. Allow the soufflé base to cool slightly.

2 **Assembling.** Tie a double layer of parchment paper around a soufflé dish to form a collar 2 inches [5 cm.] above the rim. Butter the dish and collar, then sugar them. Beat egg whites until stiff. Bring the purée to a boil and gradually beat it into the egg whites. Pour the mixture into the dish.

3 **Baking and serving.** With your finger, form a circular groove just inside the rim of the soufflé. Sprinkle the reserved berries into the groove. Bake at 375° F. [190° C.] until the soufflé puffs— 15 to 20 minutes. Remove the collar and serve the soufflé at once.

4 **Adding egg whites.** Beat egg whites until they are stiff; add sugar and whisk until they are glossy. Fold a quarter of the whites into the base to lighten it. Then fold the base into the remaining whites, gently lifting them from the bottom of the bowl to the top.

5 **Filling orange shells.** Place the orange shells on a baking sheet and spoon the soufflé mixture into them, using a second spoon to scrape the mixture from the first. Bake the soufflés in a preheated 400° F. [200° C.] oven for five minutes, or until they are puffed.

6 **Serving.** Remove the soufflés from the oven and quickly sprinkle the tops generously with confectioners' sugar. Return them to the oven and bake them for two minutes longer to brown the tops. Serve the soufflés immediately.

Fruits Broiled under Mellow Toppings

Sugar-coated cream and foamy sabayon become golden gratin toppings for fruit after just a few minutes of broiling. The fruit, insulated from the broiler's intense heat by the topping, remains cool. But the sugared cream caramelizes and the custard browns and sets.

Gratins are easy to assemble, and any fruit is a candidate, from the glamorous papaya and mango to the everyday peach and pear. Larger dried fruits such as figs and apricots may be used on their own or as embellishments to fresh fruits, but they must first be plumped by soaking them for a couple of hours.

The fruit can be used raw or, for special effects, it can be macerated in brandy ahead of time or poached in sugar syrup or wine (pages 40-43). If the fruit is enriched by either of these methods, it must then be well drained and chilled before it is broiled.

The simplest topping of all is plain cream, light or heavy, sprinkled with granulated sugar. Tangy tart cream (recipe, page 162) or sour cream coated with brown sugar produces a more richly flavored gratin (top demonstration); so, too, does whisking a bit of nutmeg, cinnamon, brandy or liqueur into the cream.

The insulating effect of cream can be augmented, if desired, by placing the dish containing the dessert in a pan of cracked ice while it is under the broiler. An added advantage of the ice is that it keeps the dish cool to the touch, facilitating removal from the oven and eliminating the need for a trivet when the gratin is served.

A gratin that is made with fruit and sabayon (bottom demonstration) can be embellished with whole or chopped nuts, ground spices or, as here, candied fruit-peel julienne. This sabayon is made with Sauternes, but any sweet, fortified or sparkling wine would be suitable—from Marsala and sherry to Champagne and Asti spumante.

A Tangy Berry Gratin

1 Preparing fruits. Pick over and rinse raspberries—both red and black raspberries are used here. Layer the berries in a shallow baking dish—in this case, a gratin dish.

A Wine-Custard Cover for Mixed Fruits

1 Assembling fruits. Rinse raspberries and set them aside. Peel and segment an orange; peel a kiwi fruit and a mango and slice them into wedges. Arrange the fruit pieces attractively in individual gratin dishes set on a baking sheet (above, left). Halve, pit and slice a nectarine and add it to the fruit in the dishes (right).

2 Ladling on custard. In a large bowl, prepare sabayon with Sauternes. Use a ladle to distribute the custard over the fruit in the gratin dishes. Ladle in just enough custard to cover the fruit. Strew the raspberries over the custard.

2 **Topping the berries.** Whisk sour cream until it is soft and fluffy. Then spread the cream over the berries in an even layer about ½ inch [1 cm.] thick. Sprinkle a ¼-inch [6-mm.] layer of brown sugar—light brown sugar is used here—over the cream.

3 **Broiling the berries.** Place the dish in a baking pan filled with cracked ice. Immediately put the pan on a shelf approximately 4 inches [10 cm.] from the heat source of a preheated broiler. Broil the dessert until the sugar caramelizes—about four minutes.

4 **Serving.** Remove the dish from the pan of ice. Serve the gratin at once, while the raspberries are cool and the cream topping is warm.

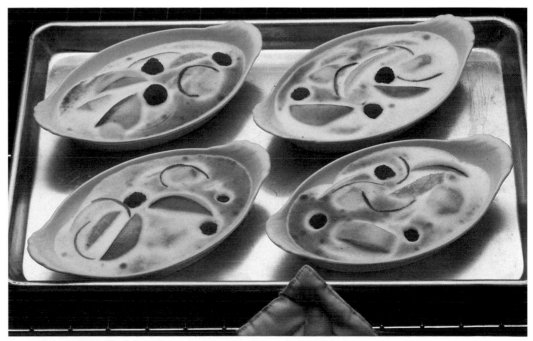

3 **Garnishing.** Cut orange peel into julienne. Pour crème de menthe into one small pot and grenadine into another; add half of the julienne to each pot, and cook over medium heat until the peel is slightly candied— about 10 minutes. Drain the julienne and scatter them over the sabayon.

4 **Gratinéing the fruit.** Place an oven shelf 6 inches [15 cm.] from the heat source and preheat the broiler. Broil the sabayon-topped fruits until they are lightly gratinéed—about one minute. Remove the gratins from the oven and serve them at once.

5

Molded and Frozen Desserts

From Simple Jellies to Opulent Assemblies

The many molded and frozen desserts featuring fruit span a gamut of culinary delights. The simplest of these is a cool jelly—fruit juice and gelatin blended to form a limpid showcase for exquisite small fruits *(opposite and pages 74-75)*. The most ambitious is baked Alaska, a seeming miracle of artifice in which meringue encases an assembly of fruit ice cream, poached fruit and cake.

Between the pristine jelly and the extravagant Alaska lies a wealth of options applicable to almost any single fruit or combination of fruits. Whipping egg whites with the fruit juice and gelatin of a basic jelly, for example, will yield a foamy dessert known as snow *(pages 76-77)*. Blending fruit juices or purées with eggs, milk and cream that have been nurtured into a custard will produce delicate puddings and mousses *(pages 76-79)*. When frozen with sugar syrup, fruit juices or purées become refreshing water ices *(pages 82-85)*; when churned with custard, fruits in any form yield mouth-watering ice creams *(pages 86-87)*.

Any of these preparations can be shaped in molds. As a rule, frozen ices and ice creams respond best to molding and unmolding in plain bowls and rings. Jellies or puddings, on the other hand, readily conform to the patterns of intricate molds, and the gelatin in these concoctions gives them enough solidity to hold their shape during unmolding. For refrigerator or freezer use, the molds may be glass, ceramic or nonreactive metal. Because metal conducts cold well, it speeds the setting process—an important consideration when assembling successive layers. Whatever the shape or material, always fill a mold to within ½ inch [1 cm.] of the rim: If the dessert has any farther to slide when unmolded, it will land on the plate with a thump that may damage it.

To ease unmolding, some cooks like to coat a mold lightly with sweet almond oil or a flavorless vegetable oil. The technique is best suited to opaque puddings or mousses; oil will dull the surface of clear jellies.

Oiled or not, a mold will release its contents most smoothly if the sides are first loosened by running a knife tip around the rim. Then the bottom of the mold can be dipped in warm—never hot—water before it is inverted onto a plate. Alternatively, the mold can be set upside down on a plate and wrapped briefly with a towel that has been well moistened in warm water and wrung dry: The dessert should slip out easily.

A mold containing peeled grapes and sliced strawberries suspended in alternating layers of orange and wine jelly is augmented by a ladleful of the orange liquid. More grapes and more wine jelly will complete the assembly, which will then be chilled until set and unmolded for serving.

A Shimmering Ring of Fruit and Jelly

A fresh-fruit jelly, made by combining fruit juice with unflavored gelatin, is a delectably light dessert that melts in the mouth. Yet the setting power of gelatin is such that the jelly can take on the shape of an ornate mold while keeping pieces of fruit suspended in an artful pattern.

Gelatin is commercially available in two forms—as a powder or in the thin sheets shown here. Ratios can be varied slightly, but as a rule you will need 4 sheets of leaf gelatin or 1 tablespoon [15 ml.] of powder to set each 2 cups [½ liter] of liquid. Whichever type you use, first soften the gelatin in just enough cool liquid to cover it, then dissolve it over low heat or in hot liquid before mixing it with cool ingredients.

In the multitiered aspic demonstrated at right *(recipe, page 166)*, gelatin is mixed with red wine as well as with orange juice to make two separate jellies that are then assembled in alternating layers containing sliced strawberries and peeled grapes. White, sparkling or a fortified wine such as sherry could replace the red wine. And any fruit that produces clear, brightly colored juice—berries, currants or pomegranates, for example—would make a good substitute for the oranges. For a gleaming jelly, the juice is strained through cloth to trap bits of pulp and fiber.

Fruits to be suspended in jelly should be firm enough to retain their shape; in addition to the grapes and strawberries used here, citrus-fruit segments, peach and banana slices or melon cubes are good candidates for this treatment. Do not use raw pineapple, papaya, kiwi, prickly pear or fig. These fruits contain protease enzymes that destroy the protein in gelatin and keep it from setting.

To prevent the fruits from being dislodged when successive layers are added, each piece is dipped in partially set jelly before it is positioned in the mold. Before starting, pat sliced or peeled pieces of fruit dry so that excess juices will not retard the setting of the jelly. And chill them well—warm bits of fruit can soften already-firm jelly.

1 Softening the gelatin. Soak gelatin in cold water until it is soft—10 to 30 minutes for the leaf gelatin shown here. Prepare medium sugar syrup *(recipe, page 162)*. Take the pan off the heat and add the softened gelatin to the syrup, stirring the mixture until the gelatin dissolves and the liquid is clear—about five minutes.

2 Making the jelly. Using a sieve lined with dampened muslin or cheesecloth, strain fresh orange juice into a bowl. Pour red wine into a separate bowl. Stirring constantly, pour half of the gelatinized syrup into the juice and the rest into the wine.

6 Adding orange jelly. Chill the mold for 15 minutes to set the first layer. Pour some orange jelly into a small bowl placed over ice and chill it until syrupy. Return the mold to its bowl of ice. Ladle in some of the thickened orange jelly. Tilt the mold and turn it rapidly to coat the sides to a depth of about 1 inch [2½ cm.].

7 Arranging strawberries. Using tweezers or two skewers, dip one strawberry slice at a time into the small bowl of partially set orange jelly. Gently press the slices, cut sides outward, into the jelly clinging to the sides of the mold. Chill for a minute, or until set.

3 **Preparing the fruits.** Starting at the stem end of each grape, lift the skin with a knife tip and peel the skin off in sections. If the grapes are not seedless, halve them lengthwise and remove the seeds, or seed them whole *(page 11)*. Hull strawberries *(page 11)*, pat them dry and cut them lengthwise into thin slices. Refrigerate the fruits.

4 **Coating the mold.** Stand the mold in a large bowl of ice and ladle in a small amount of red-wine jelly. Rotate the mold at a slight angle until the jelly coats the bottom evenly. Then tilt the mold at a sharper angle to coat the sides to a depth sufficient to cover the grapes.

5 **Setting grapes.** Pour wine jelly into a small bowl placed over ice and chill it until syrupy. With tweezers or two thin skewers, dip a grape in the syrupy jelly and set it in the mold. Repeat the process to form a circle of grapes. Refrigerate until the jelly sets—about a minute. Gently ladle in liquid wine jelly from the large bowl to cover the grapes.

8 **Finishing the second layer.** Dip the remaining strawberries in the syrupy orange jelly and arrange them, cut sides upward, in the center of the mold. Chill the mold for a minute, then ladle liquid orange jelly from the large bowl over the fruit to complete the layer. Refrigerate the mold for 15 minutes, or until the jelly sets.

9 **Completing the assembly.** Ladle a little wine jelly from the large bowl into the mold; rotate it until the jelly begins to set around the sides. Dip grapes into the small bowl of syrupy wine jelly and set them around the sides and in the center of the mold. Chill for a minute, then ladle in enough liquid wine jelly to fill the mold; cover it with plastic wrap.

10 **Unmolding.** Refrigerate the jelly for at least four hours. Tilt the mold; if the jelly stays firm, it is ready. Run a knife tip around the rim, and briefly dip the mold in warm water. Hold an upturned chilled dish tightly over the mold, invert them and lift off the mold. Rechill the jelly briefly before serving.

Foamy Fruit Puddings

When gelatin and fruit juice are mixed with eggs, the jelly takes on new textures, depending on whether only the whites of the eggs or the whites plus the yolks are used. Beaten egg whites transform the jelly into an airy snow *(top demonstration; recipe, page 133)*, a felicitous balance between the assertive tang of acidic fruits such as cranberries, lemons or currants and the bland taste of the egg whites.

The secret of a perfect snow lies in chilling the gelatinized fruit juice sufficiently before adding it to the beaten egg whites. The jelly should be just on the verge of setting—a state it has reached when it is the consistency of raw egg whites. If the jelly becomes too thick to pour, warm it over low heat until it liquefies, then rechill it until it reaches the proper consistency.

Attempting to beat too firm a jelly mixture into the whites will only shred it into tiny particles. If, on the other hand, the jelly mixture is too runny when added, it will deflate the egg whites and result in the formation of such a transient bond that the ingredients will separate into layers as the dessert sets.

Paradoxically, this very reaction is vital to the success of a honeycomb pudding *(bottom demonstration; recipe, page 132)*. The gelatin—softened in cream that lends extra richness to the dessert— is cooked with milk and egg yolks to form a custard, which is then flavored with the juice of blood oranges.

After the warm custard has been folded into the beaten egg whites, it is poured into a mold to set. As the pudding chills, the elements separate according to density. The heavy gelatin sinks to the bottom of the mold; the custard floats just above it. The tiny air bubbles in the whipped whites make them rise to the surface, where they dry and firm. When the pudding is inverted and unmolded, a cap of clear fruit jelly rests on an opaque custard, which blends into the spongy base that gives the concoction its name.

A Frothy Cranberry Snow

1 **Adding gelatin.** Cover the gelatin—in this case, powdered—with water and set it aside to soften. Mix cranberry juice *(page 21)* with water and sugar in a small, nonreactive saucepan, and stir over medium heat until the sugar dissolves. Set the pan on a trivet. Add the softened gelatin to the hot liquid and stir until the gelatin dissolves.

2 **Cooling the mixture.** Pour the hot liquid into a large metal bowl set over ice. Stir the mixture with a rubber spatula, frequently scraping the bottom and sides of the bowl. When the mixture is syrupy—it should coat the spatula— remove the bowl from the ice.

A Three-tiered Honeycomb Pudding

1 **Preparing custard.** Sprinkle gelatin over cream and let it soften. Combine egg yolks, grated orange peel and sugar in a metal bowl and whisk them together. Add the gelatin and cream. Scald milk and pour it slowly into the egg-yolk mixture, whisking until the gelatin dissolves.

2 **Cooking the custard.** Set the custard over simmering water and stir it until it thickens—about five minutes. To test the consistency, draw your finger across the back of the spoon. If it leaves a clear trail, the custard is ready. Remove it from the heat and stir in strained blood-orange juice.

3 **Beating in egg whites.** Beat egg whites until they form stiff peaks. Place the bowl containing the gelatinized cranberry juice over ice once more. If the mixture has become runny, stir it until it thickens again. Add the egg whites to the bowl and beat the ingredients together.

4 **Firming the snow.** Continue to beat the snow mixture until it triples in volume and drops in stiff mounds when the beater is lifted—about 10 minutes with an electric mixer, 15 to 20 minutes by hand. Spoon the snow into lightly oiled ramekins. Smooth the contents of each ramekin with the back of the spoon.

5 **Serving the snow.** Refrigerate the molded snow until it has set—about two hours. At serving time, unmold each dessert onto a chilled plate and garnish it. Here, the snow is served with poached whole cranberries in a sauce of sweetened cranberry purée thinned with a little juice.

3 **Straining the custard.** Beat egg whites until they form stiff peaks. Strain the custard into the whites, and gently fold the ingredients together with a rubber spatula. Pour the mixture into a mold and refrigerate it overnight.

4 **Serving the pudding.** Unmold the dessert onto a chilled serving dish and garnish it with fresh fruit. Here, the three-tiered pudding—crowned with the orange jelly that sank to the bottom of the mold—is surrounded by segments of blood orange and moistened with strained blood-orange juice.

A Multi-textured Assembly

One of the most sumptuous of all molded desserts is Bavarian cream—a rich fusion of gelatin, egg custard and whipped cream *(recipe, page 164)*. Substituting fruit juices for all or part of the water used to soften and dissolve the gelatin can add flavor and even color to the cream without changing its silken texture. Enhancing the cream ingredients with puréed fruit, on the other hand, can transform the Bavarian cream into a mousse—a dessert that is meltingly light on the tongue yet firm enough to set in a mold.

The base of the apple mousse demonstrated here *(recipe, page 95)* is a simple pouring custard *(pages 22-23)* fortified with gelatin. The jellied custard is blended into an apple purée, and whipped cream is added just before the mixture is turned into the mold and chilled.

With a mousse of this type, peaches, pears, berries, cherries, plums, nectarines and rhubarb all would make fine substitutes for the apples. Indeed, any puréed fruit would be usable except for the handful—pineapple, papaya, prickly pear, kiwi and figs—containing enzymes that destroy the setting power of gelatin.

Timing and temperature are crucial when using gelatin in a mousse. If softened gelatin comes into contact with a cold mixture, it begins to set, forming lumps and strings. Because of this, the custard must be hot when the gelatin is added. Once the jellied custard and fruit purée are thoroughly mixed, they must be chilled until they are on the verge of setting before the whipped cream can be blended in.

To combine successfully, the whipped cream and the jellied custard must be of a similar consistency. If the custard is too stiff, soften it by placing it over a pan of warm water and stirring it briefly.

A fruit mousse invites an attractive garnish. Among the most appealing and appropriate garnishes are poached and puréed fruits, such as the port-flavored peaches and puréed-apricot sauce shown here. A final accompaniment of fluffy poached meringues *(box)* matches the airy texture of the mousse.

1 **Preparing peaches.** Blanch and peel peaches, cut them in half and pit them *(page 9)*. In a nonreactive pan, poach the peach halves in a medium sugar syrup *(recipe, page 162)* until they are tender—five to 10 minutes. Use a slotted spoon to transfer them to a bowl. Pour port over the peaches and let them macerate for several hours.

2 **Making custard.** Peel and core apples *(page 7)*; slice them. Put them in a nonreactive saucepan with a little water and a cinnamon stick. Cook the apples over medium heat until soft—about five minutes—then remove the cinnamon. Purée the apples. Make a pouring custard, add softened gelatin to it and stir the custard into the purée.

Airy Puffs of Poached Meringue

1 **Sifting in sugar.** Combine milk, sugar and a vanilla bean in a wide, shallow pan and bring to a simmer over medium heat. Off the heat, let the milk infuse for 15 minutes. Beat egg whites until stiff, then gradually sift in confectioners' sugar, beating frequently. Remove the vanilla bean and return the milk to a simmer.

2 **Poaching the meringues.** Scoop up beaten egg white in one spoon and use another spoon to push this meringue into the simmering milk. Poach half a dozen or so meringues at a time for four minutes, turning them once with a perforated spoon. Drain them in a drum sieve set over a plate.

3 **Incorporating cream.** Chill the apple mixture in the refrigerator or over ice, stirring it frequently. While the custard chills, beat heavy cream until it forms soft peaks. When the custard has reached about the same consistency as the whipped cream, gently blend the two ingredients together.

4 **Filling the mold.** Lightly coat the inside of a ring mold with sweet almond oil or flavorless vegetable oil. Fill the mold with the apple mixture. To settle the contents, tap the mold on the work surface. Refrigerate the custard until firm—at least four hours.

5 **Making apricot sauce.** Cook halved and pitted apricots (page 9) in water until tender—about five minutes. Then drain and purée them. Drain the macerated peaches and transfer them to a plate. Add the port in which the peaches steeped to the apricot purée. Add sugar and, if you like, lemon juice to taste.

6 **Assembling the dessert.** Within about an hour of serving the dessert, prepare poached meringues (box, left) and set them on a drum sieve to drain. When the mousse is firm to the touch, indicating that it is fully set, unmold it onto a large, chilled serving plate. Arrange the peaches in the center of the mousse and spoon a ribbon of apricot sauce around the rim.

7 **Completing the dish.** Coat the peaches with a few spoonfuls of apricot sauce, and pour the rest of the sauce into a sauceboat. Just before serving, set the drained meringues on the border of apricot sauce.

Brilliant Colors in a Formal Pattern

The heartiest of molded desserts—and the most flamboyant—are upside-down cakes composed of sponge layers and pastry cream crowned with slices of brightly colored translucent fruits. When the cake is unmolded, the fruit makes up a lovely stained-glass pattern, giving the dessert its name of *rosace,* the French word for the spectacular rose windows that adorn European cathedrals.

Any kind of thin fruit slices may be used for the base and sides of the mold: Raw figs, nectarines or papaya all are candidates; so too are poached mangoes, peaches or pineapple. For the corners, though, the fruit must be soft enough to bend to the conformation of the mold, but firm enough to stay intact. The best choices are citruses—pink grapefruits, blood oranges or the navel oranges combined with kiwi fruits in the cake demonstrated here *(recipe, page 137).*

When making this dessert, it is a good idea to carry out the preliminaries well in advance so that the different elements are ready to be assembled at the last moment. The spongecake should be baked and cooled so that it can be easily cut into two layers; the pastry cream and the sugar syrup used to moisten the cake should be prepared and flavored.

The fruit that lines the mold must be cut into thin, uniform slices for appearances' sake. A rounded, shallow bowl into which layers of spongecake will fit snugly is the most logical mold; fruit slices cannot follow ridged contours. Coating the mold with almond oil and superfine sugar aids in unmolding and provides an attractive, glazed finish.

Once assembled, the dessert is weighted to compact the layers and make the cake easier to cut. Use a flat plate that just fits inside the rim of the mold and place kitchen weights or canned goods on top. The *rosace* will be at its best if it is left in the refrigerator overnight to become firm and allow its flavors to blend.

1 Combining eggs and sugar. Pour 2 inches [5 cm.] of hot water into a pan and set it over low heat. In a large, heatproof bowl, whisk eggs and sugar together until lightly blended. Place the bowl in the pan without letting the bowl touch the water. Begin whisking the mixture with a steady motion or beat it with an electric mixer.

2 Testing the consistency. Beat the mixture for five to 10 minutes—until it thickens into a pale, creamy mass. Turn off the heat and continue beating until the mixture triples in bulk and falls from the whisk in a thick ribbon. This will take about 20 minutes by hand or 10 minutes with an electric mixer.

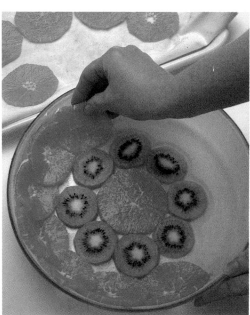

6 Lining the mold. Lightly oil and sugar a large, plain mold. Place an orange slice in the center of the mold. Surround the orange with a ring of sliced kiwi fruits. Line the rest of the mold with the remaining orange slices; overlap the slices slightly and press them gently against the bottom and sides of the mold.

7 Adding pastry cream. Prepare pastry cream *(page 23),* let it cool, then fold in whipped cream and the chopped oranges. Spoon half of the pastry cream into the mold, using the back of the spoon to spread it in a smooth layer. Fill in the gaps in the fruit lining, taking care not to disturb the pattern.

3 **Adding flour and butter.** Melt butter in a small pan and let it cool. Sift a little flour into the egg-and-sugar mixture and fold it in gently with a spoon. Add some of the cooled, melted butter and blend it in. Stir in small amounts of flour and butter alternately, until all of the ingredients are fully blended.

4 **Filling the pan.** Line the bottom of a buttered and floured cake pan with buttered parchment paper, and pour in the batter. Bake the cake in a preheated 350° F. [180° C.] oven for 35 to 40 minutes, or until it feels springy to the touch. Then cool the cake for 10 minutes. Turn the cake out onto a rack and peel off the paper.

5 **Preparing the fruits.** Peel seedless oranges (page 15) and slice them into thin rounds. Reserve the largest slices to line the mold. Chop the rest into small pieces and put them in a bowl. If you like, stir in some orange-flavored liqueur—here, Grand Marnier is used. Peel and slice kiwi fruits.

8 **Halving the cake.** Cut the cake in half horizontally with a serrated knife. Prepare medium sugar syrup (recipe, page 162). Stir in a little orange juice and orange liqueur. Brush the cut side of a cake layer with this syrup and place the layer in the mold, cut side down. Moisten the top surface with more syrup.

9 **Completing the dessert.** Spoon more fruited pastry cream into the mold, leaving enough space for the second layer of cake. Brush the cut side of the second layer with syrup and place it, moistened side down, in the mold. Brush the top of the layer with syrup, cover it with a plate and weight it.

10 **Serving.** Refrigerate the assembly for at least four hours, then remove the weights and plate. Invert the dessert onto a serving plate and lift off the mold. Moisten the blade of a long, sharp knife and cut the dessert into wedges, each with a whole slice of kiwi fruit.

Water Ices with a Tropical Tang

Fruit-flavored water ices are among the easiest of desserts to make. Fruit juice or purée is merely mixed with sugar syrup and frozen in shallow containers.

Any fruit that can be reduced to a purée or from which the juice can be extracted can be used to make a water ice. Fruits with a sharp, acidic flavor, such as tangelos, raspberries, blackberries and currants, make particularly refreshing ices. More exotic water ices can be made with puréed rhubarb, mangoes, passion fruits or quinces.

For a unique taste, juices or purées can be blended, as in the demonstration at top right—pineapple-orange ice served in a pineapple shell. Or two ices can be layered and frozen together as in the second demonstration, where orange shells are pressed into service as containers for guava and prickly-pear ices.

The base for a water ice is usually a light or medium sugar syrup *(recipe, page 162)*—the choice depending on the sweetness of the fruit and on personal taste. Either syrup should be combined with the juice or purée in a ratio of 1 to 1, although for extra flavor the sugar syrup may be made with fruit juice.

Any water ice can be enhanced with a soupçon of a liqueur, wine or spirit that complements the fruit. But add wine or spirits only after the mixture has begun to freeze. Otherwise the alcohol will act like antifreeze to retard the process.

Water ices can, of course, be frozen in an ice-cream maker if a velvety consistency is desired. But freezing water ices in shallow metal ice trays and stirring or processing them periodically will ensure a pleasantly grainy texture: The Italian word for such ices is *granita*.

For a chunky-textured, rustic water ice, the liquid mixture is frozen only until ice crystals first begin to form around the edges and bottom of the trays. The frozen areas are then stirred into the center to break up and distribute the crystals. For a more refined granita, the liquid is frozen solid in the trays. These slabs are then spun in a food processor until smooth. By either technique, the more frequently and thoroughly the mixture is crushed and frozen, the smaller the crystals will be.

Pineapple-Orange Ice in a Pineapple Shell

1 **Extracting juice.** Hollow out a pineapple *(pages 28-29)*, scooping the flesh into a glass or ceramic bowl. Scrape the remaining flesh from the inside of the shell and the underside of the leafy lid. Reserve the core. Purée the flesh, then pour the purée into a cloth *(page 21)* and squeeze out the juice into another bowl. Discard the pulp.

2 **Adding orange juice.** In a nonreactive pan, combine some of the pineapple juice with sugar and, for extra flavor, the pineapple core. Boil the mixture until the sugar dissolves, then let this syrup cool. Pour fresh orange juice into the remaining pineapple juice. Discard the core and mix the cooled syrup into the blended juices.

Refreshing Ices from Guavas and Prickly Pears

1 **Hollowing out oranges.** Cut the stem end out of each orange with a melon baller, then use the melon baller to scoop out the pulp and scrape the inside of the orange clean. Set the hollow orange shells on a tray and put them in the freezer. Reserve the orange juice and pulp for another use.

2 **Preparing the ices.** Make 2 cups [½ liter] of guava purée and 1 cup [¼ liter] of prickly-pear purée in a food mill fitted with a fine disk *(page 20)*. Add 2 cups of cold medium sugar syrup *(recipe, page 162)* to the guava purée and 1 cup to the prickly-pear purée. Pour the purées into separate metal trays and freeze them.

3 **Filling ice trays.** Ladle the fruit-juice mixture into shallow metal ice trays, and set the ice trays in a freezer. Chill the pineapple shell and its lid in the freezer at the same time.

4 **Stirring the ice.** After about an hour, or when the mixture has a slushy texture, remove the ice trays from the freezer. Stir the partially frozen mixture with a fork, turning the frozen edges into the center and mashing them into the liquid. Put the trays back in the freezer. Then stir the ice once or twice more during the next three hours

5 **Serving the ice.** When the ice is just firm—after about four hours—take the ice and pineapple shell out of the freezer. Stand the pineapple shell in a bowl of crushed ice and spoon the water ice into the shell. Fit the pineapple lid on top and serve at once.

3 **Forming a guava base.** Break up the guava ice with a spoon, drop it into a food processor and process the ice until it is soft and smooth. With an iced-tea spoon, fill each orange shell one third full with guava ice. Tap each filled orange on a work surface to settle the ice, then smooth its surface. Freeze the oranges and guava ice until solid.

4 **Layering pear ice.** Process the prickly-pear ice until it is soft and smooth. Remove the orange shells from the freezer and spoon a layer of prickly-pear ice over the guava ice. Freeze this layer, then reprocess the remaining guava ice and use it to fill the oranges to the top. Refreeze the oranges to firm the final layer of ice.

5 **Serving the layered ices.** Slice each frozen orange in half vertically with a serrated knife. Arrange the ice-filled halves on a chilled plate and serve immediately. If left to stand, the ices will melt and overflow their containers.

Peach Ice in a Tulip-shaped Cup

Coupes glacées—the elegant French precursors of America's beloved sundaes—are assemblies of raw or poached fruit and water ice or ice cream topped with a purée, a sauce or whipped cream and served in the crystal or silver goblets known as coupes.

Opportunities for improvisation and invention are limitless: Although some classic coupes combine different fruit flavors—raspberry ice with crushed pineapple, lemon ice with chopped cherries—others just as impressive feature a single fruit. Among these are coupes of crushed pineapple with pineapple ice, strawberry ice cream with fresh strawberries and strawberry purée, or orange ice with orange sections and an orange liqueur.

In the all-peach assembly demonstrated at right, peach ice is accompanied by poached peach halves and sauced with peach syrup. The peaches are poached in their skins to tint the flesh with their blush marks; to intensify the flavor of the glaze, the peach peelings are cooked in the syrup as it is reduced.

Instead of being presented in a coupe, the dessert is served in a so-called tulip wafer—a pair of thin almond cookies shaped to resemble an open flower *(recipe, page 166)*. While still warm from the oven and pliable, the cookies are flipped face down, one overlapping another on a small bowl. A second bowl is pressed over the top to mold them.

It is essential to work quickly when making tulip wafers. As they cool, the cookies become too brittle to mold. It is best, at least until you become adept at shaping them, to bake only four cookies at a time. The tulip wafers can be made up to about two days in advance, but they must be stored in an airtight container to prevent them from absorbing moisture and softening. However, if they do lose their crispness, they can be dried out by returning them to a 350° F. [180° C.] oven for two or three minutes.

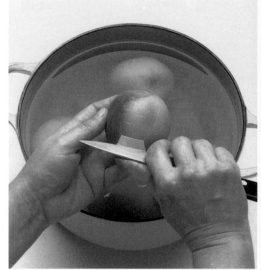

1 **Preparing the peaches.** Poach peaches in a medium sugar syrup *(recipe, page 162)* until they are tender—eight to 15 minutes. Peel the peaches, put them in a bowl and cover them with syrup. Add the peelings to the remaining syrup and boil until the syrup is reduced by half; strain it. Refrigerate the peaches and syrup.

5 **Baking cookies.** Spread softened butter in large circles on a baking sheet. Sprinkle the buttered surfaces with flour and lightly tap the baking sheet to remove the excess. Spoon a heaping tablespoonful of batter onto the center of each circle and use the back of the spoon to spread the batter; it will spread farther while it bakes. Bake the cookies in a preheated 450° F. [230° C.] oven for eight minutes, or until lightly browned.

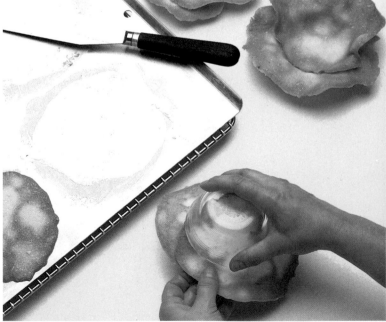

6 **Molding tulip wafers.** Take the cookies out of the oven and loosen them with a metal spatula. Working quickly, flip two cookies upside down onto an inverted small bowl, overlapping them slightly. Fit another bowl of the same size as the first on top of the cookies and gently press down to shape them into a cuplike shell. Repeat with the other cookies. If they become too brittle to mold, return them to the oven for a moment to soften.

2 **Forming balls of ice.** Make peach ice *(recipe, page 167)*, processing it at least twice. Using an ice-cream scoop, form smooth balls of the finished ice and place them on a chilled metal tray or baking sheet. Put the tray in the freezer to harden the ice balls.

3 **Peeling almonds.** Blanch almonds for one minute, then drain them. When cool enough to handle, squeeze each one firmly at the base to pop it from its loosened skin. Cool the almonds completely and grind them to a fine texture in a food processor, operating the machine in short bursts so that the almonds do not become oily.

4 **Making wafer batter.** Whisk egg whites until they are frothy, then whisk in sugar. Stir the ground almonds into the mixture, then stir in flour. Pour in clarified butter and blend all of the ingredients thoroughly. Let the batter rest for about 20 minutes.

7 **Assembling the dessert.** Halve and pit the poached peaches and drain them well. Put a ball of peach ice in each tulip wafer, and prop two overlapping peach halves against the ball. Transfer the filled tulips to individual serving plates and spoon just enough of the reduced peach syrup over the fruit to glaze it. Garnish the dessert, if you like, with fresh mint leaves—a sprig of orange mint is shown here.

A Cherry Ice-Cream Baked Alaska

The custard base that makes ice cream so much richer than water ice also makes it freeze into a denser mass that resists melting when used as the centerpiece of a baked Alaska. Protected from below by a layer of cake and insulated on the top and sides by a coating of meringue, the ice cream remains cold while the assembly turns golden brown in the oven's heat.

Although plain cake and ice cream will do, fruits contribute a flourish of color and added flavor to this easily varied old-fashioned treat. In the version demonstrated at right and on page 88, for example, a hemisphere of homemade cherry ice cream tops poached cherries that have been laid on spongecake moistened with kirsch-flavored syrup.

The ice cream can be shaped in a bowl, as shown here, or in a loaf pan or charlotte mold. Instead of resting on the fruit, the molded ice cream could be hollowed out and filled with fruit. Whole blueberries or grapes, sliced figs or plums, or chunks of pineapple or mango could all take the place of the cherries.

Though ready-made ice cream can be obtained in a profusion of flavors, none can match the product you churn at home in a hand- or electric-powered ice-cream maker. To speed the churning process, the freezer's canister and dasher are refrigerated before the custard mixture is added. Because solid pieces of fruit would impede the dasher or become crushed to a pulp, the fruit should not be added until the ice cream is almost done.

The finished ice cream then is frozen solid in a simple mold at least an inch [2½ cm.] smaller all around than the pan that will be used to bake the spongecake base. Lining the mold with plastic wrap facilitates removing the frozen ice cream.

The meringue that will cover the ice cream should be sweetened highly to give it a stiff, dense consistency—allow ¼ cup [50 ml.] of sugar for each egg white—and should be applied in a layer about ¾ inch [2 cm.] thick. The 2-quart [2-liter] ice-cream mold shown here required a meringue made with eight egg whites.

1 Poaching cherries. Prepare a medium sugar syrup *(recipe, page 162)* and flavor it with a little kirsch. Pit 4½ cups [1⅛ liters] of cherries *(page 9)*, poach them in the syrup for two minutes, then drain them. Return 1½ cups [375 ml.] of the cherries to the syrup and refrigerate them. Chop the remaining cherries coarse and refrigerate them too.

2 Filling the canister. Prepare custard for the ice cream *(recipe, page 167)* and refrigerate it. Refrigerate the canister and dasher of an ice-cream maker until they are frosty. Pour the chilled custard into the canister. Seat the canister in the freezer bucket, fit the dasher inside and put the lid on top.

6 Cleaning the dasher. Take the canister out of the bucket, wipe it off well with a dry towel and remove the lid. Lift out the dasher and use a rubber spatula to push the ice cream clinging to it back into the canister.

7 Molding the ice cream. Line the mold—here, a 2-quart [2-liter] metal bowl—with plastic wrap. Spoon the ice cream into the mold, packing it down firmly with the back of the spoon to make sure there are no air bubbles trapped inside. Smooth the surface. Cover the ice cream tightly with aluminum foil and freeze it overnight.

3 **Adding water.** Attach the motor to the dasher and switch on the machine. Keeping the motor running, pack the bucket to the top of the canister with layers of ice and rock salt. Pour about 1 cup [¼ liter] of cold water over the ice to start the freezing process.

4 **Testing consistency.** Churn the custard for 10 to 15 minutes, adding ice and salt as needed to keep the bucket full. When the motor sounds labored— an indication that the custard is thickening—turn it off. Wipe the lid and open the canister. Scoop out a spoonful of the mixture—it should be as thick as stiffly whipped cream.

5 **Adding fruit.** Spoon the chopped cherries into the canister, pressing them down into the custard so they will be evenly distributed through the ice cream. Replace the canister lid and motor and churn the ice cream for two more minutes.

8 **Preparing the cake base.** Bake a spongecake, cool it and cut it into two layers (page 81, Step 8). Place one layer, cut side up, on a large, ovenproof platter. (Save the second layer for another use.) Prepare a thick sugar syrup—flavored, if you like, with kirsch. Using a pastry brush, moisten the surface of the cake with the syrup.

9 **Arranging a fruit layer.** Drain the reserved poached whole cherries. Crowd them together in a single layer in the center of the cake. Leave a 1-inch [2½-cm.] margin of cake uncovered.

10 **Unmolding the ice cream.** Take the foil off the molded ice cream. Invert the mold, center it over the circle of cherries and set it down gently. Carefully lift off the mold and peel away the plastic wrap. Put the platter in the freezer to keep the ice cream frozen solid while you make the meringue. ▶

11 **Applying meringue.** Beat egg whites until frothy, then gradually beat in sugar until this meringue is stiff. Set the dessert on a cake-decorating stand and spread a thick layer of meringue over the ice cream. Hold the tip of a spatula at an angle to the meringue, and rotate the stand to form spiraled ridges.

12 **Piping a border.** Spoon the remaining meringue into a pastry bag fitted with a No. 0 plain tube. Pipe large, teardrop shapes around the edge of the dome; the piped border should form an airtight seal. At this stage, the dessert can be stored in the freezer for about two hours if necessary.

13 **Baking the Alaska.** Lightly dust the meringue with confectioners' sugar. Set the assembly on a baking sheet and put it in a preheated 500° F. [260° C.] oven. Bake the dessert for three to five minutes, until the ridges brown lightly.

14 **Serving.** Remove the dessert from the oven and set it on a trivet. Slice it into wedges with a sharp knife that has been dipped in hot water to prevent the meringue from sticking to it. Use a wide pastry server to lift the slices, taking care not to let the top layer of meringue slide off the surface of the ice cream.

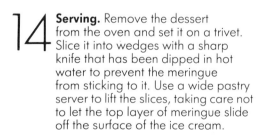

Anthology of Recipes

Drawing upon the cooking literature of more than 25 countries, the editors and consultants for this volume have chosen 213 recipes for the Anthology that follows. The selections include simple dishes such as applesauce as well as elaborate ones—for example, pineapple and frangipane fritters, made by coating pineapple slices with a thick nut paste, chilling them, then dipping them in a batter and deep frying the slices.

Many of the recipes were written by world-renowned exponents of the culinary art, but the Anthology also includes selections from rare and out-of-print books and from works that have never been published in English. Whatever the sources, the emphasis in these recipes is always on fresh, natural ingredients and on techniques that are practical for the home cook.

Since many early recipe writers did not specify amounts of ingredients or cooking times, the missing information has been judiciously added. In some cases, clarifying introductory notes have also been supplied; they are printed in italics. Modern recipe terms have been substituted for archaic language and some instructions have been expanded. But to preserve the character of the original recipes and to create a true anthology, the authors' texts have been changed as little as possible.

Only fully ripe fruits should be selected for these recipes. Berries, currants, grapes and persimmons should be rinsed gently before use, dates and figs should be wiped clean with a damp cloth and rhubarb should be scrubbed clean with a brush. All other fruits should be washed well under running water.

In keeping with the organization of the fruit guide at the beginning of the book, the recipes in the Anthology are categorized according to type of fruit, with additional categories for dried-fruit and mixed-fruit dishes. Standard preparations—sauces and doughs among them—appear at the end of the Anthology. Unfamiliar cooking terms and uncommon ingredients are explained in the combined General Index and Glossary.

Apart from the primary fruits, all ingredients are listed within each recipe in order of use, with both the customary U.S. measurements and the metric measurements provided in separate columns. To make the quantities simpler to measure, many of the figures have been rounded off to correspond with the gradations on U.S. metric spoons and cups. (One cup, for example, equals 237 milliliters. However, wherever practicable in these recipes, the metric equivalent of 1 cup appears as a more readily measured 250 milliliters—¼ liter.) Similarly, the weight, temperature and linear metric equivalents have been rounded off slightly. Thus the American and metric figures do not exactly match, but using one set or the other will produce the same good results.

Apples, Pears and Quinces

Danish Apple Cake

To serve 6

1 ½ lb.	apples, peeled, cored and sliced	¾ liter
3 tbsp.	butter	45 ml.
4 to 6 tbsp.	granulated sugar	60 to 90 ml.
½ cup	almonds, blanched, peeled and chopped	125 ml.
1 cup	dried bread crumbs	¼ liter
⅓ cup	Demerara or turbinado sugar	75 ml.
2 tsp.	sherry (optional)	10 ml.
⅔ cup	heavy cream, whipped	150 ml.
	red currant jelly	

In a nonreactive pan, cook the apple slices slowly with enough water to cover the bottom of the pan. When they are soft, mash them to a purée with a fork, or in a blender. Add 2 tablespoons [30 ml.] of the butter and add sugar to taste. Allow the purée to cool. Melt the remaining butter in a skillet, add the almonds, bread crumbs and Demerara or turbinado sugar, and fry the mixture until it is golden brown, stirring it often with a wooden spoon. Let the mixture cool.

When both the apple purée and crumb mixture are cool, arrange them in a glass bowl in alternate layers, starting and finishing with the crumbs. If you like, sprinkle a little sherry on top. Spread the whipped cream over the top and decorate the cake with swirls of melted currant jelly.

PAMELA WESTLAND
A TASTE OF THE COUNTRY

Applesauce

To serve 4

6 to 8	tart apples, peeled, cored and sliced	6 to 8
2 tbsp.	water	30 ml.
	sugar	
	ground cinnamon	
	ground allspice	

Place the apples in a nonreactive saucepan with the water. Cover and simmer over low heat until the apples are soft—about five to eight minutes.

Mash the apples with a fork or put them through a food mill. While the sauce is still warm, add sugar, cinnamon and allspice to taste.

HELEN MENDES
THE AFRICAN HERITAGE COOKBOOK

Spun Apples

Black sesame seeds can be purchased at Asian food stores or health-food stores.

To serve 4 to 6

2	large, firm apples, peeled, cored and cut into eighths	2
⅓ cup	water-chestnut powder or plain flour	75 ml.
1	egg, lightly beaten	1
3 cups, plus 2 tbsp.	peanut oil for deep frying	¾ liter, plus 30 ml.
1 cup	sugar	¼ liter
	water	
	ice cubes	
1 tbsp.	black sesame seeds	15 ml.
2 tsp.	white sesame seeds	10 ml.

Mix the water-chestnut powder or flour and the egg together in a bowl. For the first frying, dip the apple pieces into the batter and let the excess batter drip away. Deep fry a few pieces at a time in 3 cups [¾ liter] of peanut oil to crisp the batter. Drain the pieces on paper towels and set them aside. (This can be done hours in advance.)

When you are ready to serve the apples, put the sugar and 2 tablespoons [30 ml.] of peanut oil into a heavy saucepan. Prepare a large bowl of ice water. At the same time, reheat the deep-frying oil in a wok. After the deep-frying oil is hot, adjust the burner under it to keep the heat constant.

Put the saucepan with the sugar over moderately high heat. Within a couple of minutes, the sugar will dissolve and begin to caramelize. Add the sesame seeds to the caramel. Turn off the heat under it.

As soon as the caramel is ready, refry the apple pieces until they are crisp—about one and one half minutes. One by one, dip them into the caramel to coat them thoroughly. Then dip them immediately into the ice water to harden the caramel. Serve the caramelized apples immediately.

KEN HOM
CHINESE TECHNIQUE

Fried Apple Dumplings

To make about 50

1	medium-sized tart apple, peeled, cored and finely chopped	1
½ cup	raisins	125 ml.
½ cup	dried currants	125 ml.
⅓ cup	candied lemon peel	75 ml.
2 cups	flour	½ liter
¼ oz.	package active dry yeast or ⅗ oz. [18 g.] cake fresh yeast, softened in 3 tbsp. [45 ml.] tepid milk for 10 minutes	7½ g.
1 cup	milk	¼ liter
1½ tbsp.	fresh lemon juice	22 ml.
	oil for deep frying	
2 tbsp.	superfine sugar	30 ml.

Put the flour in a large bowl and mix in the apple, raisins, currants and candied lemon peel. Add the softened yeast, the milk and lemon juice, and mix to a stiff dough. Knead the dough well for about two minutes, then leave it in a warm place to rise until doubled in bulk—about one hour.

In a heavy skillet, heat a layer of oil about 2 inches [5 cm.] deep until it is very hot—375° F. [190° C.]. Drop the dough into the oil by the tablespoonful, frying two or three dumplings in each batch. Turning them once, fry the dumplings until they are golden all over—about three minutes. Drain them on paper towels, sprinkle them with the sugar and serve them immediately.

ELIZABETH GILI
APPLE RECIPES FROM A TO Z

Apple Fritters
Frittelle di Mele

If possible, choose green apples that are not too sweet. For more deluxe fritters, moisten the apple rings with a drop or two of Marsala before coating them with batter.

To serve 4

4	apples, peeled, cored and sliced into rings	4
2	eggs	2
1 tbsp.	sugar	15 ml.
3 tbsp.	flour	45 ml.
	salt	
	oil for deep frying	
	superfine sugar	

Mix together the eggs, sugar, flour and a pinch of salt in a large bowl. Dip a few apple rings at a time into this batter and deep fry them in oil that has been heated in a heavy pan. Drain the pieces on paper towels and then serve them liberally sprinkled with superfine sugar.

GIOVANNI RIGHI PARENTI
LA GRANDE CUCINA TOSCANA

Apple Omelet
Frittata alle Mela

To serve 4

2	eating apples, peeled, cored and thinly sliced	2
3 tbsp.	butter	45 ml.
1 tbsp.	lard	15 ml.
½ tsp.	ground mixed spices	2 ml.
8	eggs, beaten	8
¼ cup	heavy cream	50 ml.

Melt half of the butter and all of the lard, add the apples and mixed spices to the fats, and cook over low heat until the apples are almost soft—about five minutes. Cool them a little and mix them with the eggs and cream.

Melt the remaining butter in a large skillet, pour in the egg mixture and cook over medium heat for four to five minutes, or until the omelet is browned on the bottom. Turn the omelet over and brown it on the other side.

VINCENZO CORRADO
IL CUOCO GALANTE

Apples Cooked in Butter

Pommes au Beurre

To serve 4

2 lb.	hard, sweet apples, peeled, cored and thinly sliced	1 kg.
4 tbsp.	butter	60 ml.
3 to 4 tbsp.	superfine or vanilla sugar	45 to 60 ml.

Melt the butter in a frying pan. Put in the apple slices, add the sugar and cook gently until the apples are pale golden and transparent. Turn the slices over very gently, so as not to break them and, if they are very closely packed, shake the pan rather than stir the apples. Serve them hot.

ELIZABETH DAVID
FRENCH PROVINCIAL COOKING

Spicy Apple Crisp

This crisp may also be made with other firm-textured moist fruits—pears, peaches, nectarines, cherries, plums or the rhubarb shown on pages 64-65.

To serve 6 to 8

5	medium-sized tart apples, peeled, cored and sliced	5
¾ cup	firmly packed brown sugar	175 ml.
½ tsp.	grated nutmeg	2 ml.
1 tbsp.	fresh lemon juice	15 ml.
1 cup	rolled oats	¼ liter
⅓ cup	flour	75 ml.
½ tsp.	salt	2 ml.
4 tbsp.	butter, melted	60 ml.

Combine the apples with ¼ cup [50 ml.] of the brown sugar and ¼ tsp. [1 ml.] of the nutmeg. Arrange them in a buttered, shallow 1-quart [1-liter] baking dish or deep 9-inch [23-cm.] pie plate. Sprinkle the lemon juice over the slices.

In a small bowl, combine the oats, flour, the remaining brown sugar and nutmeg, the salt and the melted butter. With a fork, mix the ingredients until crumbly; spread them over the apples.

Bake in a preheated 350° F. [180° C.] oven for 30 minutes, or until the apples are fork-tender and the topping is brown and crisp. Serve warm with ice cream or whipped cream.

IDA BAILEY ALLEN
BEST LOVED RECIPES OF THE AMERICAN PEOPLE

Apple Crisp or Crumble

This recipe may also be made with rhubarb or other fruits. If the fruit is very sour, it should have extra sugar sprinkled on before it is topped with the crumble.

To serve 3 or 4

1 lb.	tart apples, peeled, cored and thinly sliced	½ kg.
¼ tsp.	ground cinnamon	1 ml.
¼ cup	water	50 ml.
¾ cup	flour	175 ml.
¼ cup	sugar	50 ml.
2 tbsp.	butter	30 ml.

Place the apples in a baking dish. Sprinkle them with the cinnamon and add the water. Combine the flour and sugar, and rub in the butter until the mixture has the consistency of fine crumbs.

Sprinkle the crumble on top of the fruit and bake it in a preheated 325° F. [160° C.] oven until the crumble is golden brown—about 40 minutes. Do not have the oven too hot or the juice will bubble up and spoil the top.

BEE NILSON
THE PENGUIN COOKERY BOOK

Baked Apples in Pastry

Douillon Normand

The technique of baking whole apples in pastry is shown on pages 62-63. Instead of filling the apples with the butter mixture given below you can use ¼ cup [50 ml.] of honey, brown sugar or jam. Slitting the apples around the middle will help them to keep their shape, but is not essential for pastry-wrapped fruit.

The apples can be peeled before being enclosed in the dough. They can also be baked first, in which case the baking in pastry will only take 15 minutes.

To serve 4

4	large, firm apples, cored	4
1 lb.	rich short-crust dough (recipe, page 164)	½ kg.
8 tbsp.	butter, softened and beaten with 2 tbsp. [30 ml.] of sugar and a pinch of ground cinnamon	120 ml.
1	egg, beaten	1

Roll out the dough to a thickness of ⅛ inch [3 mm.]. Using an 8-inch [20-cm.] plate as a template, cut four rounds in the dough with a sharp knife. Use a small fluted pastry cutter to stamp four circlets from the remaining dough.

Cut a slit around the middle of each apple to prevent the skin from bursting. Place each apple on a round of dough and fill the cored center of the apple with the butter-and-sugar mixture. Enclose the apples in the dough, brush the circlets with a little water and put them on top of the wrapped apples. Place the apples on a baking sheet, brush them with the beaten egg and—using the tip of a knife—score decorative lines down the sides of each apple. Bake in a preheated 400° F. [200° C.] oven for 30 minutes or until brown. Serve the apples piping hot.

PROSPER MONTAGNÉ
THE NEW LAROUSSE GASTRONOMIQUE

Apple Turnovers

To make 6

4	medium-sized tart apples, peeled, cored and sliced	4
2 cups	flour	½ liter
½ tsp.	salt	2 ml.
½ tbsp.	baking powder	7 ml.
12 tbsp.	shortening, cut into pieces	175 ml.
5 tbsp.	milk	75 ml.
⅓ cup	firmly packed brown sugar	75 ml.
1 tsp.	ground cinnamon	5 ml.
¼ tsp.	grated nutmeg	1 ml.
2 tbsp.	butter, cut into small pieces	30 ml.

Sift together the flour, salt and baking powder. Cut in the shortening. Stir in the milk to moisten the dough. Roll it out on a lightly floured surface to a thickness of ¼ inch [6 mm.]. Cut the dough into six 5-inch [13-cm.] squares. Put equal amounts of sliced apple in the center of the squares. Mix together the brown sugar, cinnamon and nutmeg, and sprinkle this over the apples. Dot with butter. Fold one corner of each square over the apple to make a triangle; press the edges together with a fork.

Place the turnovers ½ inch [1 cm.] apart on a baking sheet, and put them into a preheated 450° F. [230° C.] oven. Immediately reduce the heat to 375° F. [190° C.] and bake the turnovers for 35 minutes, or until golden brown.

IDA BAILEY ALLEN
BEST LOVED RECIPES OF THE AMERICAN PEOPLE

Tipsy Black Apple Fool

To serve 8

1 lb.	cooking apples, peeled, cored and sliced	½ kg.
½ lb.	prunes	¼ kg.
½ lb.	mixed dried fruits (pears, peaches, apricots)	¼ kg.
1 cup	red wine	¼ liter
1 tbsp.	sweet liqueur	15 ml.
1 cup	heavy cream	¼ liter

Put the apples in an ovenproof dish that has a tight-fitting lid. Add the prunes and wine, cover and put the dish in a preheated 250° F. [130° C.] oven. Bake for three to four hours, or until the fruits are very soft. After two hours, put the mixed dried fruits in another ovenproof dish with a tight-fitting lid, cover the fruits with water, put on the lid and bake them for about one hour.

Remove the prunes from the first dish and pit them. Rub the prunes through a sieve along with the apples and the wine (if there is any left). Drain the dried fruits well, rub them through the sieve, and stir them well into the prune-and-apple mixture. Chill the purée. Just before serving, stir in the liqueur. Accompany the purée with the cream.

ELIZABETH GILI
APPLE RECIPES FROM A TO Z

Baked-Apple Ice Cream

To make 1 quart [1 liter]

1 cup	sieved baked-apple flesh	¼ liter
1 cup	pouring custard (recipe, page 163)	¼ liter
1 cup	heavy cream, whipped	¼ liter
½ tsp.	vanilla extract	2 ml.
about ¾ cup	confectioners' sugar	about 175 ml.

Gently but thoroughly blend together the sieved apple, the custard and whipped cream; then add the vanilla extract and fold in confectioners' sugar until the mixture is sweetened to taste—do not add too much sugar or the mixture will not freeze easily. Turn the mixture into two refrigerator trays and freeze it for about one hour, then stir it to break up the large crystals, return it to the refrigerator and freeze it for three hours longer.

L. P. DE GOUY
ICE CREAM AND ICE CREAM DESSERTS

Apple Soufflé

Almafelfújt

To serve 6		
6 to 8	apples, peeled, halved lengthwise and cores cut out	6 to 8
1 cup	sugar	¼ liter
1	lemon, the peel grated, the juice strained	1
¾ cup	flour	175 ml.
4 tbsp.	butter, melted	60 ml.
2 cups	milk	½ liter
4	eggs, the yolks separated from the whites, the whites stiffly beaten and the yolks beaten	4
¼ cup	dry bread crumbs	50 ml.
⅓ cup	apricot jam	75 ml.
about ¼ cup	seedless white raisins	about 50 ml.
1 to 2 tsp.	ground cinnamon	5 to 10 ml.

In a large, nonreactive skillet, combine the apple halves with a very little water, 2 tablespoons [30 ml.] of the sugar and the lemon juice. Cover, and cook over medium heat until the apples are just tender—about two to three minutes. Drain the apples and set them aside.

Melt the butter in a large saucepan over low heat. Stir in the flour and slowly pour in the milk, stirring continuously until the sauce is well blended. Cook for a minute or two, then remove the pan from the heat and let the sauce cool a little. Mix in ⅔ cup [150 ml.] of the sugar, the lemon peel and the egg yolks. Fold in the egg whites.

Butter a baking dish just large enough to hold the apple halves in one layer. Coat the inside of the dish with the bread crumbs. Pour about half of the sauce mixture into the dish. Fill the hollows in the apple halves with a little apricot jam and a couple of white seedless raisins. Place the apple halves, filled side upward, on top of the sauce mixture. Pour on the remainder of the sauce mixture and place the dish in a preheated 350° F. [180° C.] oven.

Mix the remaining sugar with cinnamon to taste. After the soufflé has baked for 20 minutes, sprinkle the cinnamon sugar over the top. Continue baking the soufflé for 10 to 20 minutes longer, or until it is browned and set. A cake tester inserted into the soufflé mixture—not the apples—should come out clean.

Serve the soufflé in the baking dish or unmold it and sprinkle it with more cinnamon sugar. Serve hot or cold.

FRED MAC NICOL
HUNGARIAN COOKERY

Baked Apples with Almonds

Manzanas Asadas con Almendras

As an alternative to rubbing the peeled apples with a cut lemon to prevent discoloration, you can immerse them in 4 cups [1 liter] of water acidulated with the juice of two lemons.

To serve 6		
6	large cooking apples	6
2 tbsp.	rum	30 ml.
¼ cup	dried currants	50 ml.
½	lemon	½
2	egg yolks	2
5 tbsp.	sugar	75 ml.
2 tbsp.	butter, softened	30 ml.
½ cup	almonds, blanched, peeled, toasted and chopped	125 ml.
2 to 3 tbsp.	water	30 to 45 ml.
6	candied cherries	6

Warm the rum gently in a small saucepan, taking care not to let it catch alight. Take it from the heat and add 1 tablespoon [15 ml.] of tepid water. Put in the currants to soak. Peel and core the apples and rub them with the lemon so that they do not turn brown.

Strain the currants through a sieve set over a bowl and reserve the rum. Beat the egg yolks with the sugar in a small bowl, then add the butter, almonds and drained currants. Fill the apples with this mixture and put them in a baking dish. Pour the reserved rum into the bottom of the dish along with 2 to 3 tablespoons [30 to 45 ml.] of water.

Bake the stuffed apples in a preheated 375° F. [190° C.] oven until they are tender—about 30 minutes. Serve them warm or cold, and decorate each with a cherry.

SIMONE ORTEGA
MIL OCHENTA RECETAS DE COCINA

Apple Mousse with Peaches

Mousse de Pommes aux Pêches

To serve 4 to 6

3	peaches, blanched, peeled, halved and pitted	3
3	apples, peeled, cored and sliced	3
2	medium-sized apricots, blanched, peeled, halved and pitted	2
1 ¼ cups	medium sugar syrup *(recipe, page 162)*	300 ml.
½ cup	port	125 ml.
⅔ cup	water	150 ml.
1-inch	cinnamon stick or ¼ tsp. [1 ml.] ground cinnamon	2½-cm.
2 cups	milk	½ liter
1	vanilla bean or 1 tsp. [5 ml.] vanilla extract	1
⅔ cup	superfine sugar	150 ml.
4	egg yolks	4
1 tbsp.	unflavored powdered gelatin, soaked in ¼ cup [50 ml.] cold water for 5 minutes	15 ml.
¾ cup	heavy cream	175 ml.
	sweet almond oil or vegetable oil	
1½ tbsp.	fresh lemon juice (optional)	22 ml.
	Meringues	
	salt	
2	egg whites	2
¾ cup	confectioners' sugar	175 ml.

Poach the peaches in the sugar syrup. When they are tender, transfer them to a bowl and pour the port over them; let them macerate for a few hours.

In a nonreactive saucepan over medium heat, cook the apples with ⅓ cup [75 ml.] of water and the cinnamon—stirring from time to time—until the apples are tender but not cooked to a purée. Remove the cinnamon stick, if you are using one, and pass the apples through a sieve placed over a bowl; set the cooked apples aside.

Scald the milk with the vanilla bean and the superfine sugar. If using vanilla extract, add it after scalding the milk. Remove the milk from the heat and let it infuse for 15 to 20 minutes.

To make the meringues, add a tiny pinch of salt to the egg whites and beat them until stiff. Sift the confectioners' sugar over them and mix together thoroughly but gently.

Remove the vanilla bean from the scalded milk, and re-heat the milk, regulating the heat to a bare simmer. Drop teaspoonfuls of the meringue mixture into the milk, poaching only a few at a time since they swell and should not be crowded. After two minutes, carefully turn them over in the simmering milk, let them poach for another two minutes, and remove them to a drum sieve that is set over a bowl to collect the milk draining from them. Repeat the poaching process until all are done, transferring the meringues to a plate as they are drained.

To make a custard, first combine the poaching milk with that collected from draining the meringues. Beat the egg yolks in a saucepan and, whisking constantly, slowly pour in the milk. Cook over medium heat, stirring continuously with a wooden spoon until the mixture coats the spoon. Combine the softened gelatin with 2 or 3 tablespoons [30 to 45 ml.] of the custard, then add it to the rest of the custard. Continue stirring the custard over medium heat for a few seconds so that the gelatin dissolves completely, but do not allow the custard to come to a boil.

Mix the custard and the cooked apple together and chill—keeping an eye on the mixture—until the mixture begins to jell. Whip the cream until it is fairly firm, but not stiff, then fold it well into the apple mixture.

Lightly oil a savarin mold with sweet almond oil or a flavorless vegetable oil. Fill the mold with the mixture, tap the bottom of the mold two or three times on a tabletop to settle the contents, and chill the mousse in a freezer or the freezing compartment of a refrigerator or directly over crushed ice for at least four hours.

Stew the apricots in ⅓ cup of water until they are tender—about 15 minutes—and pass them through a nylon sieve. Remove the peaches from the port, set them aside, and add the port to the apricot purée. Taste for sweetness and add sugar if necessary. Add the lemon juice, if using.

Just before serving, dip the mold into hot water for two or three seconds and unmold the mousse onto a large, round, chilled serving dish. Pour some of the apricot sauce in a circle around the mousse, distributing the meringues on top of the ribbon of sauce, fill the central cavity of the mousse with the macerated peaches, mask them with a few spoonfuls of sauce and serve the remainder in a sauceboat.

RICHARD OLNEY
THE FRENCH MENU COOKBOOK

Pears Stuffed with Roquefort Cheese

To serve 8

8	ripe but firm pears	8
1 lb.	Roquefort cheese, softened and crumbled	½ kg.
½ lb.	unsalted butter, softened and cut into chunks	¼ kg.

Wash the pears, but do not peel them. With an apple corer, remove the cores from the blossom end, leaving the stems on. Cut a slice from the bottom of each pear, so they will stand upright on dessert plates. Beat the Roquefort cheese and butter together until very creamy. Put the mixture in a pastry bag fitted with a small rose tube and use it to fill the cavities of the pears. Decorate each pear with the cheese-butter mixture, forming a ribbon up one side and down the other. Chill the pears if not serving them immediately, but remove them from the refrigerator one hour before serving.

JULIE DANNENBAUM
MENUS FOR ALL OCCASIONS

Symposium Pears

To serve 4 to 6

6 to 8	small hard pears	6 to 8
⅔ cup	sugar	150 ml.
½ cup	water	125 ml.
7 to 10	cardamoms, lightly crushed	7 to 10
½ tsp.	saffron threads, soaked in 1 tbsp. [15 ml.] boiling water for 10 minutes	2 ml.
1	strip lemon peel	1
1 cup	dry white wine or hard cider	¼ liter
1½ tbsp.	fresh lemon juice	22 ml.

Choose a small, deep, nonreactive saucepan in which the pears can stand upright. In it dissolve the sugar in the water, bring this syrup to a boil, add the cardamoms, the saffron and its soaking water, and the lemon peel. Let the syrup simmer very gently for an hour.

Peel the pears, leaving them whole with their stems on. To prevent their discoloring, put them into the syrup. Add half the wine or cider, cover the pan, and simmer the pears gently until they are tender. (The time will vary greatly with the size and variety of the pear. Do not overcook them.)

Put the pears—still upright—in a small, deep serving dish. Strain the syrup into a clean pan; if the syrup is rather thin, reduce it by boiling. Add the lemon juice and remaining wine or cider to the syrup and boil for a few minutes. Pour the syrup over the pears, cover the dish with plastic wrap, and refrigerate the pears for 12 to 24 hours so that they take on the color and flavor of the syrup.

DOROTHY BROWN (EDITOR)
SYMPOSIUM FARE

Pears with Chocolate Sauce

Poires Belle-Hélène

To serve 6

6	pears, peeled but left whole	6
½ cup	superfine sugar	125 ml.
1 cup	water	¼ liter
1 quart	vanilla ice cream, *(recipe, page 167)*	1 liter
½ cup	almonds, blanched, peeled, slivered and toasted	125 ml.

Chocolate sauce

7 oz.	semisweet baking chocolate, broken into small pieces	200 g.
1 cup	water	¼ liter
6 tbsp.	unsalted butter, cut into small pieces	90 ml.

Simmer the pears in the sugar and water for 10 to 25 minutes, or until tender. (The cooking time depends on the type, size and ripeness of the pears.) Allow the pears to cool in the syrup in which they were cooked.

To make the chocolate sauce, put the chocolate and the water into a heavy pan and stir over low heat until the chocolate melts and the mixture is smooth. Remove the pan from the heat and stir in the butter, a few pieces at a time, making sure each addition melts before adding more.

To serve, put the vanilla ice cream in a bowl, place the pears on top and sprinkle them with the almonds. Serve the hot chocolate sauce separately.

GINETTE MATHIOT
JE SAIS FAIRE LA PATISSERIE

Pears in Chocolate Sabayon

Pears and chocolate have had a long and happy relationship. I find, however, that pure chocolate sauce overpowers the flavor of the pears. This version is more delicate! For a lovely presentation, place a pear in the bottom of a tall parfait glass. Top with the sauce and then with the whipped cream. Beautiful looking but hard to eat.

To serve the sauce cold, incorporate the whipped cream into the chilled sauce and top the pears just before serving. The sauce, in that case, can be made well in advance.

To serve 4 to 6

4 to 6	Bartlett or other large pears	4 to 6
3 cups	water	¾ liter
1 cup	sugar	¼ liter
1	strip lemon peel	1
2-inch	cinnamon stick	5-cm.
1 cup	heavy cream, whipped with 2 tbsp. [30 ml.] superfine sugar and 2 tbsp. brandy	¼ liter

Chocolate sabayon sauce

3 oz.	semisweet chocolate	90 g.
¾ cup	coffee	175 ml.
4 tbsp.	granulated sugar	60 ml.
8	egg yolks	8
2 tbsp.	Cognac	30 ml.

Peel the pears, leaving 1 inch [2½ cm.] of the stem. Leave the pears whole.

In a saucepan, combine the water, sugar, lemon peel and cinnamon stick. When the sugar is dissolved, add the pears and poach them, covered, over low heat until tender. (The cooking time varies a great deal, depending on the ripeness of the fruit.)

Remove the saucepan from the heat and let the pears cool completely in the syrup. Refrigerate until serving time. Just before serving, make the sauce.

In a small saucepan, combine the chocolate and 2 tablespoons [30 ml.] of the coffee. Cook over low heat until the chocolate is completely melted and smooth.

In the top of a double boiler, combine the sugar and egg yolks. Add the melted-chocolate mixture and the remaining coffee. Whisk the mixture over simmering water with a hand beater or a balloon whisk until the mixture is creamy and thick. Do not let it come to a boil or the sauce will curdle. Remove from the heat and add the Cognac.

Drain the pears. Place them in a serving dish and pour the warm sauce over them.

Serve the pears with the flavored whipped cream on the side or pipe the cream decoratively around the pears.

PERLA MEYERS
THE SEASONAL KITCHEN

Stewed Pears with Rice

Stoofperen met Rijstebrij

To serve 6 to 8

2 lb.	hard pears, peeled, quartered and cored	1 kg.
about ⅔ cup	granulated sugar	about 150 ml.
	ground cinnamon	
1½ quarts	milk	1½ liters
1 cup	white rice	¼ liter
2 tbsp.	vanilla sugar	30 ml.
½ cup	butter	125 ml.
⅔ cup	firmly packed brown sugar	150 ml.

Place the pears in a pan, add enough water to almost cover them, then stir in ½ cup [125 ml.] of the granulated sugar and a pinch of cinnamon. Simmer the pears until they are tender. Drain the liquid from the pears and put them in a serving bowl or individual dishes. Bring the milk to a boil, add the rice and simmer until the rice is cooked—about 30 minutes. The rice pudding must be creamy. Add the vanilla sugar and more granulated sugar to taste.

Make a sauce by melting the butter, dissolving the brown sugar in it and stirring in a pinch of cinnamon. Pour the rice pudding over the pears and serve the sauce separately.

L. VAN PAREREN-BLES
ALLERHANDE RECEPTEN

Grilled Stuffed Pears

Carefully core the pears from the base with a narrow-bladed knife and a teaspoon, keeping them whole. To cook the pears in the oven, preheat the oven to 400° F. [200° C.] and bake the foil-wrapped fruit for 30 minutes.

To serve 4

4	large pears, cored	4
½ cup	ground almonds	125 ml.
2 tbsp.	sugar	30 ml.
1 tbsp.	butter, softened	15 ml.
1	large egg yolk	1
	almond extract (optional)	

Work together the almonds, sugar, butter and egg yolk to form a paste, adding one or two drops of almond extract if the almonds do not have much taste. Fill the pears with this mixture. Wrap each pear in aluminum foil. Grill the pears over charcoal for about 30 minutes, or until the pears are soft, turning them over once.

CLAUDIA RODEN
PICNIC: THE COMPLETE GUIDE TO OUTDOOR FOOD

Pears with Raspberries

To make the raspberry purée called for in this recipe, place about 2 pints [1 liter] of fresh raspberries and ¾ to 1 cup [175 to 250 ml.] of superfine sugar in a blender and blend for three to five minutes.

To serve 6 to 12

6	large, underripe pears, peeled, halved, cored and covered with acidulated water	6
1 cup	sugar	¼ liter
3 cups	water	¾ liter
2-inch	piece vanilla bean	5-cm.
3-inch	cinnamon stick	8-cm.
2 cups	raspberry purée	½ liter
½ cup	raspberry preserves	125 ml.
¼ cup	raspberry brandy	50 ml.
6 to 12	almond macaroons (depending on size), soaked in kirsch	6 to 12
	whole raspberries or macaroon powder, made by baking almond macaroons in a 300° F. [150° C.] oven for 1 hour and crushing them with a rolling pin	

Wine sauce

5	egg yolks	5
½ cup	sugar	125 ml.
¾ cup	sweet white wine	175 ml.
½ tsp.	vanilla extract	2 ml.
1 tbsp.	grated lemon peel	15 ml.
	ground cinnamon	
1 cup	heavy cream, whipped with 2 tbsp. [30 ml.] confectioners' sugar	¼ liter

To make the wine sauce, combine the egg yolks and sugar in the top part of a double boiler and beat until they are well blended and pale yellow. Add the wine. Cook the sauce over simmering water, stirring constantly, until it heavily coats a spoon. Do not let it come to a boil.

Immediately remove it from the heat. Add the vanilla extract, lemon peel and a pinch of cinnamon, and chill the sauce for one or two hours. Fold the whipped cream into the wine sauce and chill it for one more hour.

To prepare the pears, first combine the sugar and water in a large, nonreactive saucepan. Bring the syrup to a boil and add the vanilla bean and cinnamon stick. Partially covering the pan, poach a few pears at a time over low heat until they are tender. Do not overcook. Let the pears cool com-

pletely in their syrup while preparing the rest of the dessert.

Pass the raspberry purée through a fine sieve and reserve. Mix the raspberry preserves and the brandy in a small, nonreactive saucepan. Cook over low heat until the preserves dissolve. Pass through a fine sieve into the raspberry purée. If the purée is very thick, thin it out with spoonfuls of pear syrup. Pour the purée into a glass serving dish.

Shape the macaroons into small balls. Fill the cavities of the pear halves with the macaroon balls and place the halves on top of the raspberry purée.

Just before serving, spoon the wine sauce carefully over the pears. Decorate the top with macaroon powder or whole raspberries or both.

PERLA MEYERS
THE SEASONAL KITCHEN

Pears Poached in Black Currant Juice

Poires Fraîches Pochées au Cassis

As an alternative to rubbing the peeled pears with cut lemon halves to prevent discoloration, submerge them in 1 quart [1 liter] of water acidulated with the juice of two lemons.

To serve 4

6	pears	6
2 cups	black currants, stemmed	½ liter
3 cups	superfine sugar	¾ liter
1	vanilla bean, split in half lengthwise	1
½ cup	black currant liqueur	125 ml.

Blend half of the currants to a smooth purée in a blender. Strain the purée through a fine-meshed nylon or stainless-steel sieve set over a bowl; use a wooden spoon to press the purée through the sieve so that all the juice is squeezed out. You should obtain about ⅔ cup [150 ml.] of juice. Reserve it.

Pour 1½ quarts [1½ liters] of water into a large, heavy nonreactive pan; add the sugar, the vanilla-bean halves, the currant juice and the black currant liqueur. Place the pan over medium heat. Stir the mixture with a wooden spoon until the sugar has completely dissolved, bring it to a boil, and boil it for a few minutes.

While the syrup is boiling, peel the pears, remove the stems, and core the pears with an apple corer. Rub the fruit all over with the lemon halves to prevent discoloration.

Reduce the heat under the syrup and plunge the pears into it. Cook the pears for 12 minutes, add the remaining currants and cook the mixture for a further five minutes. Turn off the heat and let the pears and black currants cool in the syrup, then turn the mixture into a serving dish. Chill thoroughly before serving.

ALAIN AND ÉVENTHIA SENDERENS
LA CUISINE RÉUSSIE

Baked Pears

Poires au Gratin

To serve 6

2 lb.	pears, peeled, quartered, cored and cut lengthwise into ½-inch [1-cm.] slices	1 kg.
¼ cup	fresh orange juice	50 ml.
¼ cup	apricot preserves	50 ml.
¼ cup	dry white wine or vermouth	50 ml.
2 tbsp.	grated orange peel	30 ml.
2 cups	crumbled macaroons, lightly toasted in a 350° F. [180° C.] oven for 5 minutes	½ liter
4 tbsp.	butter, cut into small pieces	60 ml.
	heavy cream, whipped with grated orange peel	

Combine the orange juice, preserves, wine or vermouth, and the 2 tablespoons [30 ml.] of orange peel in a small bowl; mix thoroughly. Layer the pears in a buttered 9-by-13-inch [23-by-32-cm.] baking dish, sprinkling the layers with half of the macaroon crumbs and dotting them with 3 tablespoons [45 ml.] of the butter pieces as you go. Pour the orange-juice mixture over the pears. Sprinkle them with the remaining crumbs; dot them with the remaining butter. Bake in a preheated 400° F. [200° C.] oven until the top is golden brown—25 to 30 minutes. Serve hot or cold with the whipped cream.

BERT GREENE
BERT GREENE'S KITCHEN BOUQUETS

Pears in Cream

Peras a la Crema

To serve 4

4	pears, peeled, cored and cut into large cubes	4
1 cup	confectioners' sugar	¼ liter
4 tbsp.	butter, cut into small pieces	60 ml.
½ cup	heavy cream	125 ml.
¼ cup	almonds, blanched, peeled, chopped and toasted in a 350° F. [180° C.] oven for 10 minutes	50 ml.

Place the pears in a buttered baking dish. Sprinkle them with the sugar and dot them with the butter. Bake them in a preheated 425° F. [220° C.] oven for 20 to 30 minutes, or until tender, basting them several times with the cooking juices.

When the pears are brown, cover them with the cream and return them to the oven for three minutes. Before serving, sprinkle the almonds over the top.

CARLOS DELGADO (EDITOR)
CIEN RECETAS MAGISTRALES

Stuffed Pears

Pere Ripiene

To serve 4

4	Bartlett pears, peeled, halved and cored	4
½ cup	mixed walnuts and almonds, crushed	125 ml.
5 tbsp.	sugar	75 ml.
1	small egg	1
1½ cups	sweet white wine	375 ml.

Scoop out a bit more flesh from the center of each pear half; put the scooped-out flesh in a mortar or food processor and mash it. Add the nuts, 3 tablespoons [45 ml.] of the sugar and the egg to the mashed pear flesh. Mash until everything is well amalgamated.

Put the pear halves with the cored sides upward into a buttered baking dish just large enough to hold them in one layer. If any of the halves roll or tilt, cut off a small slice from the rounded side to steady the pear. Fill the pears with the nut mixture. Sprinkle them with the remaining sugar. Pour the wine over the pears and into the bottom of the dish.

Bake in a preheated 400° F. [200° C.] oven for one hour, or until the pears are tender, the filling toasted and the wine almost evaporated. Serve hot or cold; stuffed pears keep well in the refrigerator.

MARGARET AND G. FRANCO ROMAGNOLI
THE NEW ITALIAN COOKING

Caramelized Baked Pears

Pere Cotte Caramellate

Baked pears will keep for several days if refrigerated in a closed container.

To serve 4

4	large pears, unpeeled	4
4	whole cloves (optional)	4
1 cup	Demerara or turbinado sugar	¼ liter
1 cup	water	¼ liter

Stick a clove in each pear, if you like, and stand the pears upright, close to each other, in a baking dish. Place the sugar and water in a heavy saucepan, bring to a boil and let the syrup cook for five minutes over low heat. Pour the syrup over the pears and bake them in a preheated 350° F. [180° C.] oven for 25 to 30 minutes, basting them with the cooking liquid from time to time. Take them out of the oven when nicely golden and caramelized, and serve them hot or cold.

There are several variations to this recipe:

With rum. Core the uncooked pears and stuff the cavities with several crushed almond macaroons mixed with rum. When serving the baked pears, pour over them some rum that has been heated gently in a pan, then flamed.

With Grand Marnier. Core the uncooked pears and stuff them with softened butter mixed with an equal volume of sugar and a little grated orange peel. Before serving, add some Grand Marnier to the syrup.

With wine. Bake the pears whole in a mixture of 1 cup [¼ liter] of dry red wine, ½ cup [125 ml.] of sugar and a little grated lemon peel. Let them cook slowly in a 300° F. [150° C.] oven for about an hour, and moisten them at intervals with their own syrup. When the pears are done, they will be almost caramelized.

LYDIA B. SALVETTI
CENTO RICETTE SPENDENDO MENO

Baked Quinces in Honey

To serve 4

6	small quinces (or 4 large ones), peeled, quartered and cored	6
1 cup	honey	¼ liter
1 cup	fresh orange juice, fresh grapefruit juice or wine	¼ liter

Mix the honey into the fruit juice or wine. Place the quinces in a baking dish, pour the honey mixture over them and bake them, uncovered, in a preheated 325° F. [160° C.] oven until the quinces are tender. This will take two hours or a little more. If the quinces become dry while cooking, add a little water and cover the dish. Serve the quinces cold.

LORD WESTBURY AND DONALD DOWNES
WITH GUSTO AND RELISH

Poached Quinces Filled with Cream

Punjene Kuvane Dunje

To serve 6

3	medium-sized quinces	3
3 tbsp.	fresh lemon juice	45 ml.
1¼ cups	granulated sugar	300 ml.
2 cups	water	½ liter
1¼ cups	heavy cream, chilled	300 ml.
1 to 2 tbsp.	vanilla sugar	15 to 30 ml.

Half-fill a large bowl with water and pour in the lemon juice. Thinly peel each quince, cut it in half lengthwise, scoop out the core from each half with a melon baller, and immediately drop the fruit into the lemon water to prevent it from discoloring. Reserve the peel, cores and seeds.

Choose a wide, nonreactive saucepan that will hold the quince halves snugly when they are placed in one layer. Put the sugar and water in this saucepan and stir over low heat until the sugar dissolves. Increase the heat and, when the syrup comes to a boil, drain the quinces and lay them in the syrup. Cover the pan and bring the syrup to a simmer. Poach the quinces gently for 30 to 45 minutes, or until they are soft but still hold their shape. (The exact time depends on their size and ripeness.) During the poaching process, baste them from time to time with the pan juices. When they are cooked, lift them out carefully with a slotted spoon and arrange them, cut sides up, in a glass bowl. Let them cool.

Bring the poaching liquid in the saucepan back to a boil together with the reserved peels, cores and seeds, and simmer until the liquid thickens to a syrupy consistency. Strain the syrup through a fine-meshed sieve. Pour the syrup around the quinces and chill until the syrup sets into a jelly—about one hour if the bowl is embedded in a pot of crushed ice, or two to three hours in a refrigerator.

Shortly before serving, whip the cream until soft peaks form. Add the vanilla sugar and continue beating until the cream is just stiff, then spoon the cream into the cavity of each quince half.

SPASENIJA-PATA MARKOVIĆ (EDITOR)
VELIKI NARODNI KUVAR

Peaches, Apricots, Nectarines and Mangoes

Peach Cream in Coffee Cups

Pesche alla Chicchera

To serve 6

3	ripe peaches, blanched, peeled, halved and pitted	3
½ cup	superfine sugar	125 ml.
6	egg yolks	6
⅔ cup	sweet white wine	150 ml.

Press the peaches through a nonreactive sieve to make a purée. Using a wire whisk or electric mixer, beat together the sugar, egg yolks and wine, then whisk in the peach purée. Continue whisking until the cream is very thick and fluffy, then pour it into coffee cups and chill it thoroughly in the refrigerator, but do not let the cream freeze.

FELICE CÙNSOLO
LA CUCINA LOMBARDA

Peaches in White Wine

Pêches au Vin Blanc

The best peaches for this dish are the yellow-fleshed variety; do not prepare them too long ahead of serving time or the fruit will go mushy.

To serve 4

4	peaches, blanched, peeled, halved and pitted	4
2 tbsp.	superfine sugar	30 ml.
¼ to ½ cup	white wine	50 to 125 ml.

Slice the peaches into four big wine glasses, sprinkle them with the sugar and pour 1 to 2 tablespoons [15 to 30 ml.] of white wine into each glass.

ELIZABETH DAVID
FRENCH PROVINCIAL COOKING

Peaches Aswim in Rose Petals

To serve 10

10	large peaches, peeled, halved and pitted, with 5 pits reserved	10
10	highly scented roses, plus some pink rose petals—white part removed from base—for garnish	10
1	rose-geranium leaf (optional)	1
1½ cups	sugar	375 ml.
3 cups	water	¾ liter
3 tbsp.	fresh lemon juice	45 ml.
½	vanilla bean or 1 tsp. [5 ml.] vanilla extract	½
½ cup	puréed raspberries, strained	125 ml.

Remove the petals from the whole roses; tie these petals and the rose-geranium leaf, if you are using it, loosely in a cheesecloth bag.

Make a syrup by combining the sugar, water and the petal bag. Bring to a boil, then simmer for five minutes. Remove from the heat, add the lemon juice and the vanilla, and allow the syrup to steep for 10 minutes. With a spoon, press the petal bag to extract the maximum flavor, then remove the bag and, if you are using it, the vanilla bean.

Crack the reserved peach pits and remove the almond-flavored kernels. Add the peach halves and the kernels to the syrup and simmer until the peaches are tender. (Test for doneness with a fork.) Allow the peaches to cool in the syrup, then refrigerate until chilled.

With a slotted spoon, transfer the peaches to a glass bowl. Spoon out the peach kernels and peel them. Mix the remaining syrup with the raspberry purée and pour the mixture over the peaches. Chop the kernels and sprinkle them over the surface. Scatter the pink rose petals over the peaches.

JUDITH OLNEY
SUMMER FOOD

Peaches in Meursault Butter

Soupe de Pêches au Beurre de Meursault

Meursault is a full-bodied white wine from Burgundy.

	To serve 4	
4	white peaches, blanched, peeled, halved, pitted and sliced	4
4 tbsp.	butter	60 ml.
	sugar	
⅔ cup	Meursault	150 ml.
2 tbsp.	fresh lemon juice	30 ml.
4	fresh mint leaves, finely chopped	4

Melt 2 tablespoons [30 ml.] of the butter in a skillet over medium heat, quickly fry the peach slices in it and add a pinch of sugar to caramelize them. When the peaches are caramelized—after about two minutes—remove the skillet from the heat.

In a small, nonreactive saucepan, reduce the Meursault by half over low heat, and mix in the rest of the butter and the lemon juice. Arrange the peach slices in four warmed soup plates and pour the Meursault butter over them. Sprinkle with the chopped mint and serve.

LALOU BIZE-LEROY
LE NOUVEAU GUIDE GAULT MILLAU

Fried Peaches

Fritos de Melocotón

	To serve 4	
4	peaches, blanched, peeled, quartered and pitted	4
1 cup	brandy	¼ liter
	sugar	
	the thinly pared peel of 1 lemon	
¼ cup	orange-flower water	50 ml.
⅓ cup	flour	75 ml.
about 8 tbsp.	butter	about 120 ml.

In a bowl containing the brandy, ¼ cup [50 ml.] of sugar, the lemon peel and orange-flower water, macerate the peaches for two hours. Drain the peaches and pat them dry. Melt 4 tablespoons [60 ml.] of the butter in a large skillet over high heat. Dip a few of the peach quarters at a time in the flour and sauté them quickly in the butter until they begin to turn brown; add more butter as needed. Sprinkle with more sugar and serve.

MANUEL M. PUGA Y PARGA
LA COCINA PRÁCTICA

Baked Peach Pudding

The author recommends this batter for cherries as well as peaches, and suggests accompanying the pudding with pouring custard (recipe, page 163).

	To serve 4	
8	ripe peaches, blanched, peeled, halved and pitted	8
2 cups	water	½ liter
about ⅓ cup	sugar	about 75 ml.
⅓ cup	flour	75 ml.
1 quart	milk	1 liter
6	eggs, the yolks separated from the whites, and the whites stiffly beaten	6

Stew the peaches gently in water, sweetened with sugar to taste, until they are tender—about 10 minutes.

Stir the flour to a paste with ½ cup [125 ml.] of the milk and beat in the egg yolks. Bring the remaining milk to a boil and gradually stir it into the egg-yolk mixture. Keep stirring until this batter thickens, then add the egg whites, beating them in quickly.

While the peaches are still hot, place them in a baking dish and pour the batter over them. Bake in a preheated 400° F. [200° C.] oven for 30 minutes, or until the pudding is set and browned. Serve warm.

HESTER M. POOLE
FRUITS, AND HOW TO USE THEM

Baked Stuffed Peaches

Punjene Preskve

	To serve 6	
6	peaches, wiped with a cloth to remove the down, halved and pitted	6
½ cup	almonds, ground	125 ml.
6 tbsp.	superfine sugar	90 ml.
5 or 6	vanilla wafers, crushed to a powder	5 or 6
1 tbsp.	finely chopped candied citron peel	15 ml.
½ cup	white wine	125 ml.

Scoop some of the flesh from each peach half to make more room for the filling. Reserve the flesh.

Mix the almonds with 5 tablespoons [75 ml.] of the sugar, the crushed vanilla wafers, the candied citron peel and the reserved peach flesh; add enough of the wine to make a firm but pliable mixture. Divide the almond mixture into 12 equal portions and shape each portion into a ball to resemble a peach pit. Fill the peaches with the almond balls and arrange the peach halves, with their filled sides up, in a well-buttered baking dish.

Combine the remaining sugar and wine, and sprinkle the peaches with half of this mixture. Bake the peaches in a preheated 450° F. [230° C.] oven for about 15 minutes, or until tender. Halfway through the baking time, remove the dish from the oven and sprinkle the peaches with the remaining sweetened wine. Cool the peaches and refrigerate them until well chilled. Serve cold.

SPASENIJA-PATA MARKOVIĆ (EDITOR)
VELIKI NARODNI KUVAR

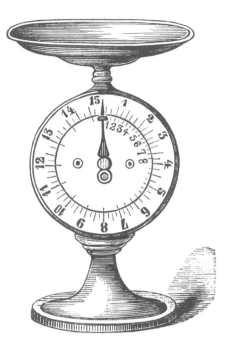

Fresh Peach Cobbler

To serve 4 to 6

2 lb.	peaches, blanched, peeled, pitted and sliced (about 4 cups [1 liter])	1 kg.
½ lb.	short-crust dough (recipe, page 164)	¼ kg.
1 tbsp.	fresh lemon juice	15 ml.
1 cup	sugar	¼ liter
3 tbsp.	flour	45 ml.
¼ tsp.	salt	1 ml.
⅛ tsp.	ground cinnamon (optional)	½ ml.
2 tbsp.	butter, cut into pieces	30 ml.
	cream or melted butter	

Roll out the dough to fit the top of a 6-cup [1½-liter] baking dish. Cut several slashes in the dough for steam vents. Set the dough aside.

Mix the peach slices and lemon juice. Combine the sugar, flour, salt and cinnamon, if you are using it. Sprinkle the sugar mixture over the peaches, and mix carefully. Butter the baking dish and spread the peach slices in it evenly. Dot the peaches with the butter pieces and cover the fruit with the rolled dough. Brush the dough lightly with cream or melted butter.

Bake the cobbler in a preheated 425° F. [220° C.] oven for 25 minutes, or until the crust is lightly browned and the peaches are tender. Serve warm or slightly cooled, plain or with whipped cream or ice cream.

JAN MC BRIDE CARLTON
THE OLD-FASHIONED COOKBOOK

Peach Granita with Poached Peaches

Neige Granitée aux Pêches Cardinalisées

To make the raspberry purée, rub 2 pints [1 liter] of raspberries through a fine-meshed nylon or stainless steel sieve and sweeten them to taste with superfine sugar.

To serve 5

10	large white peaches, blanched and peeled	10
4 cups	light sugar syrup (recipe, page 162)	1 liter
	sugar (optional)	
	apricot or peach liqueur	
1 cup	raspberry purée	¼ liter

Put the peaches into a large pan, add the sugar syrup and poach for a few minutes until tender. Remove the peaches from the syrup and leave them to cool. Reserve the syrup.

Slice five of the peaches in half and remove their pits. Pour 2 cups [½ liter] of the syrup into a blender, add the peach halves and blend until the peaches are puréed. Pour the mixture into metal ice trays and place in the freezer. When small ice crystals start to form around the edges of the mixture, remove the trays from the freezer, scoop the mixture into the blender and blend for a moment. Return the mixture to the trays. Repeat this process every 30 minutes for four hours. While the ice is still soft, add a little sugar if you wish and sprinkle in some apricot or peach liqueur.

Serve the ice coated with raspberry purée and accompanied by the whole poached peaches; or serve in individual glasses, with a poached peach on top.

ANDRÉ GUILLOT
LA VRAIE CUISINE LÉGÈRE

Peach Melba

Pêches Melba

Auguste Escoffier created Peach Melba in 1894 to honor Dame Nellie Melba, the great Australian-born opera star.

The white peaches may be replaced by yellow peaches. If the peaches are perfectly ripe and unblemished, they need not be poached: Simply peel them, rub them with the cut side of half a lemon, remove the pits and sprinkle the peaches with superfine sugar. If preferred, the peaches can be coated with puréed raspberries that have been sweetened to taste, instead of with cooked raspberry sauce.

To serve 6

6	white peaches, blanched, peeled and rubbed with a cut lemon	6
1 cup	sugar	¼ liter
1 ½ cups	water	375 ml.
1	vanilla bean	1
⅓ cup	almonds, blanched, peeled and cut into slivers	75 ml.
1 quart	vanilla ice cream *(recipe, page 167)*	1 liter
Raspberry sauce		
2 pints	raspberries, puréed through a nylon or stainless-steel sieve	1 liter
3 tbsp.	superfine sugar	45 ml.
1 tsp.	fresh lemon juice	5 ml.

In a heavy pan, combine the sugar and water with the vanilla bean and bring this syrup to a boil. Reduce the heat, add the peaches to the syrup, cover, and poach for five to six minutes. Let the peaches cool in the syrup. Drain the peaches thoroughly, halve them and remove the pits.

To make the raspberry sauce, put the puréed raspberries into a small nonreactive saucepan, and add the sugar. Taste for sweetness and add more sugar if desired. Simmer for five to six minutes, stirring with a wooden spoon, then add the lemon juice, which will enhance the flavor of the raspberries. Set the sauce aside to cool.

To serve, place spoonfuls of the vanilla ice cream in the bottom of six chilled Champagne glasses. Cover the ice cream in each glass with two peach halves. Pour the raspberry sauce over the peaches, sprinkle them with the blanched, slivered almonds and serve.

LOUISETTE BERTHOLLE
UNE GRANDE CUISINE POUR TOUS

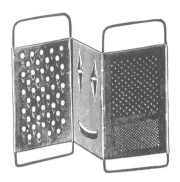

Minted Apricots

To serve 2 to 4

2 cups	sliced apricots	½ liter
¼ cup	sugar	50 ml.
¼ cup	fresh lime juice	50 ml.
¼ cup	fresh mint leaves, 2 tbsp. [30 ml.] chopped	50 ml.

Combine the sugar, lime juice and the chopped mint in a nonreactive pan. Bring the mixture to a boil; strain this sauce and allow it to cool. Add the apricots and stir to coat them with the sauce. Chill the apricots for two to three hours. Serve them in sherbet glasses garnished with the whole mint leaves.

JEAN H. SHEPARD
THE FRESH FRUITS AND VEGETABLES COOKBOOK

Apricot Ring

The purée is made from ½ pound [¼ kg.] of apricots, peeled, pitted and cooked in water until soft. Fill the center of the ring before serving with poached whole apricots if you like.

To serve 6 to 8

1 cup	apricot purée	¼ liter
2 tbsp.	apricot liqueur	30 ml.
1 ½ tbsp.	unflavored powdered gelatin	22 ml.
⅓ cup	cold water	75 ml.
2 cups	heavy cream, whipped	½ liter
5	egg whites	5
½ cup	superfine sugar	125 ml.

In a mixing bowl, combine the apricot purée and liqueur. In a small saucepan, soften the gelatin in the water for five minutes, then dissolve the softened gelatin over low heat. Blend

the dissolved gelatin into the apricot purée. Let the mixture cool and fold in the whipped cream.

In another mixing bowl beat the egg whites to the soft-peak stage. Add the sugar a little at a time, continuing the beating until the whites are stiff. Fold them into the purée mixture. Spread the mixture evenly in a 6-cup [1½-liter] ring mold rinsed in ice water and drained. Chill the apricot mixture in the refrigerator for three hours, or until it is very firm. Unmold it onto a chilled serving platter.

CHARLOTTE ADAMS AND DORIS MC FERRAN TOWNSEND
THE FAMILY COOKBOOK: DESSERT

Apricot or Peach Fritters

Gebackene Aprikosen (Pfirsiche)

To serve 4

8	apricots or 4 peaches, blanched, peeled, halved and pitted	8
	oil for deep frying	
½ cup	confectioners' sugar, mixed with 1 tbsp. [15 ml.] ground cinnamon	125 ml.
	Batter	
2	eggs	2
1 cup	milk	¼ liter
½ cup	white wine	125 ml.
1 tbsp.	confectioners' sugar	15 ml.
2 cups	flour	½ liter
	salt	

Make the batter in a large bowl by whisking together the eggs, milk, wine, confectioners' sugar, flour and a pinch of salt. Dip the fruit in the batter to coat each piece. Heat the oil in a large, heavy pan until it is very hot. Add the batter-coated fruit, a few pieces at a time, and deep fry each batch until golden—about two or three minutes. Drain the fritters well. Before serving, sprinkle the warm fritters with the cinnamon-flavored confectioners' sugar.

MARIA HORVATH
BALKAN-KÜCHE

Nectarines in Blueberry Sauce

Because many nectarines are not freestones, it is advisable to prepare them as follows: Halve each one lengthwise (through the stem end), then grasp both halves firmly and twist in opposite directions until one side pulls free of the pit. If you cannot easily pry the pit from the other half, use a grapefruit knife to cut it out neatly.

To serve 8

8	very large nectarines (or 12 medium-large ones), halved and pitted	8
1 pint	blueberries, stemmed	½ liter
2½ cups	water	625 ml.
1½ cups	sugar	375 ml.
½	lemon, thickly sliced	½
about 1 tbsp.	kirsch or mirabelle	about 15 ml.

In a 12-inch [30-cm.] nonreactive skillet or saucepan, combine the water and sugar and bring to a boil, stirring. Add the lemon slices. Set the nectarines skin side down in the syrup. Cover the pan and barely simmer for three to five minutes, or until the halves are slightly tender. Gently turn over each half and barely simmer, covered, about two minutes longer, or until the fruits are slightly softened.

Remove the fruits from the syrup with a slotted spoon. Discard the lemon pieces; reserve the syrup. When cool enough to handle, carefully pull the skin from each nectarine half. Set all the halves, cut side down, in a dish large enough to hold them in one layer. Spoon a little syrup over each half, cover, and refrigerate until serving time.

Add the blueberries to the remaining syrup. Simmer them until soft—about four minutes. With a slotted spoon, transfer the berries to the container of a food processor or blender and whirl to a fine purée. Press the purée through a fine sieve into a bowl. Add enough of the cooking syrup to produce a fairly thick, but liquid sauce. Add the kirsch or mirabelle to taste. Refrigerate until serving time.

To serve, pour the sauce into a very wide, deep serving platter. Set the nectarines into the sauce very gently (so as not to splash them with purple), placing them cut side down.

ELIZABETH SCHNEIDER COLCHIE
READY WHEN YOU ARE

Nectarine Betty

To serve 6

3 lb.	nectarines, peeled, halved, pitted and sliced	1 ½ kg.
½ cup	firmly packed light brown sugar	125 ml.
4 cups	stale bread cubes	1 liter
¼ cup	sugar	50 ml.
¼ tsp.	ground cinnamon	1 ml.
4 tbsp.	butter, melted	60 ml.

Combine the nectarines and brown sugar in a 2-quart [2-liter] baking dish. Toss the bread cubes with the sugar, cinnamon and butter until coated. Spread over the fruit. Bake in a preheated 350° F. [180° C.] oven until heated through—about 25 minutes.

JOE CARCIONE
THE GREENGROCER COOKBOOK

Mango Crisp

To serve 6 to 8

4 cups	peeled, sliced mango	1 liter
1 cup	sifted flour	¼ liter
1 cup	sugar	¼ liter
1 tsp.	baking powder	5 ml.
¾ tsp.	salt	4 ml.
1 tsp.	ground cinnamon	5 ml.
1 tsp.	grated nutmeg	5 ml.
1	egg	1
5 tbsp.	butter, melted	75 ml.
½ cup	pecans, chopped	125 ml.

Butter an 8-by-8-by-2-inch [20-by-20-by-5-cm.] baking dish and line the dish with mango slices. Sift the flour, sugar, baking powder, salt and spices together into a bowl, and work in the egg with a pastry blender until the mixture has the consistency of coarse meal. Sprinkle the mixture over the mango slices. Drizzle the melted butter over the top and add the chopped nuts. Bake in a preheated 375° F. [190° C.] oven for 45 minutes.

RARE FRUIT COUNCIL
TROPICAL FRUIT RECIPES

Mango Cream Mousse

To serve 4

2 cups	mango slices	½ liter
1 cup	heavy cream, whipped	¼ liter
¼ cup	confectioners' sugar	50 ml.
½ oz.	semisweet chocolate, finely grated	15 g.

Simmer the mango slices in enough water to cover until they are tender. Drain the slices and put them through a sieve or food mill. Cool the purée. Fold in the whipped cream and confectioners' sugar. Mound the purée in a serving dish, garnish it with the chocolate and chill before serving.

MONICA BAYLEY
BLACK AFRICA COOKBOOK

Mango Mousse

To serve 8

5	medium-sized mangoes (about 1 lb. [½ kg.] each)	5
⅓ cup	fresh lime juice	75 ml.
2	egg whites	2
	salt	
⅓ cup	sugar	75 ml.
½ cup	heavy cream, whipped	125 ml.

With a small, sharp knife, peel the mangoes and cut the flesh away from the large flat pit inside each fruit. Cut the flesh of two mangoes into ¼-inch [6-mm.] dice and set aside. Chop the three remaining mangoes fine and purée them through a food mill set over a bowl. Then stir in the lime juice.

In a large bowl, beat the egg whites with a pinch of salt until they are frothy. Sprinkle in the sugar and continue beating until the egg whites are stiff.

With a rubber spatula, fold the egg whites into the whipped cream. Stir about 1 cup [¼ liter] of this mixture into the mango purée, then pour the purée over the remaining cream and fold them together gently but thoroughly. Carefully fold in the diced mango. Spoon the mousse into individual dessert dishes or a large serving bowl. Refrigerate it for at least three hours before serving.

FOODS OF THE WORLD
THE COOKING OF THE CARIBBEAN ISLANDS

Mango Velva

To prepare the mango purée called for in this recipe, peel and slice two mangoes and rub the slices through a nylon or stainless-steel sieve set over a bowl. The technique of using an ice-cream maker is demonstrated on pages 86-87.

This may be churned, packed into freezer cartons and stored in a freezer for two to four months.

To serve 6

3 cups	puréed raw mango flesh	¾ liter
1 tbsp.	unflavored powdered gelatin	15 ml.
¼ cup	water	50 ml.
1 cup	sugar	¼ liter
2 tbsp.	fresh lemon or lime juice	30 ml.

In a heatproof bowl or measuring cup, mix the gelatin with the water and let the gelatin soften for five minutes. Stand the bowl or cup in a pan of hot water and stir the mixture until the gelatin dissolves.

In a large bowl, mix the sugar and lemon or lime juice with the mango purée. Add the dissolved gelatin and mix well. Pour into the canister of a 4-quart [4-liter] ice-cream maker and churn as for ice cream. The ice will freeze in about 15 minutes. Pack until it is ready to serve.

FLORIDA FRUIT AND VEGETABLE RECIPES

Plums, Cherries and Dates

Polish Plum Pudding

Legumina ze Świeżych Śliwek

To serve 6

1 lb.	plums, blanched and peeled	½ kg.
4 tbsp.	butter	60 ml.
1 cup	sugar	¼ liter
6	eggs, the yolks separated from the whites, and the whites stiffly beaten	6
¼ cup	dry bread crumbs	50 ml.
	sour cream	

Melt 1 tablespoon [15 ml.] of the butter in a saucepan and add the plums. When the juice starts to run, stir in half of the sugar and simmer for 20 minutes, or until the plums are tender. Cool the plums and then transfer them to a bowl. Halve the plums, remove the pits and mash the plums with a wooden pestle until they are reduced to a smooth purée. Alternatively, rub them through a fine-meshed sieve.

Melt the remaining butter in a small saucepan and let it cool. In a bowl, cream together the egg yolks, the melted butter, the rest of the sugar and two thirds of the bread crumbs. Stir this mixture into the plum purée. Gradually fold in the beaten egg whites, then transfer the pudding to a 4-cup [1-liter] mold that has been buttered and sprinkled with the remaining bread crumbs.

Bake the pudding in a preheated 425° F. [220° C.] oven for 20 minutes, or until set and browned. Unmold the pudding and serve it hot with sour cream and sugar.

IDA PLUCIŃSKA
KSIĄŻKA KUCHARSKA

Plum Dumplings

Instead of plums, you may use apricots, cherries or peaches. The Hungarians sometimes substitute 1½ cups [375 ml.] of mashed potatoes for half the flour.

To make 16 dumplings

16	Italian plums, halved, pitted and sprinkled with lemon juice	16
¼ cup	sugar	50 ml.
1 tsp.	ground cinnamon	5 ml.
⅛ tsp.	grated nutmeg	½ ml.
½ cup	ground walnuts or bread crumbs, fried for a few minutes in 4 tbsp. [60 ml.] butter	125 ml.

Dumpling dough

3 cups	flour	¾ liter
1 tsp.	salt	5 ml.
2	eggs, lightly beaten	2
¼ cup	butter, softened	50 ml.
½ to ¾ cup	milk	125 to 175 ml.

To make the dough, sift together the flour and salt into a medium bowl. Beat the eggs into the softened butter until they are well blended. Then stir the mixture into the flour, adding just enough milk to form a stiff dough. Remove the dough to a well-floured board and knead for about 10 minutes, or until it feels smooth and satiny. Roll the dough into a ball. Cover it and let it rest for 30 minutes. In a small bowl, combine the sugar, cinnamon and nutmeg, and mix.

Divide the dough in half, and roll out each section to a thickness of about ⅛ inch [3 mm.]. Use a 3-inch [8-cm.] cookie cutter to cut out circles.

Place two plum halves in the center of each circle. Sprinkle with the spice mixture and cover with another circle of dough. Seal the edges firmly by pressing down all around with the tines of a fork.

Bring a large pot of lightly salted water to a boil, and drop in eight to 10 dumplings. Simmer for 12 minutes. Remove them with a slotted spoon and place them in a well-buttered serving dish. Repeat until all the dumplings are cooked.

Top with buttered walnuts or bread crumbs and sprinkle with any remaining spice mixture. Serve the dumplings while they are still warm.

MARIA POLUSHKIN
THE DUMPLING COOKBOOK

Plum Slices

Croûtes aux Prunes

Not exactly a dish for a grand party, but all the same an excellent countrified sweet. Apricots can be cooked in the same way with good results.

To serve 2

5 or 6	plums, halved and pitted	5 or 6
4 tbsp.	butter	60 ml.
2	slices fresh bread, ½ inch [1 cm.] thick	2
¼ cup	firmly packed brown sugar	50 ml.

Butter the bread on one side and on this side put the plums, cut side up, pressing them down and into the bread with a knife. Put a little butter and brown sugar into each half plum, and put the slices into a generously buttered baking dish, plum side up. Place a piece of buttered paper over the slices, and bake in the top third of a preheated 350° F. [180° C.] oven. In about 30 minutes the bread will be golden and crisp and the plums cooked with a topping of sugary syrup.

ELIZABETH DAVID
FRENCH COUNTRY COOKING

Purple Plum Crunch

To serve 6

24	Italian plums, quartered and pitted	24
¼ cup	firmly packed brown sugar	50 ml.
3 tbsp.	flour	45 ml.
½ tsp.	ground cinnamon	2 ml.

Sugar topping

1 cup	granulated sugar	¼ liter
1 tsp.	baking powder	5 ml.
1 cup	flour, sifted	¼ liter
¼ tsp.	salt	1 ml.
1	egg, well beaten	1
8 tbsp.	butter, melted	120 ml.

Place the plums in the bottom of a shallow 2-quart [2-liter] baking dish. Sprinkle them with a mixture of the brown sugar, flour and cinnamon.

Prepare the topping by mixing the sugar, baking powder, flour, salt and egg. Strew the topping evenly over the plums. Over this pour melted butter. Bake in a preheated 350° F. [180° C.] oven for 45 minutes, or until the plums are tender and the topping crisp.

MARIAN FOX BURROS AND LOIS LEVINE
THE ELEGANT BUT EASY COOKBOOK

Chocolate Crepes with Fresh Cherry Filling

To serve 8

1 lb.	Bing cherries, stemmed and pitted	½ kg.
¼ cup	sugar	50 ml.
2 tbsp.	kirsch	30 ml.
1 tbsp.	fresh lemon juice	15 ml.
1 tsp.	vanilla extract	5 ml.
	ground cinnamon	
3 oz.	semisweet chocolate, chopped into small pieces	90 ml.
	vanilla ice cream (recipe, page 167) or sweetened whipped cream	
	cocoa powder	

Chocolate crepes

2 tbsp.	cocoa powder, preferably Dutch process cocoa	30 ml.
⅓ cup	flour	75 ml.
2 tbsp.	sugar	30 ml.
2	eggs	2
about 1 cup	milk	about ¼ liter
1 tsp.	vanilla extract	5 ml.
3 tbsp.	unsalted butter, melted and cooled	45 ml.

Place the cherries in a bowl—so as not to lose juices—and chop them. Stir in the sugar, kirsch, lemon juice and a pinch of cinnamon. Let the cherries steep for one hour.

To make the crepes, sift the cocoa powder, flour, sugar and a pinch of salt into a mixing bowl. Make a well in the middle and add the eggs, ¾ cup [175 ml.] of milk, the vanilla extract and melted butter. The batter should be the consistency of heavy cream; add more milk if necessary.

Heat a seasoned crepe pan or a lightly buttered skillet. (The pan should be hot enough so that a drop of batter sizzles when it is tested.) Add a ladleful of batter to the hot pan, quickly roll and turn the pan to spread the batter, then pour excess batter back into the bowl. Cook until brown speckles appear on top of the crepe, then turn it over briefly to cook the other side. Cook the remaining crepes similarly.

When ready to serve, stir the chocolate bits into the cherry mixture. Place a large spoonful of cherry filling down the center of a crepe and roll up the crepe. Continue to fill and roll crepes, setting two crepes on each individual plate.

Top each serving with a small scoop of vanilla ice cream or a large dollop of whipped cream. Place a little cocoa powder in a sieve and quickly dust the top of each serving.

JUDITH OLNEY
THE JOY OF CHOCOLATE

Cherry Cream

The secret of success is in having the cream, juice and eggs thoroughly chilled, and in adding the juice a little at a time to prevent curdling. A currant cream and a blackberry cream can be made in the same way. Oranges, lemons or any other fruits that have sufficient juice can also be used.

To serve 6

2 lb.	cherries	1 kg.
2 cups	heavy cream	½ liter
about 1¼ cups	sugar	about 300 ml.
2	egg whites, stiffly beaten	2

Crush the cherries without removing the pits. Sprinkle the cherries with ¾ cup [175 ml.] of the sugar and let them stand in a cool place for two hours. Strain the cherry juice through muslin or fine cheesecloth or through a fine-meshed sieve. Sweeten the juice with ½ cup [125 ml.] of sugar, or more to taste. Partly whip the cream and then gradually whip in the cherry juice and the egg whites. Continue whipping until no more froth rises. Serve at once.

HESTER M. POOLE
FRUITS, AND HOW TO USE THEM

Poached Cherries

To serve 4

1 lb.	red cherries, stemmed and pitted	½ kg.
½ cup	sugar	125 ml.
1 cup	water	¼ liter
	salt	

Bring the sugar, water and a pinch of salt to a boil in a nonreactive saucepan and boil for several minutes. Add the cherries and simmer them gently until they are just done—about five minutes. Serve warm or cold with whipped cream, ice cream or custard sauce.

JAMES BEARD
THE JAMES BEARD COOKBOOK

Cherries with Red Wine
Ciliegie al Barolo

To serve 4

1 lb.	cherries, pitted	½ kg.
1 cup	sugar	¼ liter
½ cup	black currant jelly	125 ml.
	the thinly pared peel of 1 orange, cut into strips and blanched for 5 minutes in boiling water	
½	cinnamon stick	½
2 cups	Barolo or other full-bodied red wine	½ liter
1 cup	heavy cream, whipped	¼ liter

Put the cherries in a nonreactive saucepan with the sugar, jelly, orange peel and cinnamon; cover with the wine. Set the pan over medium heat and, when the wine comes to a boil, reduce the heat and simmer very gently for 30 minutes. Let the cherries cool in their sauce. Discard the cinnamon stick and spoon the cherries and sauce into individual dishes, garnishing them with whipped cream. Refrigerate for one or two hours before serving the cherries.

LAURA GRAS PORTINARI
CUCINA E VINI DEL PIEMONTE E DELLA VALLE D'AOSTA

Fried Cherries
Chriesitütschli

To serve 6 to 8

1½ to 2 lb.	small Bing cherries, stems attached	¾ to 1 kg.
2	eggs, well beaten	2
⅔ cup	milk	150 ml.
2 tbsp.	oil or melted butter	30 ml.
1 cup	flour	¼ liter
¼ tsp.	salt	1 ml.
2 tbsp.	sugar	30 ml.
	oil for deep frying	
½ cup	sugar, mixed with 1 tbsp. [15 ml.] ground cinnamon	125 ml.

In a large bowl, beat the eggs with milk and oil or butter. Stir in the flour, salt and 2 tablespoons [30 ml.] of sugar. Beat with a rotary egg beater until smooth. Use white cotton string to tie the cherries into bundles by the stems, including five or six cherries in each bundle. Dip the bundles into the batter and fry them in oil at 380° F. [190° C.] until golden brown—two or three minutes. Then roll the cherries in the cinnamon sugar.

NIKA STANDEN HAZELTON
THE SWISS COOKBOOK

Rum Cherry Fritters

To serve 6 to 8

1 lb.	cherries, with the stems intact	½ kg.
½ cup	flour	125 ml.
2	eggs, the yolks separated from the whites	2
	confectioners' sugar	
2 tbsp.	rum	30 ml.
¼ tsp.	salt	1 ml.
½ cup	clarified butter	125 ml.
½ cup	vegetable oil	125 ml.

In a medium-sized bowl, mix together the flour, egg yolks, 2 tablespoons [30 ml.] of confectioners' sugar, the rum and salt to form a smooth batter. Cover the bowl and let the batter stand for one to two hours.

Beat the egg whites until they are stiff and fold them into the batter. In a large frying pan, heat the clarified butter and vegetable oil to 360° F. [180° C.], then turn the heat to low. Holding the cherries by the stems, dip one at a time into the batter and stand the cherry upright in the frying pan. Fry the cherries for three minutes, or until they are golden brown. Remove the cherries from the pan with a slotted spoon and drain them on absorbent paper. Dip them into the confectioners' sugar and serve.

MARIA POLUSHKIN
THE DUMPLING COOKBOOK

Cherry Cobbler

To serve 4 or 5

1 lb.	sour cherries, pitted (about 3 cups [¾ liter])	½ kg.
1 tbsp.	butter	15 ml.
¼ cup	water	50 ml.
1 cup plus 1 tbsp.	sugar	¼ liter plus 15 ml.
1 cup plus 1 tbsp.	sifted flour	¼ liter plus 15 ml.
1½ tsp.	baking powder	7 ml.
½ tsp.	salt	2 ml.
2½ tbsp.	vegetable shortening, cut into small pieces	37 ml.
about ⅜ cup	milk	about 90 ml.

In a nonreactive pan, heat together to boiling the cherries, butter and water. Mix 1 cup [¼ liter] of the sugar and 1 tablespoon [15 ml.] of the flour. Add to the cherries and heat, stirring continuously, to boiling. Turn the mixture into a 4-cup [1-liter] casserole.

Sift together the remaining flour, the remaining sugar, the baking powder and salt. Cut in the shortening until the mixture resembles coarse cornmeal. Add just enough milk to make a thick batter. Drop the batter by spoonfuls onto the cherries in the casserole. Bake in a preheated 425° F. [220° C.] oven for about 30 minutes.

RAYMOND A. SOKOLOV
GREAT RECIPES FROM THE NEW YORK TIMES

Cherry Chocolate Pudding

To serve 6

1 pint	cherries, stemmed and pitted	½ liter
6 tbsp.	butter, cut into pieces	90 ml.
1 ½ cups	firmly packed light brown sugar	375 ml.
½ tsp	ground cloves	2 ml.
⅓ cup	cocoa powder	75 ml.
⅔ cup	whole-wheat flour	150 ml.
1 tsp.	baking powder	5 ml.
½ cup	buttermilk	125 ml.
1 tsp.	maple extract	5 ml.
1 tsp.	vanilla extract	5 ml.
2	egg whites, stiffly beaten	2
	fresh orange juice	
1 tbsp.	cornstarch	15 ml.
2 tbsp.	rum	30 ml.
	heavy cream (optional)	

Butter a 5-cup [1¼-liter] baking dish and scatter 2 tablespoons [30 ml.] of the pieces of butter in the bottom. Drain the cherries, reserving any juice, and mix them with ½ cup [125 ml.] of the brown sugar and the cloves. Spread the cherry mixture evenly in the dish.

For the dough, cream the remaining butter pieces and brown sugar, and add the cocoa powder. Mix the flour and baking powder and add them to the creamed-butter mixture alternately with the buttermilk. Add the extracts and fold in the beaten egg whites last. Spoon the dough over the cherries and bake in a preheated 350° F. [180° C.] oven for 20 minutes and at 325° F. [160° C.] for another 20 minutes, or until the top is brown and a cake tester inserted into the dough comes out clean.

In a nonreactive pan, combine any juice remaining from the cherries with enough orange juice to make ⅔ cup [150 ml.]. Off the heat, blend the cornstarch with the juices, then cook until this syrup thickens and is clear. Add the rum. Turn the pudding out onto a serving plate and pour the syrup over it. Serve with cream if you like.

STELLA STANDARD
THE ART OF FRUIT COOKERY

French Cherry Custard Cake

Clafoutis

If the dish in which it is baked is an attractive one, you can serve the warm cake, sprinkled with confectioners' sugar, directly from the dish. However, I prefer to unmold it. I must caution you to expect the dessert to fall as it cools—this is basic to the nature of the batter.

To make one 8-by-8-by-2-inch [20-by-20-by-5-cm.] cake

2 cups	cherries, pitted	½ liter
4	eggs	4
1 ½ cups	milk	375 ml.
½ cup	sifted flour	125 ml.
¼ cup	granulated sugar	50 ml.
⅛ tsp.	salt	½ ml.
1 tbsp.	vanilla extract	15 ml.
	confectioners' sugar	

To make the batter in a blender, combine the eggs, milk, flour, granulated sugar, salt and vanilla in the jar. Cover the jar and blend at high speed for about a minute. Turn off the blender and scrape down the sides of the jar with a rubber spatula. Re-cover the jar and, again at high speed, blend the batter for another minute.

To make the batter by hand, beat the eggs until frothy in a medium-sized mixing bowl using an electric mixer, rotary beater or whisk. Pour in the milk, and add the flour, granulated sugar, salt and vanilla. Beat the batter for two or three minutes longer, or until it is smooth.

Thoroughly dry the cherries and spread them evenly in the bottom of a buttered baking pan measuring 8 by 8 by 2 inches [20 by 20 by 5 cm.]. Slowly pour in the batter. Bake the cake in a preheated 350° F. [180° C.] oven for about one and one half hours: The cake is done when the batter has set into a custard-like mass and a cake tester comes out clean. Let the cake cool in its pan until lukewarm.

Run the flat of a knife around the sides of the pan to free the cake. Invert a large serving platter over the pan and, grasping the pan and plate together, turn them over. Lift off the pan. Dust the top of the cake with the confectioners' sugar and serve it at once.

MICHAEL FIELD
COOKING ADVENTURES WITH MICHAEL FIELD

Dates Stuffed with Almonds

Pourmi s Bademi

To make 25

25	large, fresh dates, slit lengthwise on one side, pits removed	25
25	large almonds, blanched, peeled and toasted at 300° F. [150° C.] for 15 minutes	25
1 cup	sugar	¼ liter

Stuff a toasted almond into each date, then place the fruits, slit side up, on a wire rack positioned over a buttered pan. Put the sugar in a small frying pan or saucepan over low heat. Allow the sugar to melt to a light amber color. Immediately dribble a teaspoonful of this hot caramel over each date to cover the slit and the embedded almond. The fruits are ready to eat as soon as the caramel glaze has cooled and set. These stuffed dates will keep for at least a month in a tightly closed container.

M. TSOLOVA, V. STOILOVA AND SN. EKIMOVA
IZPOLZOUVANE NA ZELENCHOUTSITE I PLODOVETE V DOMAKINSTVOTO

Date Soufflé

To serve 6

1 cup	dates, pitted and chopped	¼ liter
½ cup	milk	125 ml.
2 tbsp.	dark rum	30 ml.
2 tbsp.	heavy cream	30 ml.
1 tsp.	vanilla extract	5 ml.
4	eggs, the yolks separated from the whites, and the yolks beaten, plus 1 additional egg white	4
½ cup	sugar	125 ml.
	heavy cream (optional)	

In a nonreactive saucepan, combine the dates with the milk; cover, and cook them for 20 minutes, or until they are very soft. Remove them from the heat and mash them in the milk to form a smooth paste. Into the mashed dates, stir the rum, heavy cream, vanilla and beaten egg yolks.

Beat the egg whites until they are stiff; gradually add the sugar until the whites stand in firm peaks. Fold a little of the date mixture into the egg whites; then fold all the whites into the dates. Spoon the batter into a buttered and sugared 4-cup [1-liter] soufflé mold and bake the dessert in a preheated 350° F. [180° C.] oven for 35 to 40 minutes, or until it is well risen and lightly browned. Serve the soufflé at once, accompanied if you wish by plain or whipped heavy cream.

ROBERT ACKART
FRUITS IN COOKING

Berries and Grapes

Blackberry Dumplings

These dumplings can be made with strawberries, raspberries, blueberries or other berries in season.

To serve 4 to 6

1 pint	blackberries	½ liter
⅓ cup	sugar	75 ml.
1½ tsp.	flour	7 ml.
	fresh lemon juice	
2 tbsp.	butter, cut into pieces	30 ml.
	heavy cream, whipped and sweetened (optional)	

Dumpling dough

1½ cups	flour	375 ml.
1 tsp.	salt	5 ml.
8 tbsp.	butter, cut into pieces and chilled	120 ml.
2 tbsp.	lard, cut into pieces and chilled, or solid vegetable shortening	30 ml.
about ⅓ cup	ice water	about 75 ml.

For the dough, first mix together the flour and salt in a medium-sized bowl. Cut in the cold butter and lard or shortening to form a mixture that is the consistency of coarse oatmeal. Add the water a spoonful or so at a time and mix it in. Use only as much water as necessary to make a dough cohesive enough to form into a ball. Cover and refrigerate for at least two hours.

In a separate bowl, mix the blackberries with the sugar and flour. Sprinkle them with lemon juice.

On a floured board, roll out the dough and cut it into six 4-inch [10-cm.] squares. Place 1 to 2 tablespoons [15 to 30 ml.] of blackberries on each square and dot with butter. Fold each square over to form a triangle. Moisten the edges with a little water, if necessary, and press down on the edges with the tines of a fork.

Arrange the dumplings on a buttered baking sheet, and bake in a preheated 375° F. [190° C.] oven until they are golden—about 25 minutes. Serve the warm dumplings plain or with sweetened whipped cream.

MARIA POLUSHKIN
THE DUMPLING COOKBOOK

Blackberry Custards

To serve 6 to 8

3 pints	blackberries	1 ½ liters
1 lb.	tart apples, peeled, cored and sliced	½ kg.
1 ½ cups	superfine sugar	375 ml.
3 tbsp.	fresh lemon juice	45 ml.
2 ½ cups	pouring custard *(recipe, page 163)*	625 ml.
	heavy cream, whipped	

Cook the apples in a nonreactive pan with very little water until soft—about 15 minutes—then add the blackberries. Continue cooking until the berries are soft. Stir in the sugar and lemon juice, then rub the fruits through a sieve. When the fruits have cooled, blend them with the custard and put the mixture into glasses. Top with the whipped cream.

GERTRUDE MANN
BERRY COOKING

Blackberry-Cream Freeze

To serve 4

1 pint	blackberries	½ liter
	sugar	
1 cup	heavy cream	¼ liter
	salt	

Crush the berries with a fork and add sugar to taste. Whip the cream—with a pinch of salt—until firm but not buttery. Fold in the berries and turn the mixture into an ice-cube tray or shallow pan. Freeze until firm but not hard.

JAMES BEARD
THE JAMES BEARD COOKBOOK

Blueberry Grunt

To serve 4

1 quart	blueberries, stemmed	1 liter
½ cup	sugar	125 ml.
1 ½ cups	flour	375 ml.
¼ tsp.	salt	1 ml.
2 tsp.	baking powder	10 ml.
¼ tsp.	grated nutmeg	1 ml.
2 tsp.	grated orange peel	10 ml.
¾ cup	milk	175 ml.
	heavy cream	

Pour the blueberries into a heavy, nonreactive skillet. Stir in the sugar and, stirring frequently, cook over low heat until the berries begin to bubble. Meanwhile, prepare the dumpling batter by first mixing the flour, salt, baking powder, nutmeg and orange peel in a bowl. Stir in the milk. Drop the batter by spoonfuls on top of the simmering blueberries to form eight dumplings. Cover the skillet and cook for about 15 minutes, or until the dumplings have doubled in size. Serve the dumplings with the blueberries and top them with the cream.

BEATRICE ROSS BUSZEK
THE BLUEBERRY CONNECTION

Blueberries in Maple and Brown-Sugar Syrup

The one thing that you should remember in making this recipe is that the blueberries should remain whole and not burst open into an indiscriminate mass. Keep the syrup at a gentle simmer and you will have perfect results. Serve the berries with a cream-based sauce, a vanilla custard or with whipped cream.

To serve 6 to 8

2 pints	plump blueberries, stemmed	1 liter
¼ cup	firmly packed light brown sugar	50 ml.
¼ cup	pure maple syrup	50 ml.
1 cup	water	¼ liter
6	strips thinly pared lemon peel	6
1	cinnamon stick	1
3-inch	piece vanilla bean, slit down the middle	8-cm.

Combine the brown sugar, maple syrup, water, lemon peel, cinnamon stick and vanilla bean in a large, heavy, nonreactive saucepan. Cover the pan and set it over low heat to dissolve the sugar. When every last bit of sugar has dissolved, uncover the pan and boil this syrup for five minutes.

Add the blueberries to the syrup and simmer slowly until they have absorbed the syrup and softened slightly, but have not become mushy. As they cook, stir the berries carefully with a rubber spatula to avoid mashing the berries.

Transfer the contents of the pot to a storage bowl. When cool, discard the lemon peel and vanilla bean. (Remember, you can wash and dry the vanilla bean and use it to flavor sugar.) Leave in the cinnamon stick if you enjoy a spicy flavor; otherwise, discard it too. Chill the blueberries briefly before serving.

LISA YOCKELSON
THE EFFICIENT EPICURE

Huckleberry Cobbler

Although the terms huckleberry and blueberry are sometimes used synonymously—and the plants are, in fact, related—the huckleberry is a wild fruit with blue or black berries that are smaller, seedier and less sweet than those of the cultivated blueberry. Either berry can be used for this recipe.

	To serve 6	
3½ cups	huckleberries	875 ml.
½ cup	honey, warmed	125 ml.
¼ tsp.	grated lemon peel	1 ml.
1 tbsp.	flour	15 ml.
	salt	
1 tbsp.	butter, cut into pieces	15 ml.
	sugar (optional)	
	Cobbler batter	
1½ cups	sifted flour	375 ml.
2 tsp.	baking powder	10 ml.
¼ tsp.	salt	1 ml.
2 tbsp.	sugar	30 ml.
4 tbsp.	vegetable shortening	60 ml.
½ cup	milk	125 ml.

Combine the berries with the honey, lemon peel, flour and a pinch of salt.

For the batter, first sift the flour, baking powder, salt and sugar together. Cut in the shortening as for biscuits, then add the milk.

Pour the berries into a buttered 8-inch [20-cm.] deep pie dish, dot them with the butter pieces, and spoon the batter over the top. Sprinkle with sugar, if desired. Bake in a preheated 425° F. [220° C.] oven for 20 to 30 minutes, or until the topping is browned. Serve hot.

HAZEL BERTO
COOKING WITH HONEY

Polish Fruit Dumplings

Ciasto na Pierogi

These dumplings can also be filled with thick jam.

	To serve 6 to 8	
1 lb.	stemmed blueberries, pitted cherries or peeled, cored and diced apples	½ kg.
1 tbsp.	fine white bread crumbs	15 ml.
	sugar	
4 tbsp.	butter, melted	60 ml.
	sour cream	
	Dumpling dough	
3 cups	flour	¾ liter
	salt	
1	egg	1
about 6 tbsp.	tepid water	about 90 ml.

To make the dough, sift the flour with a pinch of salt onto a pastry board. Make a well in the center, break the egg into it and add 4 tablespoons [60 ml.] of tepid water. Stir until all the flour is incorporated. Knead the mixture—adding more water if necessary—until you have a smooth, pliable dough that does not stick to your hands or the pastry board. Divide the dough into four parts, then roll each one out thin, keeping the dough in a bowl covered with a damp cloth until it is used so that it does not dry out. Using a teacup or wineglass, cut circles that are 2 to 2½ inches [5 to 6 cm.] in diameter from the rolled dough.

Mix the fruit with the bread crumbs and 1 tablespoon [15 ml.] of the sugar. Place some fruit mixture in the middle of each circle, fold the dough over to make a semicircle, and press the edges together firmly so that these dumplings do not open during cooking. Repeat until all of the dough and fruit is used.

Bring a wide saucepan filled with slightly salted water to a boil. Add half of the dumplings. After they rise to the surface of the water, cook them for four to five minutes, then remove them with a slotted spoon and let them drain while you poach the remaining dumplings.

To serve, arrange the dumplings on a dish, pour the melted butter over, and present sugar and sour cream on the side.

MARIA LEMNIS AND HENRYK VITRY
OLD POLISH TRADITIONS IN THE KITCHEN AND AT THE TABLE

Blueberry-Lime Soufflé

The technique of making a collar for the soufflé dish is explained on page 69.

To serve 6

1 pint	blueberries, stemmed	½ liter
1 tbsp.	grated lime peel	15 ml.
½ cup	fresh lime juice	125 ml.
2 tbsp.	unflavored powdered gelatin, softened in ¼ cup [50 ml.] water for 5 minutes	30 ml.
½ cup	sugar	125 ml.
4	eggs, the yolks separated from the whites	4
2 cups	water	½ liter
½ cup	heavy cream, whipped	125 ml.
	lime slices	

Combine the softened gelatin and half of the sugar in a nonreactive saucepan. Beat the egg yolks, mix with the water, and add to the gelatin mixture. Place over low heat and stir until the gelatin is dissolved. Remove the pan from the heat, add the lime peel and juice, and mix well. Chill until the mixture is partially thickened.

Beat the egg whites until they reach the soft-peak stage. Gradually add the remaining sugar and whip until stiff but not dry. Add the gelatin mixture and mix well. Fold in the blueberries and whipped cream, making sure they are well blended. Pour the mixture into a 6-cup [1½-liter] soufflé dish fitted with a 2-inch [5-cm.] parchment-paper collar. Chill the soufflé until firm. Remove the collar when ready to serve, and garnish the soufflé with slices of fresh lime.

CAROL KATZ
THE BERRY COOKBOOK

Frozen Cranberry Mousse

To make about 2 quarts [2 liters]

4 cups	cranberries, stemmed	1 liter
2½ cups	sugar	625 ml.
2 cups	water	½ liter
8	egg yolks, beaten until thick	8
1 tbsp.	grenadine	15 ml.
4	egg whites, beaten until frothy	4
1 cup	heavy cream, whipped	¼ liter

Combine 2 cups [½ liter] of the sugar and the water in a nonreactive saucepan and boil for five minutes. Add the cranberries and simmer them for five minutes. Remove the berries from the juice. Measure 1 cup [¼ liter] of the juice and beat the juice into the egg yolks. Transfer the mixture to a small, nonreactive saucepan and cook over moderate heat, stirring constantly until the mixture thickens enough to coat the spoon heavily. Under no circumstances allow this to boil or the eggs will curdle. Stir in the cranberries and grenadine, and pour into a bowl. Chill in the refrigerator for about one half hour until it thickens slightly.

Gradually beat the remaining sugar into the egg whites. Continue to beat until the whites form unwavering peaks on the beater when it is lifted out of the bowl. With a rubber spatula, fold the cream gently but thoroughly into the thickened cranberry mixture, then fold in the egg whites, folding until streaks of white no longer show. Pour into refrigerator trays or a 2-quart [2-liter] decorative mold or soufflé dish. Cover with foil and freeze until firm. The cranberry mousse may be served in scoops like ice cream, unmolded on a plate or served directly from a soufflé dish.

FOODS OF THE WORLD
AMERICAN COOKING: NEW ENGLAND

Cranberry Dumplings

To serve 4

2 cups	cranberries, stemmed	½ liter
1¾ cups	sugar	425 ml.
1 cup	water	¼ liter
½ cup	fresh orange juice	125 ml.
⅔ cup	flour	150 ml.
1 tsp.	baking powder	5 ml.
	salt	
¼ cup	freshly grated coconut	50 ml.
2	egg yolks	2
2 tbsp.	milk	30 ml.
2 tbsp.	butter, melted and cooled	30 ml.
	light cream	

In a heavy, nonreactive pan, combine the cranberries, 1½ cups [375 ml.] of the sugar, the water and the orange juice. Bring the mixture to a boil over medium heat, then reduce the heat to low.

Meanwhile, prepare the dumplings by first sifting together the flour, baking powder, salt and the rest of the sugar. Stir in the coconut. Combine the egg yolks, milk and butter, and stir them into the flour mixture until well blended. Drop the dumpling mixture in four or eight portions onto the simmering cranberries. Cover the skillet tightly and simmer for about 20 minutes, or until the dumplings have doubled in size. Serve hot, accompanied by light cream.

BEATRICE ROSS BUSZEK
THE CRANBERRY CONNECTION

Cranberry Steamed Pudding

To serve 6 to 8

2 cups	cranberries, stemmed and chopped	½ liter
1 cup	raisins	¼ liter
½ cup	dates, pitted and cut into pieces	125 ml.
½ cup	nuts, coarsely chopped	125 ml.
1⅓ cups	sifted flour	325 ml.
½ cup	light molasses	125 ml.
2 tsp.	baking soda	10 ml.
¼ tsp.	salt	1 ml.
⅓ cup	boiling water	75 ml.
	Hard sauce	
⅓ cup	butter, softened	75 ml.
1 cup	sifted confectioners' sugar	¼ liter
¾ tsp.	vanilla extract	4 ml.
1 tbsp.	cream	15 ml.

Mix the cranberries, raisins, dates and nuts in a large bowl. Add the flour and stir. Combine the molasses, baking soda, salt and boiling water; stir into the fruit mixture. Pour this mixture into a 6-cup [1½-liter] mold. Cover the mold tightly with foil and tie the foil in place with a string. Place the mold on a rack in a deep kettle. Pour in a layer of boiling water 1 inch [2½ cm.] deep and cover the kettle. Set the kettle over high heat and steam the pudding for one and one quarter hours, adding water if needed.

Meanwhile, prepare the hard sauce by beating the ingredients together until smooth. Refrigerate the sauce to chill it. Remove the mold from the kettle and cool the pudding for 10 minutes. Unmold the pudding and serve it warm with the hard sauce.

BEATRICE ROSS BUSZEK
THE CRANBERRY CONNECTION

Cranberry Pudding

Borówka Kisiel

The author suggests that kisiel may be made from any fruit that has a pronounced, fairly sour taste, including currants, cherries, strawberries and raspberries.

This *kisiel* may be served with sweetened milk mixed with a beaten egg yolk.

To serve 4

1½ cups	cranberries, stemmed	375 ml.
2½ cups	water	625 ml.
about ⅔ cup	sugar	about 150 ml.
6 tbsp.	potato flour	90 ml.

In a nonreactive pan, cover the cranberries with 2 cups [½ liter] of hot water. Cook until tender and press through a sieve, pouring the cooking liquid over the cranberries in the process. Pour the purée back into the pan, add ⅔ cup [150 ml.] of sugar and cook over low heat until the sugar dissolves. Remove from the heat.

Mix the potato flour with ½ cup [125 ml.] of cold water and pour slowly into the berry purée. Return to the heat. Stirring constantly, bring to a boil and cook until thick. Taste and add more sugar, if you wish. Divide the pudding into portions and sprinkle each one with a few drops of cold water. Cool before serving.

ZOFIA CZERNY
POLISH COOKBOOK

Finnish Berry Pudding

Puolukkapuuro

Cranberries replace Finnish whortleberries in this Scandinavian pudding.

To serve 4

2 cups	cranberries, stemmed	½ liter
3 cups	water	¾ liter
½ cup	sugar	125 ml.
1 cup	semolina or cream of wheat	¼ liter
½ tsp.	almond extract	2 ml.
	heavy cream, whipped	

In a nonreactive saucepan, boil the berries in the water until they are soft—about five minutes. Drain the berries, reserving the juice.

Return the juice to the pan, stir in the sugar and cook over low heat. When the sugar dissolves, gradually add the semolina or cream of wheat. Cook until thickened—about 10 minutes. Mash the berries and mix them into the pudding. Add the almond extract. Refrigerate the pudding until thoroughly chilled—about two hours.

Just before serving, whip the pudding until frothy. Spoon it into small dessert dishes and serve it with whipped cream.

CAROL KATZ
THE BERRY COOKBOOK

Gooseberry Cream

To serve 4

1½ pints	gooseberries, stemmed	¾ liter
1 tbsp.	butter	15 ml.
¼ cup	sugar	50 ml.
4	egg yolks	4

Boil the gooseberries very quickly in just enough water to cover them. Stir in the butter when the gooseberries become soft, then press them through a sieve. While the pulp is hot, sweeten it with sugar to taste and then beat in the egg yolks. Serve in cups or glasses.

JOSEPHINE DAVID
EVERYDAY COOKERY FOR FAMILIES OF MODERATE INCOME

Gooseberry Cheese

To make about 3 cups [¾ liter]

1 pint	gooseberries, stemmed	½ liter
5 tbsp.	sugar	75 ml.
½ lb.	cream cheese, softened	¼ kg.
1 cup	heavy cream	¼ liter

Cook the berries with 4 tablespoons [60 ml.] of the sugar, but without water, until soft. Pass them through the fine disk of a food mill, then allow this purée to cool.

Beat the cream cheese with the remaining tablespoon of sugar until smooth. Beat the cheese together with the gooseberry purée until completely amalgamated, then beat in the heavy cream.

GUIRNE VAN ZUYLEN
GOURMET COOKING FOR EVERYONE

Gooseberry Fool

To serve 4

1 pint	gooseberries, stemmed	½ liter
	sugar	
2 to 3 tbsp.	water	30 to 45 ml.
1 cup	heavy cream, whipped	¼ liter

Put the gooseberries in a nonreactive saucepan with ¼ cup [50 ml.] of sugar and the water. Cook very gently until the gooseberries are thoroughly done and soft enough to mash. Put them through a sieve or food mill and add sugar to taste. Fold the gooseberry purée through the whipped cream. Chill for several hours.

JAMES BEARD
THE JAMES BEARD COOKBOOK

Hot Gooseberry Soufflé

To make the gooseberry purée, combine 1 cup [¼ liter] of gooseberries, 2 tablespoons [30 ml.] of water and a sprinkling of sugar in a nonreactive pan; cover and cook over low heat for about 20 minutes until the fruit is very soft. Sieve and add more sugar if necessary.

To serve 4

¼ cup	thick, sweetened gooseberry purée	50 ml.
6 tbsp.	butter	90 ml.
½ cup	flour	125 ml.
1 cup	milk	¼ liter
3	large eggs, the yolks separated from the whites	3

In a heavy pan, melt the butter over low heat. As the butter melts, stir in the flour. Stir until smooth and blended, then gradually add the milk, stirring all the time so that the mixture remains smooth. Bring to the boiling point, still stirring, and cook for three minutes. Add the gooseberry purée and stir until thoroughly mixed.

Beat the egg yolks until they are light and combine them with the gooseberry mixture. Beat the whites until they are stiff (this means that you can turn the bowl upside down without any ill effect), and use a metal spoon to gently fold the whites into the gooseberry mixture.

Lightly oil a 5-cup [1¼-liter] soufflé dish. Turn the mixture into the soufflé dish and bake on the middle shelf of a preheated 375° F. [190° C.] oven for about 45 minutes. By this time the soufflé should be crisp on the outside and still creamy on the inside. (For a more creamy result, bake the soufflé in a water bath: Stand the soufflé dish in a pan and pour enough hot water into the pan to cover the sides of the dish by about 2 inches [5 cm.].)

Remember that the soufflé will not remain at its best for more than a few minutes after leaving the oven.

PAMELA WESTLAND
A TASTE OF THE COUNTRY

Summer Pudding

	To serve 4	
2 quarts	raspberries, blackberries, red or black currants or a mixture of berries and currants	2 liters
	butter	
6	slices stale firm-textured white bread with the crusts removed	6
2 tbsp.	water	30 ml.
about ¾ cup	sugar	about 175 ml.
	heavy cream, whipped	

Put the fruit into a nonreactive pan, add the water and sugar, and cook gently for five to 10 minutes until the fruit is soft but still bright in color. Taste and add more sugar if necessary. Remove the pan from the heat and leave it until the fruit is lukewarm.

Lightly butter a 1-quart [1-liter] pudding basin and line the base and sides with some of the bread slices. Pour the fruit and the juice into the bread-lined basin. Trim the remaining slices of bread to fit the top of the basin, dip them into the fruit so that both sides are soaked in juice, and place the bread on top of the fruit.

Stand the basin on a deep dish into which the pudding can drain. Press a plate on top of the pudding and set a 1-pound [½-kg.] weight on it. Leave the pudding in a cool place or the refrigerator overnight. Before serving, remove the plate and the weight, and drain any juices that have collected on top of the pudding. Reserve all of the drained fruit juice. Invert a serving dish over the basin and turn both over together. Give a sharp shake and remove the basin. Spoon the reserved fruit juice over the pudding. Serve with whipped cream.

PRUDENCE LEITH AND CAROLINE WALDEGRAVE
LEITH'S COOKERY COURSE

Cold Raspberry Soufflé

If you are using an electric beater to whip the egg yolks, sugar and raspberry purée, heat is not necessary.

	To serve 4	
1 pint	raspberries, stemmed, 8 berries reserved for garnish, the remaining berries puréed (about 1 cup [¼ liter] purée)	½ liter
4	eggs, the yolks separated from the whites, and the whites stiffly beaten	4
1 cup	superfine sugar	¼ liter
1 cup	heavy cream, lightly whipped	¼ liter
2 tbsp.	unflavored powdered gelatin, softened in ⅓ cup [75 ml.] of water for 5 minutes	30 ml.
	chopped pistachios	

Lightly butter a 4-cup [1-liter] soufflé dish and, to prevent spillage, tie a double layer of parchment paper around the rim with string. Place the egg yolks in a heatproof bowl with the sugar and the raspberry purée and whisk over hot water until thick and mousselike. Remove the mixture from the heat, then continue whisking until the bowl is quite cool to the touch. Fold two thirds of the cream into the mixture.

Dissolve the softened gelatin over gentle heat, add it to the raspberry mixture, set the bowl over ice and stir until the mixture begins to thicken. Fold in the whites and turn the mixture into the soufflé dish.

Refrigerate the soufflé until it is set—about three hours. When it is firm, remove the paper collar. Beat the remaining cream until it is stiff. Then decorate the top of the soufflé with the whipped cream, the reserved raspberries and chopped pistachios.

ROSEMARY HUME AND MURIEL DOWNES
CORDON BLEU DESSERTS AND PUDDINGS

Strawberries with Vinegar

Fragole all'Aceto

	To serve 2	
1 pint	fresh strawberries, hulled	½ liter
1 cup	red or white wine	¼ liter
2 tsp.	white vinegar	10 ml.
	confectioners' sugar	

Place the strawberries in a small bowl and cover them with the wine. Let the fruit stand for about five minutes, then pour off the wine completely; it serves only to wash the berries. If you were to use water instead of the wine, the strawberries would lose their taste and become watery. The result justifies the extravagant use of wine.

Fill two small bowls with the strawberries and pour 1 teaspoon [5 ml.] of vinegar into each bowl. Add sugar according to your taste. Mix well and serve. The taste of vinegar disappears; it gets overpowered by the berries. But the acidity of the vinegar brings out the taste of the berries and increases their sweetness.

HEDY GIUSTI-LANHAM AND ANDREA DODI
THE CUISINE OF VENICE

Gracious Grecian Ways with Strawberries

If fresh grapevine leaves are not available, any large edible green leaves—lettuce, romaine, kale, nasturtium, violet or lemon among them—may be substituted.

	To serve 4	
1 pint	large strawberries, preferably with stems intact	½ liter
3 oz.	cream cheese, softened	90 g.
1	egg yolk	1
¼ tsp.	almond extract	1 ml.
1 cup	confectioners' sugar	¼ liter
	light cream or half-and-half cream	
½ cup	finely chopped almonds	125 ml.
	fresh grapevine leaves, polished with a little milk	

In a mixing bowl, beat the cream cheese until it is soft and fluffy. Beat in the egg yolk, almond extract and then the confectioners' sugar. Gradually add enough cream or half-and-half to give the cheese mixture the consistency of stiffly whipped cream. One at a time, swirl each strawberry in this mixture and sprinkle it lightly with the almonds. Let the berries stand until the coating is firm. Serve them on the polished grapevine leaves.

MAGGIE WALDRON
STRAWBERRIES

Strawberries with Orange Juice

Fraises à l'Orange

	To serve 4 to 6	
2 pints	strawberries, hulled	1 liter
½ cup	superfine sugar	125 ml.
½ cup	fresh orange juice	125 ml.

Put aside about 3 cups [¾ liter] of the best strawberries. Pass the remaining strawberries through a sieve. Mix this purée with 3 tablespoons [45 ml.] of the sugar and dilute the mixture with the orange juice. Put the purée into a serving dish, arrange the reserved strawberries on top, sprinkle with the remaining sugar and serve very cold.

X. MARCEL BOULESTIN
RECIPES OF BOULESTIN

Cream Cheese Heart with Soft Summer Fruits

Coeur à la Crème

The technique of making this dessert is demonstrated on pages 34-35; there the cheese mixture is molded in individual 4-ounce [125-ml.] hearts.

	To serve 4	
	strawberries or raspberries	
½ lb.	farmer or cottage cheese	¼ kg.
1 cup	heavy cream, lightly whipped	¼ liter
2 tbsp.	superfine sugar	30 ml.
2	egg whites, stiffly beaten	2
1 cup	light cream	¼ liter

Press the cheese through a fine-meshed nylon or stainless-steel sieve and blend it with the whipped cream. Stir in the sugar, and gently but thoroughly fold in the egg whites. Turn the mixture into a 3-cup [¾-liter] muslin-lined mold, stand it on a deep plate, and leave it in the refrigerator to drain overnight. Just before serving, turn the molded cheese heart out onto a serving dish. Arrange the strawberries or raspberries around the cheese heart, and pour the light cream over it.

MARGARET COSTA
MARGARET COSTA'S FOUR SEASONS COOKERY BOOK

Enriched Molded Cream Heart

Coeur à la Crème

By using gelatin and egg yolks, you can make a rich, firm cream that sets firmly in a large heart mold or in little pottery hearts. You can quite well use cottage cheese or well-drained yogurt instead of the farmer cheese.

If you are serving *coeur à la crème* with pears, add chopped preserved ginger in syrup—about six pieces—and sweeten the cheese and egg yolks with the ginger syrup instead of sugar, using 4 tablespoons [60 ml.] of syrup to start, a little more if you like.

To serve 6

	soft raw fruit or poached fruit	
½ lb.	farmer cheese, sieved	¼ kg.
2	eggs, the yolks separated from the whites	2
¼ cup	vanilla sugar	50 ml.
2 tbsp.	unflavored powdered gelatin, softened in ½ cup [125 ml.] water for 5 minutes	30 ml.
⅓ cup	very hot water (not boiling)	75 ml.
1 cup	heavy cream or ½ cup [125 ml.] each heavy and light cream	¼ liter

Mix the cheese with the egg yolks and vanilla sugar. In a heatproof bowl, mix the softened gelatin and the hot water, stirring until the gelatin dissolves and the mixture is smooth. Leave the gelatin until it is almost cool, add the cream and whip until stiff. Fold in the cheese mixture carefully so that the ingredients are well blended but kept as light as possible. Finally, whip the egg whites until they are firm, and add to the cream mixture.

Line a 3-cup [¾-liter] mold, or little ½-cup [125-ml.] heart molds, with a double thickness of cheesecloth that has been dampened and wrung out. Ladle in the cream mixture, tapping the mold on a table to settle the mixture into the curves. Flip the ends of the cloth over the whole thing and put the cream in the refrigerator to set.

Unmold the cream onto a dish to serve and surround the heart, or hearts, with soft fruit or with poached fruit.

JANE GRIGSON
JANE GRIGSON'S FRUIT BOOK

Strawberries and Raspberries in Liqueur

Spirituele Aardbeien en Frambozen Salade

To serve 4

1 pint	strawberries, hulled	½ liter
1 pint	raspberries	½ liter
3 tbsp.	superfine sugar	45 ml.
1½ tbsp.	Armagnac	22 ml.
1½ tbsp.	Curaçao	22 ml.
½ cup	heavy cream	125 ml.
1½ tbsp.	kirsch	22 ml.

In a glass bowl, mix the strawberries and raspberries gently together with 2 tablespoons [30 ml.] of the sugar. Pour the Armagnac and Curaçao over them, cover the bowl and refrigerate the berries for one hour.

Whip together the cream and the remaining sugar until the cream is stiff. Add the kirsch and lightly fold the cream into the berry mixture. Refrigerate the cream-coated berries—either in the glass bowl or in individual dessert glasses—for one hour before serving them.

HUGH JANS
VRIJ NEDERLAND

Strawberry Shortcake

To serve 8

1½ pints	strawberries, hulled	¾ liter
3 cups	flour	¾ liter
1 cup	superfine sugar	¼ liter
1 tsp.	salt	5 ml.
4 tsp.	baking powder	20 ml.
2 tsp.	ground mixed spices	10 ml.
12 tbsp.	butter, cut into pieces	180 ml.
1 cup	walnuts, finely chopped	¼ liter
2	eggs, the yolks separated from the whites, and the whites stiffly beaten	2
⅔ cup	milk	150 ml.
⅔ cup	heavy cream, whipped	150 ml.

Butter and flour three 8-inch [20-cm.] layer-cake pans. Sift the flour, half of the sugar, the salt, baking powder and mixed spices into a mixing bowl. Rub the butter into the flour mixture until it resembles fine bread crumbs. Stir in the chopped walnuts. Beat the egg yolks and milk together, and gradually add them to the mixture until it forms a soft but not sticky dough. (This might not take up quite all of the egg mixture.)

Turn the dough onto a lightly floured board and knead until it is smooth and there are no more cracks. Divide the dough into three and press each piece with the flat of your hand into a cake pan. Bake in a preheated 450° F. [230° C.] oven for 12 to 15 minutes, until firm and golden brown on top. Turn out the shortcake rounds onto a wire rack to cool.

Reserve a few whole strawberries for the decoration. Chop the rest and sprinkle them with the remaining sugar.

Fold the beaten egg whites into the whipped cream and spread an equal amount of the mixture over the top of each shortcake round. Scatter the chopped strawberries over two rounds and place one on top of the other. Place the remaining round on top and decorate with the reserved strawberries.

PAMELA WESTLAND
A TASTE OF THE COUNTRY

Chocolate-Rum Fondue

To serve 4

2 pints	strawberries, hulled	1 liter
2 tbsp.	honey	30 ml.
½ cup	heavy cream	125 ml.
9 oz.	milk chocolate, broken into small pieces	270 g.
¼ cup	finely chopped nuts	50 ml.
3 tbsp.	rum	45 ml.

Heat the cream and honey in a fondue pot over a high flame. Lower the flame, add the chocolate pieces and stir constantly until they are melted. Stir in the nuts and rum. Spear one strawberry at a time on a small skewer or fondue fork and dip it into the fondue mixture.

CAROL KATZ
THE BERRY COOKBOOK

Strawberry Perfection Custard

To serve 8

1 quart	strawberries, cleaned and lightly sweetened with sugar	1 liter
¼ cup	anisette or other anise-flavored liqueur	50 ml.
¾ cup	flour	175 ml.
4	eggs	4
1 cup	sugar	¼ liter
1 quart	boiling milk	1 liter
1 cup	heavy cream, whipped	¼ liter

Pour the liqueur over the sweetened strawberries and refrigerate until the berries are well chilled—one to two hours.

In a saucepan, blend the flour, eggs and sugar together and slowly mix in the boiling milk. Cook over medium heat for several minutes, stirring constantly until the mixture boils. Let cool, then add the cream. Set aside eight berries for garnish and gently mix the rest of the strawberries and their juice into the custard.

To serve, spoon the custard into well-chilled Champagne glasses and garnish each portion with a reserved berry.

RALPH H. REESE
THE FLAVOR OF PITTSBURGH

Cold Strawberry Cream

Bombe aux Fraises

To serve 6 to 8

3 pints	strawberries, hulled	1½ liters
1¼ cups	sugar	300 ml.
6 tbsp.	kirsch	90 ml.
½ cup	water	125 ml.
5	egg yolks	5
2 cups	heavy cream, whipped	½ liter

Place 3 cups [¾ liter] of the strawberries with ¾ cup [175 ml.] of the sugar in an electric blender and purée. Pour the purée into a nonreactive pan and bring to a boil over medium heat. Simmer for three minutes, then strain through a fine nylon or stainless-steel sieve. Cool; mix in 2 tablespoons [30 ml.] of the kirsch and set this sauce aside.

Place the remaining strawberries and sugar and the water in a nonreactive saucepan. Bring to a boil and cook over medium heat for five minutes. Let cool, then strain the juices. Reserve the strawberries. Place the juices with the egg yolks in a heavy nonreactive saucepan. Place over very low heat and beat with a wire whisk for seven to eight minutes to produce a sabayon with the consistency of a light mayonnaise. The mixture should never be so hot that you cannot hold your finger in it. If it gets too hot during cooking, remove the pan from the heat and continue beating until the temperature lowers.

When cooked, place the pan in cold water and continue beating for a few minutes until the mixture is cold. Add the remaining kirsch and the reserved strawberries. Fold the whipped cream into the strawberry-egg mixture. Place in a 2-quart [2-liter] mold and freeze for at least five hours.

To serve, first run the mold under lukewarm water for a few seconds and unmold the bombe onto a tray. Pour a few tablespoons of the strawberry sauce on top of and around the bombe, and serve the remaining sauce on the side. The bombe should not be too cold so that it can be served easily with a spoon.

JACQUES PÉPIN
A FRENCH CHEF COOKS AT HOME

Strawberry Fritters

To serve 4 to 6

1 pint	large strawberries	½ liter
¾ cup	apricot jam	175 ml.
½ cup	almonds, blanched, peeled, toasted and finely chopped	125 ml.
2	eggs, lightly beaten	2
1 cup	fine soda-cracker crumbs	¼ liter
	vegetable oil for deep frying	
	confectioners' sugar (optional)	

Wash the berries, hull them, and drain them on paper towels until completely dry.

Force the apricot jam through a strainer. Dip the strawberries in the jam, then roll them in the almonds. Quickly dip the strawberries in the beaten eggs and roll them in the cracker crumbs. Place the strawberries, in a single layer, on a large plate or tray and refrigerate them for several hours to firm their coating.

Pour the oil into a deep skillet to a depth of at least 2 inches [5 cm.] and heat it to 360° F. [180° C.] on a deep-frying thermometer. Fry the strawberries, a few at a time, until they are golden brown—about one minute. Drain them on paper towels. Serve them while they are still warm, accompanied—if you like—with a saucer of confectioners' sugar in which to roll them.

ANN CHANDONNET
THE COMPLETE FRUIT COOKBOOK

Strawberries in Custard

Fraises de l'Etoile

To serve 4

1½ pints	strawberries, hulled	¾ liter
3 tbsp.	confectioners' sugar	45 ml.
1 split	Champagne (6½ oz. [195 ml.])	1 split
4	egg yolks	4
⅔ cup	granulated sugar	150 ml.
2 tbsp.	cornstarch	30 ml.
1½ tsp.	vanilla extract	7 ml.
1 cup	milk, scalded	¼ liter
¾ cup	heavy cream	175 ml.

Combine the strawberries and confectioners' sugar in a bowl; mix well. Pour the Champagne over the strawberries. Refrigerate, covered, at least two hours.

Beat the egg yolks with ⅓ cup [75 ml.] of the granulated sugar and the cornstarch until light and fluffy. Beat in the vanilla extract and gradually add the scalded milk. Cook in the top of a double boiler over hot water until this custard is thick. Remove it from the heat; let it stand until cool.

Whip the cream until thick; fold it into the custard. Spoon two thirds of the custard mixture into an ovenproof glass serving bowl or a soufflé dish. Drain the strawberries. Press one strawberry at a time into the custard. Spread the remaining custard over the top. Refrigerate the dessert for at least two hours; then place the bowl in the freezer while proceeding with the next step.

Melt the remaining granulated sugar in a heavy saucepan over low heat; cook until this syrup turns into a rich, brown caramel. Immediately remove the custard from the freezer and drizzle the caramel over the top in a thin lattice. (This must be done very quickly or the caramel will harden.) Refrigerate the dessert until you are ready to serve it.

BERT GREENE
BERT GREENE'S KITCHEN BOUQUETS

Strawberry Soufflé

This soufflé may be made with any kind of berry—raspberries, blackberries or the blueberries shown on pages 68-69.

To serve 6

1 pint	strawberries, hulled and puréed (about 1 cup [¼ liter] purée)	½ liter
1 tsp.	fresh lemon juice	5 ml.
1 tsp.	orange liqueur	5 ml.
⅓ cup	sugar	75 ml.
5	egg whites	5
	cream of tartar	

Pour the strawberry purée into a heavy, nonreactive saucepan. Add the lemon juice, orange liqueur and sugar. Place on medium heat and stir for a half minute or so, or until the sugar is dissolved. Keep the purée simmering while beating the egg whites.

Put the egg whites in a large mixing bowl, add a pinch of cream of tartar, and beat the whites until they are very firm. Pour in the hot purée while continuing to beat at high speed;

the volume of the beaten whites will expand considerably. Scrape in every bit of purée from the pan, and beat just enough to incorporate the sauce.

Spoon the soufflé batter into a 2-quart [2-liter] mold that has been buttered and dusted with sugar. Level off the top of the batter and use your thumb to remove a rim of batter about ¼ inch [6 mm.] wide from around the edge of the dish, thus ensuring a straight-rising crown. Bake the soufflé in a preheated 375° F. [190° C.] oven for 20 minutes, or until the top is puffed and lightly browned. Serve at once.

CAROL CUTLER
THE WOMAN'S DAY LOW CALORIE DESSERT COOKBOOK

Yogurt and Strawberry Jelly

Legumina z Kwaśnego Mleka

To serve 6 to 8

1 pint	strawberries, hulled and puréed through a nonreactive sieve	½ liter
1 quart	yogurt	1 liter
½ cup	sugar	125 ml.
2 tbsp.	unflavored powdered gelatin, softened in ⅓ cup [75 ml.] cold water for 5 minutes and warmed over low heat until dissolved	30 ml.

Stir the yogurt well, then mix in the sugar and the strawberry purée. Pour the dissolved gelatin into the strawberry-flavored yogurt and beat it in. Pour the mixture into a glass compote dish and refrigerate it until set—about two hours.

ZOFIA CZERNY AND MARIA STRASBURGER
ŻYWIENIE RODZINY

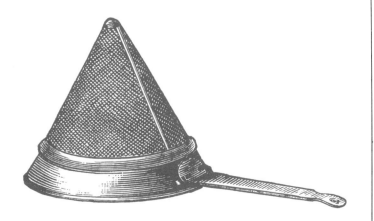

Strawberry Mousse

Mousse aux Fraises

To serve 8

2 pints	strawberries, hulled	1 liter
1¼ cups	sugar	300 ml.
6	egg yolks	6
3 tbsp.	unflavored powdered gelatin, softened in ½ cup [125 ml.] water for 5 minutes	45 ml.
	red food coloring	
2 tbsp.	strawberry or raspberry white brandy or kirsch	30 ml.
4 cups	heavy cream, whipped	1 liter
3 tbsp.	Cognac	45 ml.

With a wire whisk, mix ¾ cup [175 ml.] of the sugar and egg yolks in the top of a double boiler. Whisk over hot, but not boiling, water for approximately eight minutes, or until the mixture becomes very pale in color and thickens. Place the top pot in cold water and stir until the mixture thickens to the consistency of mayonnaise. Set the softened gelatin over hot water and stir until the gelatin dissolves, then add to the egg-yolk mixture.

Purée 1 cup [¼ liter] of the strawberries in a blender and add them to the egg-yolk mixture. Slice another cup of the strawberries and add them to the mixture, along with about 10 drops of red food coloring to give the mousse a pink color. Add the brandy or kirsch. Whip 3 cups [¾ liter] of the cream until stiff and fold it into the mousse mixture.

Line the bottom and sides of a 2-quart [2-liter] mold with wax paper. Pour in the mousse mixture. Then cover the mold with plastic wrap and place it in the refrigerator for at least five or six hours.

Set aside about 1 cup of the remaining strawberries to use as a garnish. Purée the rest of the strawberries in a blender with the remaining sugar and the Cognac. Refrigerate this sauce mixture. Whip the remaining cup of heavy cream and chill it.

Unmold the mousse and remove the wax paper. Pour some of the sauce around the mousse and garnish with the whole strawberries and reserved whipped cream. Serve with the remaining sauce on the side.

JACQUES PÉPIN
A FRENCH CHEF COOKS AT HOME

Green Grapes in Sour Cream

To serve 8

2 lb.	seedless green grapes, stemmed (about 6 cups [1½ liters])	1 kg.
¼ cup	firmly packed brown sugar	50 ml.
2 cups	sour cream	½ liter

Place the grapes in a mixing bowl. Sprinkle the sugar over them, turning the grapes to coat them evenly. Let them stand for several minutes until the sugar dissolves, then gently blend in the sour cream. Chill for several hours. Serve the grapes in sherbet glasses.

CHARLOTTE ADAMS AND DORIS MC FERRAN TOWNSEND
THE FAMILY COOKBOOK: DESSERTS

Grape Cobbler

The technique of making grape juice is shown on page 21.

To serve 6

3 cups	grapes	¾ liter
½ cup	fresh grape juice	125 ml.
1¾ cups	firmly packed light brown sugar	425 ml.
6 tbsp.	butter, 3 tbsp. [45 ml.] softened	90 ml.
1½ cups	flour, sifted	375 ml.
1 tbsp.	baking powder	15 ml.
¾ cup	milk	175 ml.
½ tbsp.	vanilla extract	7 ml.
Grape sauce		
¾ cup	fresh grape juice	175 ml.
1 tbsp.	fresh lemon juice	15 ml.
1 tbsp.	cornstarch	15 ml.
1 tbsp.	butter	15 ml.
¼ cup	cream (optional)	50 ml.

In a nonreactive pan, bring the grapes to a boil with 1 cup [¼ liter] of the brown sugar, 3 tablespoons [45 ml.] of butter and the grape juice—stirring until the sugar dissolves and the butter melts. Set the mixture aside, off the heat. Cream the softened butter and the rest of the brown sugar. Sift together the flour and baking powder and add them to the butter mixture alternately with the milk. Add the vanilla extract

and pour the batter into a buttered 8½-inch [21-cm.] baking dish. Let the batter rest for two minutes, then cover it with the grape mixture. Bake in a 350° F. [180° C.] oven for 20 minutes, then reduce the heat to 325° F. [160° C.] and bake for another 20 minutes, or until the cobbler is puffed and golden brown.

Meanwhile, for the sauce, blend the juices with the cornstarch in a nonreactive pan. Add the butter and, stirring constantly, simmer the mixture until it thickens and is clear. Then stir in the cream, if you wish.

Serve the cobbler hot, accompanied by the sauce, which may be at room temperature.

STELLA STANDARD
THE ART OF FRUIT COOKERY

Simonetta's Black-Grape Ice

Granita d'Uva Nera alla Simonetta

To serve 6

1 lb.	black grapes	½ kg.
1 cup	sugar	¼ liter
½ cup	water	125 ml.
6 tbsp.	fresh lemon juice	90 ml.
2 tbsp.	ruby port	30 ml.
	heavy cream, whipped	

The day before you plan to serve, purée the grapes in a blender and push the pulp through a sieve to remove skins and seeds. Combine the sugar and water in a saucepan and cook, stirring over medium heat, until the sugar is dissolved. Boil the syrup for five minutes. Pour the syrup into a mixing bowl and allow it to cool; then stir in the grape purée and the lemon juice. Whisk until well blended. Pour into a 6-cup [1½-liter] mold and freeze until the mixture is mushy in the center but set around the rim of the mold. Using an electric beater, beat the ice until smooth. Return to the freezer and freeze overnight.

Remove from the freezer, beat again, add the port and refreeze until firm. Turn out onto a serving dish and serve with the whipped cream.

PAULA WOLFERT
MEDITERRANEAN COOKING

Grape Jelly

Crisp almond cookies or lemon wafers should be served with this light dessert.

	To serve 6	
2 lb.	muscat or other well-flavored grapes, 12 of the largest grapes peeled, halved and seeded	1 kg.
about ½ cup	superfine sugar	about 125 ml.
2 tbsp.	unflavored powdered gelatin, softened in ¼ cup [50 ml.] water	30 ml.
3 tbsp.	fresh lemon juice	45 ml.
2 to 3 tbsp.	Grand Marnier or Curaçao, or ⅓ cup [75 ml.] fresh orange juice	30 to 45 ml.
⅔ cup	heavy cream, lightly whipped	150 ml.

Put the whole unpeeled grapes into a pan with ½ cup [125 ml.] of the sugar. Simmer until the grapes collapse—about two minutes—leaving them on the heat for as brief a time as possible. Sieve them into a 2-cup [½-liter] measuring cup. If necessary, add enough water to have 2 cups of liquid. Stir the softened gelatin into the warm grape juice. Add the lemon juice and liqueur or orange juice. Taste and add more sugar, but do not make the mixture too sweet. Refrigerate the mixture until almost set—about one hour. With a rotary beater or whisk, beat to a creamy froth. Pour the mixture into six glasses and refrigerate until firm. Decorate each serving with the reserved grape halves, placed cut side down.

Spoon the whipped cream onto the jellies just before serving, but do not cover the domed tops of the grape halves: These should show up like little islands.

JANE GRIGSON
JANE GRIGSON'S FRUIT BOOK

Grape Juice and Semolina Mold

Moustalevria

If the grape juice is not sweet enough, add some sugar or honey while cooking.

	To serve 4	
3 cups	fresh grape juice	¾ liter
4½ tbsp.	fine semolina	67 ml.
1 cup	grated walnuts	¼ liter
1 tbsp.	sesame seeds	15 ml.
	ground cinnamon	

Bring the grape juice to a boil and stir in the semolina. Cook over low heat, stirring continuously, until the mixture is thick, and big bubbles appear on the surface. Pour into individual glasses. When cold and set, sprinkle with the nuts, sesame seeds and cinnamon to taste.

MARO DUNCAN
COOKING THE GREEK WAY

Grape-Nectarine Yogurt Salad

	To serve 8	
1½ cups	peeled, diced nectarines or pears	375 ml.
1½ cups	grapes, halved and seeded	375 ml.
2 tbsp.	unflavored powdered gelatin	30 ml.
1½ cups	fresh orange juice	375 ml.
1 tbsp.	sugar	15 ml.
2 cups	yogurt	½ liter
3 tbsp.	honey	45 ml.
½ tsp.	vanilla extract	2 ml.
1 tsp.	grated lemon or orange peel	5 ml.
¼ cup	chopped walnuts or almonds	50 ml.

In a medium-sized, nonreactive saucepan, soften the gelatin in 1 cup [¼ liter] of orange juice for about five minutes. Then place over low heat. Stir until the gelatin dissolves—about three minutes. Remove from the heat. Stir in the sugar, the remaining ½ cup [125 ml.] of orange juice, the yogurt, honey, vanilla extract and lemon or orange peel. Stir until the mixture is smooth. Chill, stirring occasionally, until the mixture is the consistency of unbeaten egg whites. Fold in the nectarines, grapes and nuts. Turn into a 2-quart [2-liter] bowl or eight dessert dishes, and chill until set.

SANDAL ENGLISH
FRUITS OF THE DESERT

Melons

Cantaloupe with Port Sherbet and Raspberries

Melon avec Sorbet au Porto et Framboises

With less sugar than the recipe calls for, this sherbet can be a refreshing appetizer.

To serve 6

3	cantaloupes, halved and seeded	3
2 pints	raspberries	1 liter
3 cups	port	¾ liter
1½ cups	water	375 ml.
4 tbsp.	fresh lemon juice	60 ml.
1 tsp.	green peppercorns, rinsed if brine-packed	5 ml.
2-inch	strip orange peel	5-cm.
2-inch	strip lemon peel	5-cm.
about 3 tbsp.	sugar	about 45 ml.
	fresh mint leaves	

In a nonreactive saucepan, combine the port, water, 3 tablespoons [45 ml.] of lemon juice, the peppercorns, orange peel, lemon peel and 1 tablespoon [15 ml.] of sugar. Bring this mixture to a boil and simmer it for five minutes. Strain the mixture and cool it. Freeze the sherbet in an ice-cream maker, or pour it into a shallow pan and freeze it in the freezer—stirring it several times during the process.

In a blender, purée half of the raspberries with the remaining lemon juice and 2 tablespoons [30 ml.] of sugar. Strain. Taste, and add more sugar if necessary.

Fill each melon half with two scoops of sherbet. Coat the sherbet lightly with the raspberry sauce. Decorate the melons with the remaining raspberries and the mint leaves.

WOLFGANG PUCK
WOLFGANG PUCK'S MODERN FRENCH COOKING
FOR THE AMERICAN KITCHEN

Stuffed Melon, Leon-Style

Melón Relleno a Estilo Leonés

To serve 4

1	honeydew melon, the top sliced off, the seeds removed and the flesh spooned out, the shell reserved	1
2	peaches, blanched, peeled, halved, pitted and chopped	2
2	bananas, peeled and chopped	2
2 cups	morello cherries, pitted and chopped	½ liter
⅓ cup	fresh lemon juice	75 ml.
⅔ cup	fresh orange juice	150 ml.
2 tbsp.	sweet white vermouth	30 ml.
¼ cup	orange liqueur	50 ml.
3 tbsp.	sugar	45 ml.

In a bowl, mix the melon flesh with the other fruits, the juices, vermouth, liqueur and sugar. Stuff the melon shell with the mixture. Chill before serving.

JOSE GUTIERREZ TASCON
LA COCINA LEONESA

Frozen Honeydew Mousse

To make 1 quart [1 liter]

2 cups	puréed honeydew-melon flesh	½ liter
½ cup	sugar	125 ml.
1 tbsp.	fresh lemon juice	15 ml.
1 tbsp.	unflavored powdered gelatin, softened in ¼ cup [50 ml.] of water for 5 minutes	15 ml.
½ tsp.	vanilla extract	2 ml.
1 cup	heavy cream, whipped	¼ liter

Combine the honeydew purée, sugar and lemon juice in a nonreactive saucepan, and cook only until the mixture is hot and the sugar has dissolved. Stir in the softened gelatin and, when it has dissolved, pour the mixture into a bowl. Chill until the mixture begins to thicken. Add the vanilla extract, then fold in the whipped cream. Turn the mixture into two ice trays and freeze until it is firm. Remove the mousse from the refrigerator and let it stand for 10 minutes at room temperature before serving.

HENRI PAUL PELLAPRAT
THE GREAT BOOK OF FRENCH CUISINE

Melon Granita

Granita van Meloen

	To serve 4	
1	honeydew melon, halved, seeded and pulp scooped out	1
¼ cup	superfine sugar	50 ml.
1½ tbsp.	kirsch	22 ml.
1 tbsp.	fresh lemon juice	15 ml.
4	red candied cherries	4

Purée the melon pulp in a blender, and blend in the sugar, kirsch and lemon juice. Pour the mixture into a shallow metal tray and freeze for a total of three hours. After the first 30 minutes, remove the tray from the freezer and stir the mixture with a fork. Replace the tray in the freezer and repeat the procedure twice more at 30-minute intervals. Serve the granita in ice-cold glasses and decorate it with the candied cherries.

HUGH JANS
VRIJ NEDERLAND

Melon Fritters with Strawberry Sauce

Beignets de Melon au Coulis de Fraises

	To serve 4 to 6	
2	melons (about 1 lb. [½ kg.] each)	2
1½ pints	strawberries, hulled	¾ liter
¼ oz.	package active dry yeast or one ⅗ oz. [18 g.] cake fresh yeast	7 g.
1 cup	beer	¼ liter
1¾ cups	flour	425 ml.
	salt	
	superfine sugar (optional)	
1 quart	peanut oil	1 liter
¾ cup	confectioners' sugar	175 ml.

Place the yeast in a large earthenware bowl, pour in the beer and beat well with a whisk to soften the yeast. After 10 minutes, pour in the flour, add two pinches of salt and use a wooden spoon to stir the dry ingredients into the yeast mixture until a smooth batter is formed. Cover the bowl with a cloth and leave the batter to rest and rise until it doubles in bulk—about one to two hours.

Reduce the strawberries to a purée in a blender, then strain the purée through a fine-meshed sieve set over a bowl. Whisk the strained purée and then taste it; if it is not sweet enough, add a little superfine sugar. Pour the purée into a sauceboat and refrigerate it.

Slice each melon in half and scoop out the seeds. Cut each melon half into slices ¾ inch [2 cm.] thick and remove the rind. Set the melon slices aside.

Pour the oil into a large, heavy pan and set it over medium heat for 15 minutes. When the oil is hot, turn the heat to low. Dip two melon slices at a time into the batter and, when they are completely coated, lift them out with a fork and place them in the hot oil. You can fry about eight fritters at the same time. After three minutes, the fritters will have swelled up and become golden colored on one side. Turn them over with a wooden spoon and fry for two more minutes until the other side is also golden. Remove the fritters from the pan with a skimmer and place them on paper towels to drain. Repeat this process until all of the coated melon pieces have been fried.

Pour the confectioners' sugar into a bowl. When the fritters are thoroughly drained, roll them in the sugar until they are evenly coated; place the fritters on a buttered baking sheet. Put the baking sheet under a preheated broiler, and broil the fritters for about two minutes on each side to caramelize their surfaces. Arrange the fritters on a serving dish and serve immediately, accompanied by the chilled strawberry purée.

ALAIN AND ÉVENTHIA SENDERENS
LA CUISINE RÉUSSIE

Melon and Red Currants in Wine

Cocktail de Melon aux Groseilles

If fresh currants are unavailable, use fresh blueberries.

	To serve 4	
2	small melons (about 2 lb. [1 kg.] each), halved and seeded	2
1 pint	red currants, 4 perfect clusters set aside for garnish, the remaining currants stemmed	½ liter
½ cup	Sauternes or Barsac	125 ml.
2 tbsp.	superfine sugar	30 ml.

Using a melon baller or a small spoon with sharp edges, carve out the flesh of the melon, forming small uniform pieces. Drop them into a mixing bowl. Then scrape out the flesh that remains—taking care not to remove any green from the rind—to leave a smooth, sturdy shell. Divide this part of the flesh equally and return it to the four shells.

Add the stemmed currants to the bowl containing the melon balls. Pour in the Sauternes or Barsac. Then combine the fruits gently with the superfine sugar and divide the mixture among the melon halves. Decorate each serving with a cluster of currants.

ROGER VERGÉ
ROGER VERGÉ'S CUISINE OF THE SOUTH OF FRANCE

Ginger-sauced Melon

To serve 2 to 4

2 cups	watermelon and cantaloupe balls	½ liter
½ cup	Chablis or other white wine	125 ml.
½ cup	sugar	125 ml.
1 tsp.	whole cloves	5 ml.
2 tbsp.	fresh lime or lemon juice	30 ml.
1 tbsp.	finely chopped candied ginger	15 ml.

Combine the wine, sugar and cloves in a small, nonreactive saucepan. Simmer them for about five minutes. Strain out the cloves; add the lime or lemon juice and ginger to the wine syrup and chill it. Arrange the melon balls in sherbet glasses. Spoon the chilled wine syrup over the melon; garnish the melon with mint sprigs and serve at once.

JEAN H. SHEPARD
THE FRESH FRUITS AND VEGETABLES COOKBOOK

Chilled Stuffed Persian Melon

To serve 6

1	Persian melon	1
1 cup	stemmed blueberries, seedless grapes, pitted Bing cherries or sliced strawberries	¼ liter
1 cup	fresh orange juice	¼ liter
1 tbsp.	grenadine	15 ml.
	kirsch or Cherry Heering	

Cut out the melon top around the stem; set the top aside. Scoop out the interior to make as many melon balls as you can without piercing the rind. Combine the berries, grapes or cherries with the melon balls and spoon the fruits into the melon shell.

Lace the fresh orange juice with the grenadine and add kirsch or Cherry Heering to taste. Pour this mixture into the melon shell and replace the top. Refrigerate the melon or pack it in ice and leave it all day. Remove it a short time before serving.

ANN CHANDONNET
THE COMPLETE FRUIT COOKBOOK

Watermelon Snow

To serve 6

2 cups	cubed watermelon	½ liter
1 cup	fresh orange juice	¼ liter
3 tbsp.	fresh lemon juice	45 ml.
¼ cup	cherry syrup	50 ml.
¾ cup	Demerara or turbinado sugar	175 ml.
2	egg whites, stiffly beaten	2

Mash the watermelon to a mush. Add the orange juice, lemon juice and cherry syrup. Mix in the sugar, pour into an ice cube tray and freeze for one and one half hours. Empty the contents into a mixing bowl. Fold the egg whites into the melon mixture. Freeze in a covered freezer container.

SUZANNE TOPPER
THE FRUIT COOKBOOK

Citrus Fruits

Broiled Pink Grapefruit with Honey

Pamplemousse Rose Grillé au Miel

Be sure the honey you choose is very, very thick. If you use clear, flowing honey, it will brown and run off the grapefruit without caramelizing. I choose lavender honey for this recipe, and I prefer pink grapefruit because they are pungent and more flavorful.

To serve 1

1	pink grapefruit	1
2 tbsp.	solid lavender honey	30 ml.

So that the grapefruit may stand upright without tipping, cut off a very thick piece of skin from each end, without penetrating the flesh. Then cut the fruit in half crosswise. Slip a serrated knife between the flesh and the membrane of each section and loosen the segments from the skin with a curved knife.

Preheat the broiler to its maximum temperature. Spread each grapefruit half with 1 tablespoon [15 ml.] of thick honey and, when the broiling unit is very hot, slide the grapefruit underneath, close to the heating element. Broil the grapefruit for seven to eight minutes, or until the surface is lightly caramelized. Serve sizzling hot.

ROGER VERGÉ
ROGER VERGÉ'S CUISINE OF THE SOUTH OF FRANCE

Grapefruit Crepes Suzette

Crêpes Suzette Pamplemousse

To serve 4 or 5

2	grapefruits, the peel of 1 shredded and the juice strained, the other peeled and segmented	2
6 tbsp.	unsalted butter, or 3 tbsp. [45 ml.] unsalted butter and 3 tbsp. safflower oil	90 ml.
½ cup plus 2 tbsp.	Demerara or turbinado sugar	155 ml.
8 to 10	crepes (recipe, page 165)	8 to 10
3 tbsp.	dry sherry (optional)	45 ml.

Beat 3 tablespoons [45 ml.] of butter and 2 tablespoons [30 ml.] of the sugar in a bowl with an electric mixer until the mixture is light and fluffy; add half of the shredded grapefruit peel and beat a little longer. Spread this butter over the underside of each crepe. Fold the crepes in half, then fold them in half again.

To make the grapefruit sauce, combine the remaining 3 tablespoons of butter or the safflower oil, all of the grapefruit juice, the rest of the shredded peel, and the remaining ½ cup [125 ml.] of sugar in a nonreactive sauté pan. Stir the ingredients over low heat until the grapefruit peel becomes translucent. Let the sauce simmer gently for five minutes. Heat the sherry in a little pan, ignite, and pour it onto the sauce. Add the grapefruit segments and warm them in the sauce for just a moment.

Arrange the folded crepes, overlapping them slightly, on a serving dish. Pour the sauce over them. Serve warm.

MARION GORMAN AND FELIPE P. DE ALBA
THE DIONE LUCAS BOOK OF NATURAL FRENCH COOKING

Grilled Grapefruit

To serve 1

½	grapefruit, the central core removed, the flesh segments separated and freed from the shell	½
	firmly packed brown sugar	
½ tbsp.	butter	7 ml.

Sprinkle the grapefruit with brown sugar. Place the butter in the center of the fruit. Grill the grapefruit 4 inches [10 cm.] from the heat source of a preheated broiler until it is lightly browned—five to seven minutes.

BEE NILSON
THE PENGUIN COOKERY BOOK

Cold Grapefruit Soufflé

To serve 4

2	large seedless grapefruits, halved, flesh removed, shells reserved	2
2	eggs, the yolks separated from the whites	2
¾ cup	sugar	175 ml.
½ cup	heavy cream	125 ml.
1 tbsp.	unflavored powdered gelatin, softened in ¼ cup [50 ml.] cold water for 5 minutes	15 ml.
2 tbsp.	Cointreau or other orange-flavored liqueur	30 ml.
1 tbsp.	finely grated orange peel	15 ml.

Purée the grapefruit flesh through a fine sieve set over a bowl, pressing down hard with the back of a spoon before discarding the pulp. Set the purée aside. Meanwhile, with a wire whisk, or a rotary or electric beater, beat the egg yolks and sugar together in a bowl for about three minutes until the yolks are thick.

Pour the cream into a nonreactive saucepan and cook over medium heat until bubbles appear around the edge of the pan. Remove the pan from the heat. Stir a small amount of the cream into the egg yolks to warm them. Then, beating constantly, add the egg yolks to the cream and then stir in the softened gelatin. Return to low heat and continue to stir until the custard mixture is smooth and thick enough to coat the spoon heavily. Do not let the mixture come near the boiling point or it will curdle. Strain the custard through a fine sieve into a deep bowl and stir in the grapefruit purée and orange liqueur.

Set the bowl of custard into a larger bowl filled with crushed ice or ice cubes and water. With a metal spoon, stir the custard until it is quite cold and begins to thicken. Beat thoroughly with a whisk to be sure it is perfectly smooth. Beat the egg whites until they are stiff enough to stand in firm, unwavering peaks on the beater when it is lifted from the bowl. Scoop the egg whites over the custard and, with a rubber spatula, fold them together gently but thoroughly.

Ladle the soufflé into the reserved grapefruit shells and swirl the top into decorative peaks with the edge of the spatula. Sprinkle the soufflés with orange peel and refrigerate for at least three hours, or until the soufflés are firm and set.

FOODS OF THE WORLD
PACIFIC AND SOUTHEAST ASIAN COOKING

Spiced Grapefruit

To serve 4

2	large grapefruits, halved, segmented, seeds removed	2
1 tbsp.	honey	15 ml.
	ground ginger	
	ground cardamoms	
	ground cinnamon	
	Angostura bitters	

Set the grapefruit, cut side up, on a baking sheet. Melt the honey over low heat and add a pinch of each of the spices. Spoon the honey over the grapefruit halves and let them stand for 10 minutes to let the flavors blend. Shake a dash of bitters over each grapefruit half and broil the halves under a preheated broiler for five to 10 minutes. The fruit should be hot and spicy on top and cool underneath.

PAMELA DIXON
NEW WAYS WITH FRESH FRUIT AND VEGETABLES

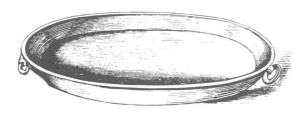

Grapefruit Sherbet with Pomegranate Seeds

Sorbetto di Pompelmo Con Melagrano

To serve 8

3 cups	fresh grapefruit juice, preferably squeezed from pink grapefruits	¾ liter
½ cup	pomegranate seeds	125 ml.
1¼ cups	sugar	300 ml.
⅓ cup	water	75 ml.
3	egg whites	3
¼ tsp.	cream of tartar	1 ml.
	pinch of salt	

Bring the sugar and water to a boil, stirring until the sugar dissolves. Without stirring, continue to boil the syrup until it reaches the hard-ball stage and registers 250° F. [120° C.] on a candy thermometer. While the sugar-water mixture boils, beat the egg whites with the cream of tartar and the salt until they hold a firm peak. Pour the hot syrup slowly into the egg whites, continuing to beat as you pour. Keep on beating for a total of five minutes, or until the egg whites are stiff and glossy.

Stir the egg whites into the grapefruit juice. Pour into a shallow metal pan and freeze until almost firm. Remove from the freezer, place in a mixing bowl, and beat briefly until smooth, fluffy and blended. Pour into eight chilled dishes and finish freezing. Remove from the freezer 15 minutes before serving and sprinkle with pomegranate seeds.

MARGARET AND G. FRANCO ROMAGNOLI
THE NEW ITALIAN COOKING

Lemon Fritters

To serve 4 to 6

2 tbsp.	fresh lemon juice	30 ml.
2 tsp.	grated lemon peel	10 ml.
2 cups	flour	½ liter
1	egg	1
1 cup	milk	¼ liter
1 tbsp.	sugar	15 ml.
¼ tsp.	salt	1 ml.
3 to 4 cups	vegetable oil for deep frying	¾ to 1 liter
	confectioners' sugar	

In a medium-sized bowl, combine the flour, egg, milk, sugar, salt and lemon juice to form a batter. Add the lemon peel and mix well. Cover and let the batter stand for one to two hours.

In a heavy pot, heat a 2-inch [5-cm.] layer of vegetable oil to 375° F. [185° C.]. Drop the batter by spoonfuls into the hot oil and fry the fritters for three to four minutes, or until they are golden brown. Do not fry more than six fritters at a time. Remove the browned fritters from the oil with a slotted spoon and drain them on absorbent paper. Repeat until all of the fritters are cooked. Sprinkle them with confectioners' sugar and serve them hot or cold.

MARIA POLUSHKIN
THE DUMPLING COOKBOOK

Stewed Kumquats and Prunes

This dish may be served hot or cold.

	To serve 4	
1 cup	prunes, soaked in cold water overnight	¼ liter
6	kumquats, sliced into rounds and seeded	6
1 tbsp.	honey	15 ml.
½ cup	fresh orange juice	125 ml.

Simmer the prunes in their soaking water for 10 minutes, or until they are tender and plump. Strain the prunes, reserving the cooking liquid, and pit them.

In a nonreactive saucepan, combine ½ cup [125 ml.] of the reserved cooking liquid, the honey and the orange juice. Bring to a boil, then immediately reduce the heat to low and add the sliced kumquats. Simmer the mixture for about five minutes, take the pan off the heat and stir in the prunes.

FAYE MARTIN
RODALE'S NATURALLY DELICIOUS DESSERTS AND SNACKS

Lemon Miracle Pudding

This pudding is well worth trying, as it produces a sponge topping with a lemon sauce underneath. Serve hot or cold.

	To serve 2 to 4	
1	lemon, the peel grated, the juice strained	1
1 tbsp.	butter	15 ml.
¾ cup	sugar	175 ml.
1 tbsp.	hot water	15 ml.
2 tbsp.	flour	30 ml.
2	eggs, the yolks separated from the whites, and the whites stiffly beaten	2
¾ cup	milk	175 ml.

Beat the butter and sugar together until white and fluffy, then add the hot water and beat again briefly. Stir in the lemon peel, juice and flour. Beat the egg yolks into the milk and stir this into the first mixture. Fold in the egg whites. Pour into a buttered 3-cup [¾-liter] baking dish and stand this in a baking pan of water.

Bake the pudding, uncovered, at 250° F. [120° C.] for one and one quarter hours.

TESS CONWAY
SEYCHELLES DELIGHTS

Lemon Fluff

	To serve 4 to 6	
¼ cup	fresh lemon juice	50 ml.
1 tbsp.	grated lemon peel	15 ml.
4	extra-large eggs, the yolks separated from the whites	4
1 cup	sugar	¼ liter
1½ tsp.	unflavored powdered gelatin, softened in ⅓ cup [75 ml.] water for 5 minutes	7 ml.
2 tsp.	butter	10 ml.
⅛ tsp.	salt	½ ml.
½ cup	heavy cream, whipped	125 ml.
¼ cup	freshly grated coconut	50 ml.
2 tbsp.	fresh orange juice	30 ml.
1 tbsp.	grated orange peel	15 ml.

In the top of a double boiler, beat the egg yolks very well. Gradually beat in ½ cup [125 ml.] of the sugar. Stir in the lemon juice and lemon peel. Stirring constantly, heat over simmering water until the mixture thickens and coats the back of the spoon.

Meanwhile, soften the gelatin and heat it gently to dissolve it. Add the butter, salt and dissolved gelatin to the lemon mixture. Cool until this mixture starts to thicken.

Beat the egg whites until frothy. Gradually beat in the remaining sugar until the whites are stiff. Fold the whites into the lemon gelatin and turn this mixture into four to six individual soufflé dishes. Refrigerate the mixture for several hours or overnight.

Decorate each serving of lemon fluff with the whipped cream. Mix the coconut with the orange juice and orange peel, and sprinkle it over the servings.

JEAN HEWITT
THE NEW YORK TIMES WEEKEND COOKBOOK

Cold Lemon Soufflé

To serve 4 to 6

2	lemons, the peel grated, the juice strained	2
1 cup	superfine sugar	¼ liter
3	eggs, the yolks separated from the whites	3
4	sheets leaf gelatin, soaked in cold water for 10 to 30 minutes and drained, or 1 tbsp. [15 ml.] unflavored powdered gelatin, softened in ¼ cup [50 ml.] water for 5 minutes	4
⅔ cup	heavy cream, lightly whipped	150 ml.
	pistachio nuts	

Stir the lemon peel and juice, the sugar and the egg yolks together in a nonreactive saucepan. Cook the mixture over low heat, stirring all the time, until it is thick enough to coat a spoon. Do not let the mixture come near to a boil lest it curdle. Set this custard aside off the heat.

Whip the egg whites to a stiff froth, then add the lightly whipped cream. Add the gelatin to the lemon mixture. Stir in lightly the whites and the cream. Pour into a mold and chill. When set, unmold and decorate with pistachio nuts.

OXFORDSHIRE FEDERATION OF WOMEN'S INSTITUTES
500 JOLLY GOOD THINGS

Honeycomb Mold

This mold may also be made with other tart fruit juice—cranberry, lime, raspberry, rhubarb or the blood-orange juice shown on pages 76-77.

To serve 6

2	lemons, the peel thinly pared, the juice strained	2
3	large eggs, the yolks separated from the whites, and the whites stiffly beaten	3
2 tbsp.	unflavored powdered gelatin, softened in ¼ cup [50 ml.] of water for 5 minutes	30 ml.
⅓ cup	sugar	75 ml.
⅓ cup	heavy cream	75 ml.
2 cups	milk	½ liter

Put the egg yolks in a large bowl or the top of a double boiler. Add the lemon peel, softened gelatin, sugar and cream. Heat the milk to just under the boiling point and whisk it into the egg-yolk mixture. Set the bowl over a pan of simmering water, and stir until you have a custard of more or less the consistency of heavy cream. Taste the custard and add more sugar if you like, but this pudding should not be very sweet. Mix in the lemon juice and strain the mixture. With a metal spoon, fold the strained custard into the beaten egg whites; turn and lift the mixture gently. Pour the pudding mixture into a 4-cup [1-liter] mold, and chill it. When the pudding is firmly set, slip a knife around the edge of the mold; it will then unmold easily. The pudding will have a cap of clear lemon jelly, then a thin band of opaque cream jelly shading off into a honeycombed spongy base that makes a slight crinkling noise as it is eaten.

JANE GRIGSON
GOOD THINGS

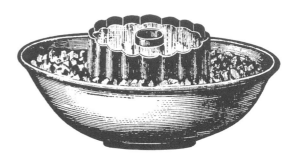

Lemon Froth with Nuts

Citroenschuim met Noten

To serve 4

2	lemons, the peel grated, the juice strained	2
1 tbsp.	unflavored powdered gelatin, softened in ¼ cup [50 ml.] cold water for 5 minutes	15 ml.
1 cup	confectioners' sugar	¼ liter
2	egg whites	2
2 tbsp.	chopped hazelnuts	30 ml.

In a nonreactive saucepan, combine the softened gelatin and the sugar. Stir over low heat until the gelatin and sugar dissolve completely; do not let the mixture boil. Remove the pan from the heat and stir in the lemon peel and juice.

Allow the mixture to cool until it begins to thicken and then whisk it—by hand or with an electric beater—until its consistency is light and frothy.

Whisk the egg whites until stiff and fold them into the lemon mixture. Pour the lemon froth into sundae glasses and refrigerate them until the froth is set. Decorate the dessert with the chopped hazelnuts and serve.

HUGH JANS
VRIJ NEDERLANDS KOOKBOEK

Lemon Snow

This snow may also be made with other tart fruit juices—orange, grapefruit, lime or the cranberry juice shown on pages 76-77.

This is a gelatin-based dessert that requires time to reach the syrupy stage and still more time to set. To hurry this up, place the bowl that holds the gelatin mixture inside a larger ice-filled bowl. Keep the bowl in this ice bath as you whip the mixture.

To serve 6		
½ tsp.	finely grated lemon peel	2 ml.
⅔ cup	fresh lemon juice	150 ml.
2 tbsp.	unflavored powdered gelatin, softened in ½ cup [125 ml.] water for 5 minutes	30 ml.
1⅓ cups	sugar	325 ml.
2½ cups	boiling water	625 ml.
6	egg whites	6

In a large bowl, mix the softened gelatin and sugar. Add the boiling water and stir well until the gelatin is completely dissolved. Add the lemon peel and juice. Chill until the mixture is syrupy, about one half hour in a bowl of ice or about one hour in the refrigerator. Beat the egg whites until stiff. Add them to the lemon mixture and stir until it begins to thicken slightly—about five minutes. Pour into a serving dish and chill for at least two hours until set.

ELEANOR GRAVES
GREAT DINNERS FROM LIFE

Cold Lime Soufflé

To serve 6		
¾ cup	fresh lime juice	175 ml.
1½ tsp.	coarsely chopped lime peel	7 ml.
1 tbsp.	unflavored powdered gelatin	15 ml.
4	eggs, the yolks separated from the whites, plus 2 additional egg whites	4
1 cup	sugar	¼ liter
	salt	
	green food coloring (optional)	
1 cup	heavy cream, whipped	¼ liter
	fresh mint leaves	

Prepare a soufflé dish as follows: Fold in half lengthwise sufficient parchment paper to go around the dish with a good margin for taping. With the folded edge as the upper edge, lightly oil the side which will face the center of the dish. Wrap the parchment paper around the dish and secure it with tape so that 4 inches [10 cm.] stand above the rim.

In a small bowl, soften the gelatin in ¼ cup [50 ml.] of the lime juice. In the container of an electric blender, whirl the remaining ½ cup [125 ml.] of lime juice with the peel until the peel is chopped into fine particles.

In the top of a double boiler, combine the egg yolks, ½ cup of sugar and a pinch of salt. Add the lime mixture and, stirring constantly, cook the mixture over simmering water until it coats the spoon. Remove it from the heat and stir in the gelatin mixture and one or two drops of food coloring, if you are using it. Continue stirring until the gelatin is dissolved.

In a mixing bowl, beat the egg whites until they hold a soft shape; gradually add the rest of the sugar, beating constantly until the whites form stiff peaks. Gently fold and blend the whipped cream and egg whites into the lime mixture. Pour it into the prepared dish and chill it for at least three hours, or until it is set. Before serving, remove the parchment paper collar and garnish the soufflé with a few fresh mint leaves.

ROBERT ACKART
FRUITS IN COOKING

Orange Yogurt

Narrangee Dhye

To serve 4		
2	oranges, peeled and segmented	2
2 cups	yogurt	½ liter
1 tbsp.	honey	15 ml.
½ tsp.	ground coriander	2 ml.
3	whole cardamoms, seeds removed and crushed to a powder	3
⅛ tsp.	ground cloves	½ ml.
¼ tsp.	salt	1 ml.

Combine the yogurt, honey, coriander, cardamom seeds, cloves and salt. Mix them well. Stir in the orange segments. Chill the mixture for several hours before serving.

FAYE MARTIN
RODALE'S NATURALLY DELICIOUS DESSERTS AND SNACKS

Deep-fried Orange Crullers
Diples

To make 6 dozen

½ tsp.	grated orange peel	2 ml.
3 tbsp.	fresh orange juice	45 ml.
2½ cups	flour	625 ml.
½ tsp.	baking powder	2 ml.
⅛ tsp.	salt	½ ml.
2	eggs, plus 1 egg yolk	2
3 tbsp.	peanut oil	45 ml.
	oil for deep frying	
1 cup	honey	¼ liter
⅓ cup	water	75 ml.
¾ to 1 cup	finely chopped walnuts	175 to 250 ml.
	ground cinnamon	

Sift the flour with the baking powder and the salt into a large mixing bowl. Lightly beat the eggs and yolk with the grated orange peel and orange juice. Press a deep hollow in the middle of the flour with your fist and pour in the egg mixture. Using your hands, gradually incorporate the flour into the center, then gather the dough into a ball. Turn out onto a floured surface and vigorously knead the dough until it is very smooth and elastic, gradually working in the peanut oil by tablespoonfuls. Cover the dough with a damp kitchen towel and put it aside to rest for at least one hour in a cool place.

Divide the dough into four parts. On a floured surface, roll one part of dough until paper thin. Cut it into strips 6 inches [15 cm.] long and about 1 inch [2½ cm.] wide. Loop them like bows or tie them into loose knots. Repeat with the remaining portions of dough.

In a deep skillet, heat the oil to a depth of 1½ inches [4 cm.]. Fry four or five crullers at a time until they are golden brown on both sides. This takes about one minute. With tongs or a slotted spoon, set the crullers on racks to drain.

Heat the honey and dilute it with the water. Dribble the mixture over the slightly cooled crullers, then sprinkle them at once with the chopped walnuts and dust them with ground cinnamon.

PAULA WOLFERT
MEDITERRANEAN COOKING

Orange Sections with Orange-flower Water
Lichine ma Zhar

In Morocco, lichine ma zhar is served as a sweet salad course, but it may also be served as a dessert.

To serve 4

4	navel oranges, peeled and segmented	4
¼ tsp.	orange-flower water	1 ml.
1 tbsp.	confectioners' sugar, mixed with ⅛ tsp. [½ ml.] ground cinnamon	15 ml.

Arrange the orange segments attractively in rows or concentric circles on a serving plate, overlapping the segments slightly. Sprinkle them with the orange-flower water, cover the plate with aluminum foil or plastic wrap, and refrigerate for at least two hours, or until thoroughly chilled. Just before serving, sprinkle the oranges with the cinnamon sugar.

FOODS OF THE WORLD
A QUINTET OF CUISINES

Hot Orange Pudding
Hsi-mi-chü-keng

To serve 4 to 6

1	large orange, peeled, segmented and broken into small pieces	1
2 cups	cold water	½ liter
¼ cup	sugar	50 ml.
½ cup	pearl tapioca, soaked in ½ cup [125 ml.] of water for at least 4 hours	125 ml.

In a 2-quart [2-liter] nonreactive saucepan, combine the cold water with the sugar. Bring to a boil over high heat, stirring until the sugar dissolves. Drain the tapioca and pour it into the pan slowly, stirring constantly. Cook over medium heat, stirring, for two minutes until the pudding thickens. Stir in the orange pieces and bring the pudding to a boil again. Serve at once.

FOODS OF THE WORLD
THE COOKING OF CHINA

Sliced Orange Compote

To serve 6

6	seedless oranges	6
2 cups	water	½ liter
½ cup	sugar	125 ml.
¼ tsp.	freshly grated nutmeg	1 ml.
½ cup	orange liqueur	125 ml.

With a swivel-bladed vegetable peeler, carefully remove the peel from the oranges, making certain that none of the white pith is included. Cut the peel into very thin julienne. Bring the water, sugar and nutmeg to a boil in a nonreactive saucepan. Add the orange-peel julienne, cover partially and simmer for 15 minutes.

Meanwhile, cut away the white pith from the oranges. On a cutting board with juice grooves or on a saucer, cut the oranges crosswise into ¼-inch [½-cm.] slices. As you work, place the slices in a deep heatproof bowl. Scrape into the bowl any juice that collects on the board or in the saucer.

Pour the orange liqueur into the boiling syrup, let it simmer for half a minute, then pour the syrup over the orange slices through a strainer that will catch the julienne. Transfer ½ cup [125 ml.] of the cooking syrup to a small pot. Tightly cover the orange slices at once, let them cool completely at room temperature, then chill them.

Add the drained orange peel to the syrup in the small pot. Place over medium heat and cook, uncovered, until all the liquid has evaporated and the strips are lightly caramelized. Scrape them into a small bowl, cover and refrigerate. To serve, transfer four or five orange slices to a dessert plate, spoon a little of the syrup over them, then garnish with a little of the caramelized orange peel.

CAROL CUTLER
THE WOMAN'S DAY LOW-CALORIE DESSERT COOKBOOK

Souffléed Oranges

Oranges Soufflées

The technique of making souffléed oranges is demonstrated on pages 68-69. Instead of flavoring the soufflé base with vanilla extract, a vanilla bean may be added to the milk before it is scalded and removed before the milk is incorporated into the egg mixture.

The soufflé base can be prepared three to four hours ahead. Brush the surface of the mixture with melted butter to prevent the formation of a skin, and keep the mixture at room temperature. Half an hour before serving, heat the base until very hot but not boiling.

	To serve 4	
5	large navel oranges, 4 cut in half crosswise, peel of 1 grated	5
1 cup	milk	¼ liter
3	eggs, the yolks separated from the whites, plus two additional whites	3
¼ cup	granulated sugar	50 ml.
2½ tbsp.	flour	37 ml.
3 tbsp.	Grand Marnier or other orange liqueur	45 ml.
1 tsp.	vanilla extract	5 ml.
2 tbsp.	confectioners' sugar, sieved	30 ml.

Scoop out the flesh from the orange halves without piercing the peels and reserve it for another use. To make the soufflé base, first scald the milk in a heavy saucepan. Remove it from the heat. Put the egg yolks, grated orange peel and half the granulated sugar in a bowl and beat until thick; stir in the flour. Whisk in the scalded milk and pour the mixture into the saucepan. Bring to a boil, then simmer for two minutes, whisking the mixture constantly. Remove the saucepan from the heat and stir in the liqueur and vanilla.

Whisk the egg whites until stiff, add the remaining granulated sugar and continue whisking until the egg whites are glossy. Stir one quarter of the whites into the orange mixture; then add this to the remaining whites and fold the mixture together as lightly as possible. Use a pastry bag with a star tube to fill the orange halves, or spoon the soufflé mixture into them. Bake in a preheated 400° F. [200° C.] oven for five minutes, or until the soufflés are puffed and brown. Sprinkle the tops with the confectioners' sugar and return to the oven for two minutes. Serve at once.

FAYE LEVY
LA VARENNE TOUR BOOK

Orange Brandy Fritters

To serve 8

5	large oranges, 4 peeled and segmented, the peel of 1 grated and the juice strained	5
2 cups	water	½ liter
⅓ cup	brandy	75 ml.
1 cup	sugar	¼ liter
	oil for deep frying	
	Brandy batter	
1 cup	flour	¼ liter
4 tsp.	sugar	20 ml.
¼ tsp.	salt	1 ml.
4 tsp.	butter, melted	20 ml.
about ⅓ cup	warm water	about 75 ml.
2	egg yolks, beaten, plus 1 egg white, stiffly beaten	2
3 tbsp.	brandy	45 ml.

To make the brandy batter, first sift the flour, sugar and salt together in a large bowl. Add the melted butter and enough warm water to form a smooth batter. Stir in the egg yolks and add the brandy. Fold in the egg white just before using.

Combine the water, brandy and sugar in a nonreactive saucepan. Bring to a boil and simmer for five minutes. Add the drained orange segments and simmer for 10 minutes. Skim the segments out of the syrup with a slotted spoon and cool them. Set the syrup aside in the saucepan.

Heat oil to 370° F. [185° C.]. Dip a few orange segments at a time into the brandy batter and fry them until light golden brown—about two minutes. Drain on absorbent paper.

In the meantime, cook the syrup until it spins a thread and reaches a temperature of about 225° F. [110° C.] on a candy thermometer. Add the grated peel and orange juice. Serve the syrup hot, over the fritters.

JEAN GORDON
ORANGE RECIPES

Hot Orange Soufflé

Soufflé Chaud à l'Orange

The orange mixture can be prepared three to four hours ahead of time and kept, covered, at room temperature. In this case, the mixture should be warmed until hot to the touch before it is mixed with the egg whites.

To serve 4

½ cup	fresh orange juice	125 ml.
1 tbsp.	grated orange peel	15 ml.
4 tbsp.	butter, plus 2 tsp. [10 ml.] softened butter	60 ml.
⅔ cup plus 1 ½ tbsp.	granulated sugar	150 ml. plus 22 ml.
4	egg yolks	4
5	egg whites, stiffly beaten	5
	confectioners' sugar	
1 to 2 tbsp.	Grand Marnier (optional)	15 to 30 ml.

Butter a 4-cup [1-liter] soufflé dish with the 2 teaspoons [10 ml.] of softened butter, sprinkle in 1½ tablespoons [22 ml.] of the granulated sugar, and discard the excess sugar. Set the dish aside.

In a heavy, nonreactive pan, heat the remaining butter with ¼ cup [50 ml.] of the granulated sugar and all of the orange juice until the butter and sugar melt. Take the pan from the heat and beat in the egg yolks, one by one. Add the orange peel. Return the pan to the stove and, stirring constantly, cook the mixture very gently until it thickens to the consistency of heavy cream.

Add the remaining sugar to the beaten egg whites and beat for 10 seconds, or until the whites are glossy. Stir about a quarter of the egg whites into the orange mixture. Add this combination to the remaining whites and fold the ingredients together as lightly as possible. Gently pour the mixture into the prepared soufflé dish and bake at once in a preheated 425° F. [220° C.] oven for 12 to 15 minutes, or until the soufflé is puffed and brown. Dust the top with confectioners' sugar, sprinkle with Grand Marnier—if you are using it—and serve the soufflé at once.

ANNE WILLAN
LA VARENNE'S PARIS KITCHEN

Upside-down Orange Cake

Rosace à l'Orange

The techniques of assembling an upside-down cake appear on pages 80-81. If the peel and pith are removed (page 15) before the oranges are sliced, it will be unnecessary to simmer the slices in sugar syrup, which eliminates the bitterness of the pith. Two kiwi fruits, peeled and thinly sliced, may be substituted for one of the oranges. The author recommends serving the cake within 48 hours of assembly.

To serve 6

4	unpeeled oranges, thinly sliced	4
4 cups	light sugar syrup (recipe, page 162)	1 liter
1 cup	pastry cream (recipe, page 165)	¼ liter
1 cup	heavy cream, flavored with 1 tsp. [5 ml.] vanilla sugar and stiffly whipped	¼ liter
	superfine sugar	
1	spongecake (recipe, page 166)	1
⅔ cup	medium sugar syrup (recipe, page 162), flavored with 2 tbsp. [30 ml.] Grand Marnier	150 ml.

In a nonreactive saucepan, simmer the orange slices in the sugar syrup over very low heat for two hours. Pour the oranges and syrup into a bowl and leave overnight. Drain the orange slices, set half of them aside for decorating the cake and chop the remaining slices into small pieces. Mix the pieces with the pastry cream, then fold the pastry cream mixture very gently into the whipped cream.

Butter or oil a 7-cup [1¾-liter] round mold and sprinkle in superfine sugar; turn the mold so that the whole inner surface is covered with sugar. Place an orange slice in the center of the mold and surround it with more orange slices, making sure that each slice overlaps its neighbor and that the slices cover the sides of the mold. Half-fill the mold with the orange-flavored pastry cream.

Using a serrated knife, slice the spongecake into two layers. Combine the orange juice with the liqueur-flavored sugar syrup. Brush both sides of each layer of cake with the sugar syrup. Place one layer on top of the pastry cream, trimming the layer if necessary to fit the mold. Cover the layer with the remaining pastry cream and place the second layer of cake on top. Put a plate over the cake, press the plate down and place a small weight on top of the plate. Refrigerate the cake for at least two hours.

Just before serving, take the cake out of the refrigerator, remove the weight and the plate, dip the base of the mold into hot water, place a serving plate over the cake and turn the cake out of the mold.

GASTON LENÔTRE
LENÔTRE'S DESSERTS AND PASTRIES

Orange Butterscotch Pudding

To serve 4 to 6

½ cup	fresh orange juice	125 ml.
¾ cup	orange segments, seeded	175 ml.
½ cup	honey	125 ml.
2½ tbsp.	cornstarch	37 ml.
⅛ tsp.	salt	½ ml.
1½ cups	milk	375 ml.
2	eggs, the yolks separated from the whites	2
¼ cup	firmly packed brown sugar	50 ml.

In the top of a double boiler set over boiling water, mix the honey, cornstarch and salt; add the milk and then the orange juice slowly, stirring well until thickened. Beat the egg yolks and slowly dribble them into the mixture. After a couple of minutes of further cooking, remove this orange custard from the heat and let it cool to room temperature.

In a mixing bowl, beat the egg whites, gradually adding the brown sugar during the beating process. Continue to beat until the whites are stiff. Fold the whites into the custard mixture.

Refrigerate the pudding until set and well chilled—about three hours. Garnish it with the orange segments before serving.

SUZANNE TOPPER
THE FRUIT COOKBOOK

Tangerine Mousse

To serve 2

2	tangerines, the peel cut into strips, 1 tbsp. [15 ml.] juice strained	2
2 tbsp.	sugar	30 ml.
1	egg	1
1½ tbsp.	orange liqueur	22 ml.
⅓ cup	heavy cream, whipped, or 2 egg whites, stiffly beaten	75 ml.

Mash the tangerine peel and sugar together to extract the flavor from the peel. Add the tangerine juice to dissolve the sugar. Discard the peel. Add the egg to the sugar and beat until a ribbon forms—about five minutes—then beat in the orange liqueur. Mix one quarter of the whipped cream or beaten egg whites into the tangerine base, and fold in the remainder of the cream or whites. Freeze until ready to use.

MADELEINE KAMMAN
DINNER AGAINST THE CLOCK

Tangerine-Apricot Bavaria

To serve 8 to 10

1¾ cups	fresh tangerine juice	425 ml.
1½ cups	fresh apricot juice	375 ml.
2 tsp.	grated tangerine peel	10 ml.
2 tbsp.	unflavored powdered gelatin	30 ml.
½ cup	sugar	125 ml.
	salt	
3	egg whites	3
½ cup	heavy cream, chilled	125 ml.

Banana-cream dressing

2	bananas, peeled and mashed	2
1 cup	sour cream	¼ liter
2 tbsp.	firmly packed brown sugar	30 ml.
2 tbsp.	honey	30 ml.

In a nonreactive saucepan, first combine the gelatin, sugar, salt and tangerine juice. Let stand for five minutes, then cook and stir over medium heat until the gelatin dissolves. Stir in the apricot juice and tangerine peel. Chill until the mixture is partially set—about three hours.

Beat the egg whites until stiff peaks form. Fold the whites into the gelatin mixture, then chill it again until partially set. Whip the cream until soft peaks form. Add to the partially set gelatin mixture and continue beating until well blended. Pile into a 6-cup [1½-liter] mold or eight to 10 individual molds and refrigerate until firm.

To make the banana-cream dressing, whip the sour cream until fluffy. Stir the sugar and honey into the mashed bananas and mix until smooth. Fold this banana mixture into the whipped sour cream.

Unmold the Bavaria and serve with the dressing.

ANN CHANDONNET
THE COMPLETE FRUIT COOKBOOK

Citrus Salad

Citrussalade

To serve 4

2	grapefruits	2
2	oranges	2
2	tangerines	2
3 to 4 tbsp.	sugar	45 to 60 ml.
2 tbsp.	Grand Marnier	30 ml.
	ground cinnamon	

Halve the grapefruits, remove the segments with a grapefruit knife—cutting away the white membrane—and chop the flesh coarse. Scrape the inside of the empty grapefruit shells clean. Set them aside after cutting off a thin slice from the bottoms for better balance.

Grate the peel of one of the oranges, without removing any of the pith, and reserve the grated peel. Peel the oranges and divide them into segments; chop them coarse. Peel the tangerines, then remove any pith from the segments and chop them coarse.

Combine the chopped fruits and loosely fill the four grapefruit shells with the mixture. Sprinkle the fruits with sugar to taste and the grated orange peel. Sprinkle with the Grand Marnier, cover with plastic wrap and refrigerate. Serve cold, sprinkled with a pinch of ground cinnamon.

HUGH JANS
VRIJ NEDERLAND

Tangerine and Apple Tapioca

To serve 4

¾ cup	fresh tangerine segments, seeded	175 ml.
2	medium-sized apples, peeled, cored and sliced	2
½ cup	Demerara or turbinado sugar	125 ml.
2 tbsp.	butter	30 ml.
1 tbsp.	fresh lemon juice	15 ml.
⅛ tsp.	ground cinnamon	½ ml.
⅛ tsp.	grated nutmeg	½ ml.
⅛ tsp.	salt	½ ml.
2 cups	apple juice	½ liter
¼ cup	quick-cooking tapioca	50 ml.
1½ cups	milk	375 ml.
2	egg whites, stiffly beaten (optional)	2

Combine the apples, sugar, butter, lemon juice, cinnamon, nutmeg, salt and apple juice in a deep, nonreactive saucepan and bring the mixture just to the boiling point. Then cover, and simmer over low heat for 25 minutes. Baste the ingredients with a little juice from the bottom of the pot, occasionally adding water or more juice, if needed. Set the apple mixture aside at room temperature.

Combine the tapioca and milk in another saucepan and cook over medium heat, stirring constantly, until the milk comes to a boil and the tapioca thickens. Blend the apple mixture and tangerine segments into the thickened tapioca. Refrigerate until the pudding is thoroughly chilled—about three hours. If you like, fold stiffly beaten egg whites into the mixture shortly before serving it.

SUZANNE TOPPER
THE FRUIT COOKBOOK

Guavas, Prickly Pears, Kiwi Fruits and Figs

Guava Pudding

To serve 4

8	large, soft guavas, peeled and halved	8
¼ cup	sugar	50 ml.
1	large banana, peeled and sliced	1
	cream or grated coconut	

Scoop the soft pulp out of the guava halves and set the shells aside. Press the pulp through a coarse sieve to remove the seeds. Mix the pulp with the sugar. Cut up the guava shells and put them into a serving dish with alternating layers of the sliced banana. Pour the pulp over the fruits in the dish. Cover the dish and chill for two to three hours. Serve with cream, grated coconut or both.

SELMA AND W.J.A. PAYNE
COOKING WITH EXOTIC FRUIT

Stewed Guavas

To serve 6

20	firm guavas, peeled and cut lengthwise into halves	20
1½ cups	sugar	375 ml.
3 cups	water	¾ liter
	fresh lemon juice	
	milk or cream (optional)	

Boil the sugar and water in a nonreactive saucepan, stirring until the sugar dissolves. Put the guavas in this syrup and cook slowly until they are tender. Add a squeeze of lemon juice. Remove the guavas carefully. Press them through a sieve or strainer into a bowl. Add a little of the syrup to the guava purée and whip it up. Milk or cream may be added at this point. Chill the purée and serve it in glass dishes.

E. CHAPMAN NYAHO, E. AMARTEIFIO AND J. ASARE
GHANA RECIPE BOOK

Cactus Cobbler

To serve 4

4 cups	puréed prickly pears	1 liter
1 tsp.	ground cinnamon	5 ml.
½ tsp.	grated nutmeg	2 ml.
1 tbsp.	quick-cooking tapioca	15 ml.
4 tbsp.	butter	60 ml.
¾ cup	sugar	175 ml.
1 tsp.	vanilla extract	5 ml.
½ cup	lemonade, made with 1 tbsp. [15 ml.] fresh lemon juice, 1½ tbsp. [22 ml.] sugar and ½ cup [125 ml.] water	125 ml.

Cobbler dough

1 cup	flour	¼ liter
½ tsp.	baking powder	2 ml.
	salt	
4 tbsp.	butter, cut into pieces	60 ml.
⅓ cup	milk	75 ml.

For the dough, first mix the flour, baking powder and salt. Cut in the butter until the mixture has the consistency of cornmeal. Add the milk and mix until a dough forms. Turn it onto a floured board and roll the dough into a large round. Cut it into four wedges.

Spread the puréed prickly pears over the four pastry pieces and sprinkle the purée with the cinnamon, nutmeg and tapioca. Roll up the wedges and place them in a buttered 6-by-10-inch [15-by-25-cm.] baking dish.

In a small pan, combine the butter, sugar and vanilla extract. Add the lemonade. Stirring often, heat this mixture until the butter melts and the sugar dissolves. Pour the sauce over the cobbler. Bake in a preheated 350° F. [180° C.] oven for one hour, or until the crust is brown. Serve the cobbler either warm or cold.

SANDAL ENGLISH
FRUITS OF THE DESERT

Festive Prickly-Pear Jellied Salad

To make the prickly-pear juice called for in this recipe, peel, slice and purée in a blender 1½ pounds [¾ kg.] of prickly pears, put the purée in a cheesecloth-lined sieve and squeeze the cloth to extract the juice.

To serve 8 to 10

1½ cups	prickly-pear juice	375 ml.
2 cups	small fresh fruit pieces, prepared for eating and cut as necessary	½ liter
2 tbsp.	unflavored powdered gelatin	30 ml.
1 cup	fresh orange juice	¼ liter
⅓ cup	sugar	75 ml.
¼ tsp.	salt	1 ml.
½ cup	dry red wine	125 ml.
⅓ cup	fresh lemon juice	75 ml.

Soften the gelatin in ½ cup [125 ml.] of the orange juice for five minutes. Combine the remaining orange juice and the prickly-pear juice with the sugar and salt, and heat it almost to boiling. Add the softened gelatin and stir to dissolve. Add the wine and lemon juice. Chill until the mixture is slightly thickened. Add the fruit pieces and pour the mixture into a 6-cup [1½-liter] ring mold. Chill the mold until the gelatin is set—about three hours. Unmold the jellied salad onto a large, round platter.

SANDAL ENGLISH
FRUITS OF THE DESERT

Kiwi Cream

To make the coconut milk called for in this recipe, pour about 1½ cups [375 ml.] of boiling water over ¾ cup [175 ml.] of freshly grated coconut. After five minutes, strain the mixture through cheesecloth to extract all of the milk.

To serve 6 to 8

4	kiwi fruits, peeled and mashed in a food mill or processor	4
¼ cup	tapioca flour	50 ml.
½ cup	water	125 ml.
1½ cups	coconut milk	375 ml.
2 tsp.	grated lemon peel	10 ml.
1 cup	heavy cream, whipped	¼ liter

Combine the tapioca flour and water in a nonreactive saucepan. Stir in the coconut milk and heat slowly, stirring constantly with a wire whisk until the sauce is thick. Then add the kiwi fruits to the warm mixture along with the lemon peel. Bring the mixture to a boil, then set it aside to cool. Chill for one hour. Fold the whipped cream into the kiwi mixture and serve immediately.

GAIL L. WORSTMAN
THE NATURAL FRUIT COOKBOOK

Burnt Cream with Kiwi Fruits

Crème Brulée aux Kiwis

Burnt cream has been made in England since the 17th Century, but it gained a new reputation when a chef at Trinity College, Cambridge, took it up at the end of the last century. Being a rich pudding, it was usually served with fruit. Not long ago, someone had the idea of putting grapes underneath the pudding. Why not? And kiwi fruits taste even better than grapes. Raspberries and poached sliced peaches and pears do well, too.

Some people stand the gratin dish in a tray of crushed ice before broiling the sugar. This prevents the custard from overheating underneath and bubbling up through the sugar.

The success of burnt cream depends partly on the flavor of the cream you use. *Crème fraîche* is ideal. If you are in a hurry, you can use it whipped, instead of making a custard.

To serve 10 to 12

1½ lb.	kiwi fruits, peeled and sliced	¾ kg.
4	large eggs, plus 4 large egg yolks	4
4 cups	heavy cream	1 liter
	the thinly pared peel of 1 lemon	
2-inch	cinnamon stick	5-cm.
	sugar	

Choose a large gratin dish with a capacity of at least 6 cups [1½ liters]. Cover the bottom with the sliced kiwi fruits.

Beat the eggs and extra egg yolks together in a large heatproof bowl. Bring the cream, lemon peel and cinnamon slowly to just under the boiling point. Strain the hot cream into the beaten eggs, whisking them together vigorously at first, then more gently until you have a smooth custard. Put the bowl over a pan of barely simmering water, and stir with a wooden spoon until the custard is very thick—the back of the spoon should be coated. Should the custard begin to show a hint of graininess, rapidly pour it into a processor or blender and whizz at top speed for a few minutes. Pour the custard over the fruit and chill it for several hours.

A couple of hours before serving, sprinkle enough sugar over the whole thing to make a layer almost ¼ inch [6 mm.] deep. Preheat the broiler to its highest setting. Slip the dish underneath. Do not turn your back on it, but watch as the sugar melts to a marbled brown glassiness—within two or three minutes. If the broiler heat is uneven, you will have to turn the dish.

JANE GRIGSON
JANE GRIGSON'S FRUIT BOOK

Hot Fried Figs

Frittura di Fichi Ruspoli

	To serve 4	
8	firm black figs, peeled	8
½ cup	dark rum	125 ml.
⅓ cup	flour	75 ml.
½ cup	water	125 ml.
	vegetable oil, olive oil or lard	

Soak the figs in the rum for one hour, turning them often.

In a shallow bowl slowly stir the flour into the water; beat this batter until smooth and creamy. In a heavy skillet, heat enough oil or lard to form a layer about ½ inch [1 cm.] deep. When the fat is very hot but not smoking, dip the figs one at a time into the batter, then into the hot fat. Fry the figs until they are golden brown on both sides—about two minutes. Drain, and serve the figs very hot.

PAULA WOLFERT
MEDITERRANEAN COOKING

Fresh Figs with Raspberries

Figues Fraîches Rafraîchies aux Framboises

	To serve 4	
12	firm ripe black figs	12
1 pint	raspberries	½ liter
¼ cup	red currant jelly	50 ml.
6 tbsp.	tart cream (recipe, page 162) or 1 cup [¼ liter] heavy cream, stiffly whipped	90 ml.
2 tbsp.	raspberry brandy	30 ml.
2 tbsp.	confectioners' sugar	30 ml.
12	candied violets	12

Barely stroking the flesh of the figs, use a small sharp knife to pull back the skin. Cut off the stem, stand each fig upright and cut a cross at the stem end—splitting the fruit through to the middle. Then, with a slight pressure of your thumb and index finger, open each fig like a blossom with four petals. Arrange the figs on a plate and keep them cold in the refrigerator.

Pick over the raspberries and drop them into a bowl. Melt the currant jelly, without letting it become hot, and gently stir it into the raspberries. Set the bowl of raspberries aside in the refrigerator.

Just before serving, combine the tart cream or whipped cream with the raspberry brandy and sugar. Mix with a wire whisk until thickened.

Spread equal portions of the cream mixture over the centers of four chilled dessert plates. Then arrange three figs on each plate—bursting open like flowers. Place a heaping tablespoon [15 ml.] of raspberries glazed with jelly in the center of each fig, and decorate it with a candied violet.

ROGER VERGÉ
ROGER VERGÉ'S CUISINE OF THE SOUTH OF FRANCE

Bananas

New Orleans Flaming Bananas

Flaming bananas is a specialty dessert in New Orleans, where colorful banana boats from Central and South America have unloaded their valuable cargoes for over a century.

	To serve 4	
2	medium-sized bananas, peeled and cut in half lengthwise and then crosswise	2
¼ cup	light brown sugar	50 ml.
2 tbsp.	butter	30 ml.
2 tbsp.	water	30 ml.
2 tsp.	fresh lemon juice	10 ml.
3 tbsp.	Cognac, warmed	45 ml.
	whipped cream or vanilla ice cream (recipe, page 167)	
	flaked coconut (optional)	

Stirring constantly, melt the brown sugar and butter in a chafing dish over direct heat or in an electric skillet set at moderate. Stir in the water and lemon juice and continue stirring until the sugar is melted.

Add the banana quarters and cook until they are hot and tender, turning them once. Add the warmed Cognac, ignite it, and shake the pan until the flame dies. Serve the bananas immediately, topped with whipped cream or ice cream and sprinkled with coconut, if you like.

JAN MC BRIDE CARLTON
THE OLD-FASHIONED COOKBOOK

Candied Sesame Bananas

Kluay Tord Lad Nam Chuam

This recipe gives good results with a variety of fresh fruits including apples and peaches. The cooking method is slightly complicated and requires the use of a candy thermometer to ensure that the temperature of the syrup remains near, but not over, 290° F. [150° C.].

To serve 4

4	firm bananas, peeled and cut into diagonal slices	4
¼ cup	fresh lime juice	50 ml.
	sesame seeds	
	oil for deep frying	
1½ cups	water	375 ml.
2 cups	sugar	½ liter
⅛ tsp.	cream of tartar	½ ml.

Place the banana slices in a mixing bowl and sprinkle them with the lime juice. Fill another mixing bowl with equal parts of ice cubes and water. Spread the sesame seeds in a shallow bowl. Butter a serving platter and set it aside.

In a wok, heat a layer of oil about 2 inches [5 cm.] deep until it just begins to vaporize. Quickly pat several of the banana slices at a time dry with a paper towel and deep fry them until they brown—about one minute. Drain the slices and set them aside.

Boil the water in a small saucepan, remove the pan from the heat, and add the sugar and cream of tartar, stirring until the sugar dissolves. Set this syrup over medium heat, cover and cook for two to three minutes. (This allows the water vapor to wash the partially dissolved sugar crystals down from the sides of the pan.) Uncover the syrup and place a candy thermometer in the pan. Stirring occasionally, let the temperature of the syrup increase to 290° F. [150° C.]; this will require at least three minutes over high heat.

Remove the syrup from the heat and place it in a pot partly filled with hot water. Set the pot over low heat to maintain the water temperature so that the syrup does not cool and thicken. In production-line fashion, drop a banana piece into the syrup, remove it with a long-handled fondue fork and roll it in the sesame seeds. Dunk it then directly into the ice water and place it on the buttered platter. Repeat until all the bananas are coated. Serve at once.

JENNIFER BRENNAN
THE ORIGINAL THAI COOKBOOK

Chestnut and Banana Roll

Režnjevi od Kestena i Banana

To serve 8 to 10

3 lb.	chestnuts	1½ kg.
2	bananas, peeled	2
1 cup	sugar	¼ liter
1 cup	water	¼ liter
10 tbsp.	butter, softened	150 ml.
2 cups	heavy cream, chilled	½ liter
1 to 2 tbsp.	confectioners' sugar	15 to 30 ml.

Chocolate glaze

5 oz.	semisweet or milk chocolate, broken into chunks	150 g.
3 tbsp.	strong, freshly made coffee	45 ml.
1 to 2 tbsp.	milk, scalded	15 to 30 ml.
1½ tbsp.	butter	22 ml.

Boil the chestnuts for 10 minutes in salted water. Cool them slightly. Peel them, removing both the outer shells and inner skins. Cover the chestnuts with water and simmer them until tender—about an hour. While they are hot, purée them through a fine sieve or food mill. Put the sugar and water into a large saucepan and heat gently, stirring until the sugar dissolves. Increase the heat and boil this syrup for a few minutes. Add the chestnut purée and blend it in well. Then remove the mixture from the heat and let it cool.

Cream the butter and add it to the cooled chestnut mixture. Stir it in thoroughly. Rinse a loaf pan in cold water and let it drain. Turn the chestnut mixture onto a work surface and roll it out into a fairly thick, neat rectangle three times the width of the pan. Place the bananas side by side on the short side of the rectangle nearest you, parallel with the edge, then roll up the rectangle like a jelly roll. Put the roll into the pan with the loose edge facing downward. Leave the pan embedded in a bowl of crushed ice or in a refrigerator for a few hours, or until the chestnut roll is firm.

To make the chocolate glaze, put all the glaze ingredients except the butter into a small saucepan and place it over low heat. Stir the mixture continuously until the chocolate melts to a smooth paste. Take the pan off the heat and stir in the butter. Let the glaze cool slightly.

Unmold the chestnut and banana roll and place it carefully on a long dish or tray. Pour the chocolate glaze over the roll to cover it completely, then refrigerate it.

While the glaze is hardening, whip the cream until it forms soft peaks, then add the confectioners' sugar and continue to whip the cream until it is stiff. Chill the whipped cream. Just before serving, heap the cream over the top and sides of the glazed roll, bring it to the table and slice it thin.

SPASENIJA-PATA MARKOVIĆ (EDITOR)
VELIKI NARODNI KUVAR

Drunken Bananas

Maia Ona

	To serve 6	
6	small, firm bananas, peeled	6
½ cup	rum	125 ml.
2 tsp.	fresh lemon juice	10 ml.
1	egg, beaten	1
⅔ cup	freshly grated coconut or chopped almonds, walnuts or macadamia nuts	150 ml.
	oil for frying	

Soak the bananas in the rum and lemon juice for about one hour, turning them frequently. Then dip them in the egg and roll them in the coconut or chopped nuts. Heat ½ inch [1 cm.] of oil in a frying pan and fry the bananas slowly until they are brown on all sides and tender—about five minutes. Drain them on paper towels and serve hot.

ROANA AND GENE SCHINDLER
HAWAIIAN COOKBOOK

Bananitos

	To make 16	
2	bananas, peeled	2
1	egg	1
½ cup	milk	125 ml.
½ cup	flour	125 ml.
1 tsp.	baking powder	5 ml.
	honey	
	fresh mint leaves	
	fresh pineapple chunks	

Mash the bananas in a bowl. Beat in the egg. Add the milk. Combine the flour with the baking powder, add to the batter and mix thoroughly.

Pour the batter in small amounts onto a greased griddle and brown the fritters on both sides. To serve them, drizzle with the honey and garnish with the mint leaves and pineapple chunks.

CAROL COLLVER THURBER
THE CALYPSO COOKBOOK

Baked Bananas

Salatka z Bananów Pieczonych

	To serve 4	
5	bananas, peeled	5
⅓ cup	rum	75 ml.
½ cup	heavy cream, mixed with 2 tbsp. [30 ml.] vanilla sugar	125 ml.
1 tbsp.	chopped walnuts	15 ml.

Place the bananas in a flat buttered baking dish, and bake them in a preheated 350° F. [180° C.] oven for 15 minutes, or until soft. Take them out and let them cool. Then slice them and arrange them on a plate. Sprinkle with the rum, pour the cream over them and, finally, scatter the walnuts on top.

ZOFIA ZAWISTOWSKA
SURÓWKI I SAŁTKI

Banana Soufflé-Pudding

Flamèri aux Bananes

	To serve 6	
4	bananas, peeled, sliced, soaked in 3 to 4 tsp. [45 to 60 ml.] kirsch and puréed through a sieve	4
1 cup	milk	¼ liter
7 tbsp.	butter	105 ml.
¾ cup	flour	175 ml.
6	eggs, the yolks separated from the whites, and the whites stiffly beaten, plus 2 egg yolks	6
	confectioners' sugar	

In a saucepan, bring to a boil the milk and the butter. Gradually add the flour. Working the mixture with a wooden spatula, cook over medium heat until the paste pulls away from the spatula.

Remove the saucepan from the heat and very gently incorporate the egg yolks, one at a time. Stir in the banana purée, then fold in the stiffly beaten egg whites. Pour the mixture into a buttered 2-quart [2-liter] soufflé dish. Bake in a preheated 325° F. [160° C.] oven for 25 minutes. Remove the dish from the oven and sprinkle the top of the soufflé with confectioners' sugar. Serve at once.

PAUL BOUILLARD
LA CUISINE AU COIN DU FEU

Baked Banana Halves

To serve 6

6	bananas, peeled and cut in half lengthwise	6
½ cup	firmly packed brown sugar	125 ml.
3 tbsp.	fresh orange juice	45 ml.
2 tbsp.	rum	30 ml.
2 tbsp.	butter, melted	30 ml.
¼ cup	raisins, soaked in warm water for 15 minutes and drained	50 ml.
	heavy cream	

Combine two thirds of the sugar, the orange juice, rum and melted butter.

Place the banana halves in a shallow, buttered baking dish; sprinkle them with the raisins and pour the sauce over them. Sprinkle over the remaining sugar and bake in a preheated 375° F. [190° C.] oven until the bananas are soft and the sauce is syrupy—about 20 minutes. As they bake, baste the bananas occasionally with the sauce. Serve the bananas piping hot, accompanied by heavy cream.

PAMELA DIXON
NEW WAYS WITH FRESH FRUIT AND VEGETABLES

Banana Brown Betty

For a more elaborate dessert, the author suggests making a meringue mixture from two egg whites stiffly beaten with 2 tablespoons [30 ml.] of sugar, spreading it on top of the cooked pudding and browning it quickly in a 400° F. [200° C.] oven.

To serve 6

6	bananas, peeled and thinly sliced	6
½ cup	sugar	125 ml.
6 tbsp.	butter, cut into small pieces	90 ml.
3 tbsp.	orange marmalade or guava jelly	45 ml.
½ cup	dry bread crumbs	125 ml.
½ tsp.	ground cinnamon	2 ml.
	heavy cream	

Arrange half of the sliced bananas in a layer in a buttered baking dish. Add half of the sugar, half of the butter pieces and all of the marmalade or guava jelly. Cover with a layer of bread crumbs and sprinkle with the cinnamon. Add the remaining bananas, sugar, butter and crumbs. Bake in a preheated 325° F. [160° C.] oven for 45 minutes, or until the top is crisp and brown. Serve hot, accompanied by cream.

AGNES B. ALEXANDER
HOW TO USE HAWAIIAN FRUIT

Pineapples, Papayas, Passion Fruits and Pomegranates

Pineapple Gratin with Rum

Gratin d'Ananas au Rhum

To serve 6 to 8

½	pineapple, peeled, quartered, cored and coarsely chopped	½
1 cup	granulated sugar	¼ liter
2	large eggs, plus 4 egg yolks	2
1 cup less 3 tbsp.	flour	¼ liter less 45 ml.
2 cups	milk, scalded	½ liter
1 tsp.	vanilla extract	5 ml.
1 cup	heavy cream	¼ liter
½ cup	dark rum	125 ml.
½ cup	almonds, blanched, peeled, cut into slivers and toasted	125 ml.
3 cups	sifted confectioners' sugar	¾ liter

Make a thick *crème pâtissière:* Place the granulated sugar and egg yolks in a heavy saucepan and beat until the mixture is pale yellow and forms a ribbon—about 10 minutes. Beat in the two whole eggs, then the flour. Place over very low heat and, stirring constantly, cook until the mixture is lukewarm. Meanwhile bring the milk to a boil. Pour the milk into the egg mixture, stirring vigorously with a wire whisk. Continue to cook, stirring, for about three minutes, or until the custard mixture is thick and smooth. Remove from the heat and stir in the vanilla extract, then add the cream and the rum. Strain the custard into a bowl.

Butter a shallow baking dish and pour in half the custard mixture. Cover with the pineapple chunks and top with the rest of the custard. Sprinkle with the almonds and the confectioners' sugar, and run under a preheated broiler for a minute or two to brown the top.

ELISABETH LAMBERT ORTIZ
THE COMPLETE BOOK OF CARIBBEAN COOKING

Pineapple and Frangipane Fritters

Beignets d'Ananas à la Frangipane

The author recommends keeping the batter at the consistency of thick cream. This will ensure the crispness and delicacy of the fritters, but it will also result in a greater loss of batter during the frying process.

The frangipane and the pineapple should be prepared a few hours ahead of the batter, which should be prepared an hour or so before the meal. The batter must relax to lose its elasticity, or it will refuse to coat the pineapple and frangipane properly.

	To serve 4	
½	pineapple	½
	oil for deep frying	
	superfine sugar	

Frangipane

1 cup	milk	¼ liter
1	vanilla bean	1
3 tbsp.	sugar	45 ml.
⅓ cup	flour	75 ml.
1	egg, plus 1 egg yolk	1
2	amaretto cookies, crumbled	2
2 tbsp.	butter	30 ml.
1 tbsp.	pistachios, blanched, peeled and chopped	15 ml.

Batter

¾ cup	flour	175 ml.
	salt	
1 tsp.	sugar	5 ml.
1	egg, the yolk separated from the white	1
⅓ cup	tepid beer	75 ml.
2 tbsp.	butter, melted	30 ml.
4 to 6 tbsp.	water	60 to 90 ml.

To make the frangipane, bring the milk to a boil with the vanilla bean and sugar; let the milk cool slightly. Sift the flour into a pan, add the whole egg and the egg yolk and stir with a wooden spoon, keeping the motion to the center so that the flour is gradually absorbed into the egg. Remove the vanilla bean from the milk and slowly add the milk to the flour-and-egg mixture, stirring all the time. Cook over medium heat, continuing to stir vigorously, until the mixture becomes very thick. Remove from the heat, add the crumbled cookies, butter and the chopped pistachios, mix well and let the mixture cool.

Cut the pineapple into slices ⅓ to ½ inch [8 mm. to 1 cm.] thick; cut each slice into quarters, slice off the rind and woody core. Butter a plate, spread half the frangipane over the surface, arrange the pineapple pieces on top in regular rows, and cover with the remaining frangipane so that each pineapple piece is coated. Chill until needed.

To make the batter, put the flour, a pinch of salt and the sugar in a bowl, add the egg yolk and stir in the beer, adding it at two or three intervals. Stir only until a regular consistency is achieved. Do not beat the batter. Stir in the melted butter and enough water to bring it to the consistency of heavy cream. Cover the batter with a plate and leave it at room temperature until needed. Just before using, beat the egg white until stiff and fold it gently into the batter.

Heat the oil; when it sizzles at contact with a drop of batter, it is ready. Using a spatula, carefully cut through the frangipane and lift out each piece of coated pineapple. Drop the pineapple pieces one at a time into the batter, lift them out and drop them into the hot oil. Do not fry too many at a time. Carefully turn over the pineapple pieces with the tines of a fork, and when they are golden and crisp on both sides, scoop them out with a large skimming spoon. Drain them on paper towels and transfer them to the folded napkin on which they will be served. When all are fried, sprinkle the surface with superfine sugar and serve immediately.

RICHARD OLNEY
THE FRENCH MENU COOKBOOK

Pineapple Ambrosia

This 19th Century dessert is a classic in American cooking.

	To serve 6	
1	large pineapple, peeled, quartered, cored and coarsely grated	1
1 cup	sugar	¼ liter
4	eggs, 2 left whole, the yolks of 2 separated from the whites	4
	salt	
2 cups	milk, scalded and partially cooled	½ liter
1 tsp.	vanilla extract	5 ml.

In a soufflé dish, combine the pineapple with ½ cup [125 ml.] of the sugar and chill the mixture for two hours.

In the top of a double boiler, beat together the whole eggs, the two extra yolks, ¼ cup [50 ml.] of the remaining sugar and a little salt. Set over simmering water and gradually stir in the milk. Stirring constantly, cook the custard until it thickens and coats the spoon—about three minutes. Allow the custard to cool, then stir in the vanilla extract.

Pour the custard over the chilled pineapple. Beat the two remaining egg whites until they are frothy; gradually add the remaining ¼ cup of sugar and beat the whites until they are stiff. Spread this meringue over the dessert and bake it in a preheated 425° F. [220° C.] oven for five minutes, or until the top is golden. Chill the dessert well before serving.

ROBERT ACKART
FRUITS IN COOKING

Pineapple Ice

Granité à l'Ananas

The technique of preparing a pineapple to make pineapple ice is demonstrated on pages 28-29.

Once it has been put into its shell, the pineapple ice may be returned to the freezer for another hour or so and allowed to become slightly firmer—but if it is served frozen solid, it loses all its quality.

	To serve 4	
1	large pineapple	1
¾ cup	sugar	175 ml.
1½ cups	fresh orange juice	375 ml.

Cut off and discard the base of the pineapple. Remove the top of the pineapple, cutting in at an angle all around so as to form a lid, then pare the flesh from the inside of the lid. Put the pineapple flesh into a bowl and reserve the lid.

To remove all the flesh from the inside of the pineapple, use a long, sharp, pointed knife to cut around the edge of the fruit to about halfway down, keeping close to the skin, but being careful not to pierce it. Cut a similar circle around the hard central core and make spokelike incisions between the two circles. Use a tablespoon to remove the wedges of pineapple flesh, then place them in the bowl with the flesh from the lid. Repeat this process with the lower half of the pineapple. Scrape around the core until all the flesh has been removed and the shell is empty except for the upright core. Cut into the base of the core with the point of the knife and break it off as cleanly as possible. Reserve the pineapple shell.

Mash the pineapple flesh with a pestle. Then, to extract as much juice as possible, push it through a sieve set over a bowl. Mix about 1 cup [¼ liter] of the pineapple juice with the sugar and boil to form a syrup. When it is cool, mix it with the rest of the pineapple juice and the orange juice. Ladle the mixture into shallow metal trays and place them in the freezer with the pineapple shell and lid. After about an hour, remove the trays from the freezer and stir the mixture, scraping all the frozen parts from the sides and bottoms of the trays and mashing these pieces into the liquid. Return the trays to the freezer and repeat this process a couple of times during the next three hours, or until the ice has a slightly firm but still mushy consistency when stirred. Spoon the ice into the chilled pineapple shell and serve.

RICHARD OLNEY
THE FRENCH MENU COOKBOOK

Passion-Fruit Salad

Passievrucht Salade

	To serve 4	
4	passion fruits, halved	4
½ cup	strawberries, hulled and halved	125 ml.
½ cup	raspberries	125 ml.
Cream sauce		
½ cup	heavy cream	125 ml.
1 tbsp.	fresh lemon juice	15 ml.
1 tbsp.	confectioners' sugar	15 ml.
1 tbsp.	sweet white wine	15 ml.

Divide the strawberries evenly among four small dishes and cover them with the raspberries. Spoon out the passion-fruit flesh and distribute it over the raspberries. Whip together all the sauce ingredients and pour the sauce over the fruits. Serve chilled.

E. NAKKEN-RÖVEKAMP
EXOTISCHE GROENTEN EN VRUCHTEN

Passion-Fruit Delicious

	To serve 4	
2 tbsp.	fresh passion-fruit juice	30 ml.
2 tbsp.	butter, softened	30 ml.
¾ cup	sugar	175 ml.
2	eggs, the yolks separated from the whites, and the whites stiffly beaten	2
½ cup	flour, sifted with 1 tsp. [5 ml.] baking powder	125 ml.
1¼ cups	milk	300 ml.
	pouring custard *(recipe, page 163)*	

Cream the butter and sugar; add the egg yolks, flour, milk and passion-fruit juice. Fold in the egg whites. Pour the mixture into a buttered 9-inch [23-cm.] piepan, stand in a pan of hot water, and bake in a preheated 425° F. [220° C.] oven for 10 minutes. Reduce the heat to 350° F. [180° C.] and bake until set. Serve cold with pouring custard.

RARE FRUIT COUNCIL
TROPICAL FRUIT RECIPES

Papaya Compote with Pineapple and Strawberries

To serve 6

3	papayas, halved and seeded	3
½	pineapple, peeled, quartered, cored and diced	½
1 pint	strawberries, hulled and halved	½ liter
	sugar	

In a mixing bowl, combine the pineapple chunks and the strawberries; add sugar to taste and stir the fruits gently. Arrange the papaya halves on a serving platter. Fill the cavities of the papayas with the pineapple mixture, and chill the compote for one hour.

ROBERT ACKART
FRUITS IN COOKING

Baked Papaya Dessert

To make the coconut milk called for in this recipe, pour about 1½ cups [375 ml.] of boiling water over 1½ cups of freshly grated coconut. After about five minutes, strain through a cloth, pressing to extract all of the milk.

To serve 4

2	small, ripe papayas (about ¾ lb. [350 g.]), peeled, halved lengthwise and seeds removed	2
½ cup	sugar	125 ml.
¼ cup	water	50 ml.
1½ cups	coconut milk	375 ml.

Arrange the papaya halves cut side upward in a shallow baking-serving dish large enough to hold them in one layer. Sprinkle the fruit with the sugar and pour the water down the sides of the dish. Bake uncovered in the middle of a preheated 375° F. [190° C.] oven for one and one half hours, or until the papayas are tender but still intact, basting them every 20 minutes with the syrup that will accumulate in the dish. Increase the heat to 400° F. [200° C.] and bake for five minutes more until the syrup thickens and browns to a caramel color. Turn off the heat, pour the coconut milk into the cavities of the papayas, and let them rest in the oven for five minutes until the milk is warm. Serve at once, or refrigerate and serve chilled.

FOODS OF THE WORLD
PACIFIC AND SOUTHEAST ASIAN COOKING

Papaya-Sauce Cake

To make one 8½-by-4½-by-2½-inch [21-by-11-by-6-cm.] loaf

1 cup	diced papaya	¼ liter
3 tbsp.	water	45 ml.
4 tbsp.	butter, softened	60 ml.
1 cup	sugar	¼ liter
1	egg, beaten	1
1¼ cups	flour	300 ml.
1¼ tsp.	baking powder	6 ml.
½ tsp.	salt	2 ml.
½ tsp.	ground cinnamon	2 ml.
½ tsp.	grated nutmeg	2 ml.
¼ tsp.	ground ginger	1 ml.
½ tbsp.	fresh lemon juice	7 ml.
½ cup	seedless raisins (optional)	125 ml.

In a nonreactive pan, stew the papaya in the water until a smooth sauce is obtained; press the mixture through a coarse sieve if necessary. Cream the butter. Add the sugar and mix well. Add the egg. Sift the flour, baking powder, salt and spices. Add the cooled papaya sauce and the dry ingredients alternately to the egg mixture. Fold in the lemon juice and the raisins, if you are using them. Pour the batter into a buttered loaf pan and bake in a preheated 350° F. [180° C.] oven for 50 to 60 minutes.

FLORIDA FRUIT AND VEGETABLE RECIPES

Papaya Milk Sherbet

To make 1 quart [1 liter]

1½ cups	puréed raw papaya pulp	375 ml.
3 tbsp.	fresh lemon or lime juice	45 ml.
½ cup	fresh orange juice	125 ml.
1 cup	sugar	¼ liter
1½ cups	milk	375 ml.

Combine the papaya with the fruit juices. Dissolve the sugar in the milk, add the fruit mixture gradually to the milk and freeze in an ice-cream maker.

RARE FRUIT COUNCIL
TROPICAL FRUIT RECIPES

Pomegranate Ice

To serve 6

2 cups	pomegranate juice	½ liter
¼ cup	fresh lemon or tart orange juice	50 ml.
1 tbsp.	unflavored powdered gelatin	15 ml.
¼ cup	cold water, plus ¾ cup [175 ml.] boiling water	50 ml.
¾ cup	sugar	175 ml.

In a heatproof bowl, soften the gelatin in the cold water for five minutes. Add the boiling water and stir to dissolve the gelatin. Stir in the sugar; add the fruit juices. Cool the mixture. Freeze it in an ice tray.

SANDAL ENGLISH
FRUITS OF THE DESERT

Rhubarb and Persimmons

Rhubarb Delight

Monukka raisins are small black raisins, and are available at health-food stores.

To serve 6 to 8

1 lb.	rhubarb, the leaves and root ends removed, the stalks cut into ½-inch [1-cm.] pieces	½ kg.
¾ cup	*monukka* raisins	175 ml.
¾ cup	chopped dates	175 ml.
2	oranges, halved, seeded and ground with peel, juice reserved	2
2 quarts	boiling spring water	2 liters
1 tsp.	sea salt	5 ml.
¼ tsp.	cayenne pepper	1 ml.

Combine the rhubarb, raisins, dates, ground oranges and their juice in a nonreactive saucepan. Pour the boiling water over all. Add the salt and cayenne.

Bring the mixture to a boil and simmer four to five minutes. Pour into a porcelain or glass bowl and let stand in a cool place overnight.

JEAN HEWITT
THE NEW YORK TIMES NATURAL FOODS COOKBOOK

Rhubarb Fool

To serve 8 to 10

1 lb.	rhubarb, leaves and root ends removed, cut into 2-inch [5-cm.] chunks	½ kg.
1 cup	sugar	¼ liter
2 tbsp.	chopped candied ginger	30 ml.
2 cups	heavy cream, whipped	½ liter

In a heavy, nonreactive pan with a tight-fitting lid, combine the rhubarb, sugar and ginger. Cook over gentle heat until the rhubarb is tender—about 10 minutes. Drain the rhubarb and purée it in a blender or food mill. Cool the purée completely. Combine the whipped cream with the rhubarb purée and spoon it into parfait glasses or a glass bowl. Chill before serving.

THE GREAT COOKS COOKBOOK

Small Rhubarb Creams

To serve 4 to 6

1½ lb.	rhubarb, leaves and root ends removed, stalks cut into ½-inch [1-cm.] pieces	¾ kg.
⅔ cup	water	150 ml.
1 cup	sugar	¼ liter
3 tbsp.	unflavored powdered gelatin, softened in ¾ cup [175 ml.] of water for 5 minutes	45 ml.
⅔ cup	heavy cream	150 ml.
	red food coloring (optional)	
	pouring custard (recipe, page 163)	

Put the rhubarb pieces into a nonreactive saucepan with the water and sugar. Simmer gently for a few minutes until the juice flows freely, then stir in the softened gelatin. Continue to simmer the mixture gently until the rhubarb is tender and the gelatin dissolved, after which stir in the cream and, if you wish, a few drops of food coloring. Pour the preparation into small fancy molds that have been previously rinsed with cold water.

Chill the creams. When they are firmly set, unmold the creams into a glass dish. Pour between—not upon—them some good thick custard.

M. K. SAMUELSON
SUSSEX RECIPE BOOK

Rum Persimmons

To serve 4

4	persimmons, stems removed, halved lengthwise	4
1/3 cup	medium rum or dark Jamaica rum	75 ml.
1/3 cup	firmly packed light brown sugar	75 ml.
4 tbsp.	sour cream	60 ml.

Arrange the persimmons, cut side up, on shallow dessert plates. Top each half with rum, sugar and 1 tablespoon [15 ml.] of sour cream. Spoon out of the shell to eat.

VICTOR J. BERGERON
TRADER VIC'S RUM COOKERY AND DRINKERY

Persimmon Pudding

The persimmons must be almost translucent, soft and ripe.

To serve 4 to 6

3	large persimmons, peeled and sliced	3
2	bananas, peeled and sliced	2
1/2 cup	firmly packed brown sugar	125 ml.
3 tbsp.	whole-wheat flour	45 ml.
4 tbsp.	butter, softened	60 ml.
2 tbsp.	fresh lime juice	30 ml.
1/4 cup	honey	50 ml.
	heavy cream	

Mix the brown sugar, flour and butter to form crumbs. In a buttered 4-cup [1-liter] baking dish arrange alternate layers of the fruits and the sugar mixture. Sprinkle the lime juice and dribble the honey over the top. Bake in a preheated 350° F. [180° C.] oven for 30 minutes until the top is brown and bubbly. Serve with heavy cream.

STELLA STANDARD
THE ART OF FRUIT COOKERY

Persimmon Ice

In making persimmon ice, special care should be used to select thoroughly ripe fruit. The ice may be made in either an ice-cream maker or a freezer.

To serve 6 to 8

3 cups	puréed raw persimmon flesh	3/4 liter
2 tbsp.	unflavored powdered gelatin	30 ml.
2 1/2 cups	water, 2 cups [1/2 liter] boiling	625 ml.
1 3/4 cups	sugar	425 ml.
3 cups	fresh grapefruit juice	3/4 liter

In a heatproof bowl, soften the gelatin in the 1/2 cup [125 ml.] of cold water for five minutes. Add the boiling water and sugar, stir well and let cool. Then add the grapefruit juice and freeze the mixture in an ice-cream maker until it is like mush. Fold in the persimmon purée and continue freezing until the ice is firm. Pack and allow the ice to stand for several hours before serving.

BERTHA MUNKS
FLORIDA'S FAVORITE FOODS

Persimmon Gelatin

To prepare the persimmon purée called for in this recipe, peel one soft, ripe persimmon and cut it into small chunks. Rub the chunks through a nylon or stainless-steel sieve set over a bowl.

To serve 4

3/4 cup	puréed raw persimmon pulp	175 ml.
1 tbsp.	unflavored powdered gelatin, softened in 1/4 cup [50 ml.] cold water for 5 minutes	15 ml.
1/3 cup	hot water	75 ml.
1 tsp.	fresh lemon juice	5 ml.
2	egg whites, stiffly beaten	2

Place the softened gelatin in a large bowl. Add the hot water and stir until the gelatin dissolves. Mix in the persimmon purée and lemon juice. Refrigerate the mixture until it is on the verge of setting, then fold in the egg whites. Pour the jelly into sherbet glasses and refrigerate it until firm and thoroughly chilled—about one more hour.

RARE FRUIT COUNCIL
TROPICAL FRUIT RECIPES

Dried Fruits

Dried Apricot and Fresh Pear Compote

Grated almonds can be added at the last minute, or ¼ cup [50 ml.] of pine nuts. Serve with or without cream.

To serve 4

3 cups	dried apricots, covered with about 3 cups [¾ liter] boiling water (or half water and half orange juice) and soaked overnight	¾ liter
2 or 3	hard pears (4 or 5 if small), peeled, quartered or cut into eighths and cored	2 or 3
	sugar	

One hour before serving, drain off the liquid from the apricots and poach the pears in the liquid until they are soft but not mushy—approximately 20 minutes. Add more water if there is not enough liquid. Remove the pears from the heat, add the apricots and allow the mixture to cool, but do not chill it. Add sugar to taste.

LORD WESTBURY AND DONALD DOWNES
WITH GUSTO AND RELISH

Apricot-Ginger Ice Cream

To make 3 pints [1 ½ liters]

1 cup	dried California apricots	¼ liter
¾ cup	water	175 ml.
¼ cup	syrup-packed preserved ginger, drained and chopped	50 ml.
1 tbsp.	fresh lemon juice	15 ml.
½ tsp.	almond extract	2 ml.
2 cups	heavy cream, preferably not ultrapasteurized	½ liter
2 cups	milk	½ liter
¾ cup	sugar	175 ml.
⅛ tsp.	salt	1 ml.

Combine the apricots and water in a small, heavy, nonreactive saucepan and cook over low heat, covered, until the fruit is very soft—about 25 minutes. Pour the fruit into the container of a processor or blender; add the ginger and whirl to a very fine purée. Add the lemon juice and mix. Scrape the purée into a bowl; cool it somewhat. Add the almond extract; cover and refrigerate.

Heat together in another heavy saucepan the cream, milk, sugar and salt, stirring occasionally until the sugar dissolves and the mixture comes just to a simmer. Cool, cover, then refrigerate it.

When both the apricot purée and the cream mixture are thoroughly chilled, gradually stir the cream mixture into the purée. Turn into the container of an ice-cream machine and freeze according to the manufacturer's directions.

Pack the ice cream into a freezer container and let it ripen—or mellow—for a day or two in the freezer. Before serving the ice cream, let it soften for about an hour in the refrigerator.

ELIZABETH SCHNEIDER COLCHIE
READY WHEN YOU ARE

Cold Apricot Soufflé

To serve 6 to 8

16	dried apricots, soaked in warm water overnight	16
½ cup	apricot liqueur	125 ml.
	vegetable oil	
1 cup	milk	¼ liter
4	eggs, the yolks separated from the whites, plus 3 additional egg whites	4
½ cup	sugar	125 ml.
1 tbsp.	unflavored powdered gelatin, softened in ¼ cup [50 ml.] cold water for 5 minutes	15 ml.
¼ cup	fresh lemon juice	50 ml.
1 cup	heavy cream	¼ liter
½ cup	crushed almond-macaroon crumbs	125 ml.

Apricot cream

½ cup	tart apricot jam, sieved, or puréed poached apricots	125 ml.
1 cup	heavy cream, chilled	¼ liter

Drain the apricots, place them in a small bowl and pour on the apricot liqueur.

Fold a long strip of aluminum foil lengthwise and rub one side with the vegetable oil. Tie it neatly around a 4-cup [1-liter] glass soufflé dish, oiled side of the foil facing inward, to make a collar standing 3 inches [8 cm.] above the top.

Heat the milk in the top of a double boiler. In a bowl, beat the egg yolks with the sugar until they are light and lemon-colored—about 10 minutes—and pour the hot milk over them. Beat. Return the mixture to the top of the double boiler and add the softened gelatin.

Stirring or whisking constantly, cook the mixture over hot water until it is thick and creamy; be careful that the mixture does not boil. Remove the pan from the heat and let the mixture cool.

Rub the apricots in the liqueur through a fine sieve and stir the purée into the cooled custard. Stir in the lemon juice. Refrigerate the mixture until it begins to thicken. Whip the cream until it is thick but not stiff and fold it into the apricot-custard mixture. Refrigerate the mixture again until it is just beginning to set.

Beat the egg whites until they are stiff but not dry and fold them gently into the mixture with a large metal spoon. Spoon the soufflé into the prepared soufflé dish and chill it for at least three hours.

Remove the collar before serving and pat the crushed macaroon crumbs over the sides.

To make apricot cream: Add the strained jam or the purée to the chilled cream. Beat the mixture until it is the right consistency for piping through a pastry bag fitted with a No. 7 star tube. Decorate the top of the soufflé with rosettes of apricot cream.

THE GREAT COOKS COOKBOOK

Dried-Fruit Souffléed Pudding

The author suggests that dried pears or prunes may be substituted for the apricots. In such cases, replace the almond extract and kirsch; use vanilla extract and pear brandy for the pears, and use lemon extract and rum or prune brandy for the prunes.

To serve 8

¾ lb.	dried apricots, soaked in water overnight	350 g.
⅔ cup	heavy cream	150 ml.
½ cup	firmly packed brown sugar	125 ml.
5 tbsp.	cornstarch	75 ml.
4	eggs, the yolks separated from the whites, and the whites stiffly beaten	4
1 tsp.	almond extract	5 ml.
	pouring custard *(recipe, page 163)*	
2 tbsp.	kirsch	30 ml.

Drain the fruit, purée it in a blender and sieve it, if you wish a very fine-textured pudding. Mix the fruit purée, cream,

brown sugar and cornstarch in a heavy, nonreactive saucepan. Stirring, cook over medium heat until the mixture thickens enough to coat a spoon. Add the egg yolks, one by one, whisking well after each addition. Add the almond extract. Then fold in the beaten egg whites. Turn the mixture into a buttered 2-quart [2-liter] soufflé set in a pan of hot water. Bake in a preheated 325° F. [160° C.] oven for 40 to 45 minutes, or until a knife inserted in the center of the pudding comes out clean.

Unmold the pudding onto a serving platter. Flavor the custard with liqueur and pour it over the pudding. Serve lukewarm or chilled.

MADELEINE KAMMAN
THE MAKING OF A COOK

Fig Pudding

The technique for making fig pudding is demonstrated on pages 48-49. The author recommends serving the pudding with pouring custard (recipe, page 163).

To serve 6

½ lb.	dried figs, chopped	¼ kg.
1 cup	flour	¼ liter
¼ lb.	suet, finely chopped (about 1 cup [¼ liter])	125 g.
2 cups	fresh bread crumbs	½ liter
1 tsp.	baking powder	5 ml.
½ cup	superfine sugar	125 ml.
	salt	
	grated nutmeg	
2	eggs	2
about ¾ cup	milk	about 175 ml.

In a large bowl, mix together the figs, flour, suet, bread crumbs, baking powder, sugar and a pinch each of salt and nutmeg. Beat the eggs with ½ cup [125 ml.] of the milk and stir into the fig mixture. Add more milk as necessary until the mixture is soft enough to fall from a spoon.

Butter a 4- or 5-cup [1- or 1¼-liter] pudding basin; cut a circle of parchment paper the size of the bottom of the basin and fit it into the basin. Spoon the pudding mixture into the basin. Sprinkle dampened muslin or cheesecloth with flour and place it over the basin, floured side down. Pleat the cloth to allow the pudding to rise during cooking and tie the cloth with string beneath the ridge of the basin.

Place a trivet in a large pan and lower the pudding onto it. Pour boiling water into the pan until the basin is two thirds submerged. Cover the pan and simmer for two and one half hours. Unmold the pudding onto a plate and serve hot.

MRS. BEETON
MRS. BEETON'S ALL ABOUT COOKERY

Figs Villamiel
Higos Villamiel

To serve 8

1 lb.	dried figs	½ kg.
½ lb.	walnuts (2 cups [½ liter])	¼ kg.
2 cups	red wine	½ liter
2 cups	port	½ liter
½ cup	honey	125 ml.
¾ cup	fresh orange juice	175 ml.
1 cup	heavy cream, whipped	¼ liter

Cut a lengthwise opening in each fig and stuff it with as many walnuts as it will hold. Place the stuffed figs in a nonreactive saucepan with the wine, port, honey and orange juice. Bring the mixture to a boil, reduce the heat to low and cook the figs uncovered for about an hour. When the figs are tender, transfer them to a serving plate and decorate them with the whipped cream.

LUÍS BETTÓNICA (EDITOR)
COCINA REGIONAL ESPAÑOLA

Pear Dumpling

Wrapping the plate in muslin helps to retain the shape of the dumpling and keep the fruits on the plate, and makes it easier to lift the plate out when the dumpling is cooked.

To serve 6

1 lb.	dried pears, soaked in water overnight and drained	½ kg.
1 lb.	prunes, soaked in water overnight and drained	½ kg.
½ lb.	stale white bread	¼ kg.
1 cup	self-rising flour	¼ liter
¼ tsp.	salt	1 ml.
¼ tsp.	grated nutmeg	1 ml.
1½ tsp.	ground cinnamon	7 ml.
⅔ cup	finely chopped suet	150 ml.
1	egg, beaten	1
1⅓ cups	brown sugar	325 ml.
2 tbsp.	red wine	30 ml.

Cut off the crusts from the bread and grate them. Soak the rest of the bread in water until quite soft, then squeeze dry. Sift the flour, salt, nutmeg and half of the cinnamon into a bowl. Add the soaked bread, the grated crust crumbs, suet

and egg. Mix thoroughly and then beat the mixture until it is smooth. Roll it into a dumpling and place it on a round heatproof plate.

Arrange the fruits around the dumpling, then sprinkle the fruits and dumpling with the brown sugar, the red wine and the rest of the cinnamon. Wrap the plate loosely in muslin, gathering the corners of the cloth above the dumpling and knotting them to form a handle. Place the wrapped plate in a large pan. Add cold water to cover the dumpling, then cover the pan with a tightly fitting lid and bring the water to a boil. Cook for two hours, boiling constantly. Lift the plate with its contents from the pan, remove the muslin and serve the dumpling and fruits on the plate.

MADELEINE MASSON
THE INTERNATIONAL WINE AND FOOD SOCIETY'S
GUIDE TO JEWISH COOKERY

Prunes in White Wine
Pruneaux au Vouvray

Instead of being cooked, the prunes in this recipe can be loosely packed in a jar, covered with wine and left to soak for a week or more. Be sure to keep them constantly submerged. Red wine can be substituted for the white wine.

To serve 6

1 lb.	prunes	½ kg.
3 cups	Vouvray or other dry white wine	¾ liter
½ cup	sugar	125 ml.
Chantilly cream		
1 cup	heavy cream	¼ liter
2 tsp.	sugar	10 ml.
1 tsp.	vanilla extract	5 ml.

Three or four days ahead, wash the prunes and put them in a large bowl. Pour the wine over them, cover and let them soak overnight at room temperature.

The next day, transfer the prunes and wine to a large, nonreactive pot, add the sugar and bring to a boil, stirring occasionally. Simmer over low heat until the prunes are just tender—20 to 25 minutes. Let the prunes cool. Refrigerate the prunes for two or three days; they will absorb some of the remaining wine.

Just before serving, make the Chantilly cream: In a chilled bowl, beat the cream until it starts to thicken. Add the sugar and vanilla, and continue beating until the cream is stiff enough to cling to the whisk. Put the prunes with their liquid in small dessert dishes. Serve cold and pass the Chantilly cream separately.

ANNE WILLAN
FRENCH REGIONAL COOKING

Christmas Eve Compote
of Prunes and Figs

Wigilijny Kompotz z Suszonych Śliwek i Fig

If you prefer the prunes to be more tender, lower the heat and simmer them for 10 minutes after bringing them to a boil.

	To serve 6	
½ lb.	prunes, pitted and soaked in 2 cups [½ liter] warm water overnight, soaking water reserved	¼ kg.
½ lb.	dried figs, soaked in 2 cups [½ liter] warm water overnight, soaking water reserved	¼ kg.
2 tbsp.	sugar	30 ml.
2-inch	cinnamon stick	5-cm.
1	small lemon, one strip of peel thinly pared, the juice strained	1

Pour the prunes and their soaking water into a nonreactive pan, add 1 tablespoon [15 ml.] of sugar and the cinnamon stick and bring to a boil. Remove from the heat.

Pour the figs and their soaking water into another nonreactive pan. Add the remaining sugar, the lemon juice and peel, and cook for five minutes. Remove the cinnamon stick and lemon peel from the fruits and combine the separately cooked fruits. Serve the compote at room temperature.

MARIA LEMNIS AND HENRYK VITRY
OLD POLISH TRADITIONS IN THE KITCHEN AND AT THE TABLE

Stuffed Prunes

Pruneaux Farcis

To make the almond paste, mix ½ cup [125 ml.] of blanched, peeled and ground almonds with ¼ cup [50 ml.] of sugar. Pour in a beaten egg yolk, a little at a time, stirring with a fork or knife until the mixture becomes moist enough to mix with your hand. Gather the mixture into a ball and knead it quickly with your hand until the paste has a smooth consistency.

	To serve 6	
1 lb.	prunes	½ kg.
½ cup	raisins	125 ml.
	Armagnac	
½ cup	almond paste	125 ml.
1 tbsp.	grated orange peel	15 ml.
1 tbsp.	sugar	15 ml.
	hazelnuts, toasted	

Immerse the prunes and raisins in water to which a generous dash of Armagnac has been added, and let them soak for 12 hours, or until plump. Combine the orange peel and sugar, and let the mixture stand for at least 12 hours.

With a slotted spoon, transfer the soaked raisins to another bowl and set them aside. Pour the prunes and their soaking liquid into a nonreactive pan. Poach the prunes for 15 minutes, or until soft, then let them cool in the liquid. Make a stuffing from the raisins, the almond paste and the orange-peel mixture. Add a dash of Armagnac.

When they have cooled, remove the prunes from the liquid and pat them dry. Make an incision on one side of each prune, remove the pit and fill the cavity with some of the stuffing. Decorate each prune with a toasted hazelnut.

COEN HEMKER AND JACQUES ZEGUERS
DE VERSTANDIGE KEUKEN

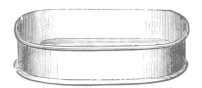

Fruit Compote, Bilbao-Style

Compota a la Bilbaina

	To serve 6	
⅔ cup	prunes, soaked in warm water overnight	150 ml.
⅓ cup	dried peaches, soaked in warm water overnight	75 ml.
1 cup	dried figs, soaked in warm water for 1½ hours	¼ liter
1 cup	raisins, soaked in warm water for 1½ hours	¼ liter
3	large apples, peeled, cored and cut into cubes	3
1 quart	red wine	1 liter
1 cup	sugar	¼ liter
2-inch	cinnamon stick	5-cm.
	thinly pared peel of 1 lemon	

Drain the dried fruits. Cut the peaches into large pieces and pit the prunes, taking care not to open them too much. Place the peaches, prunes, figs and raisins in a deep, nonreactive saucepan with the wine, sugar, cinnamon stick and lemon peel. Add enough water to cover the fruits completely and bring the liquid to a boil. Reduce the heat and let the fruits simmer, uncovered, for 20 minutes. Then add the apples. Continue to simmer until all of the fruits are tender.

The liquid should become syrupy. If it does not, remove the fruits, and boil the liquid until it thickens; then pour it over the compote of fruits.

JUAN CABANÉ AND ALEJANDRO DOMÉNECH
NUESTRA MEJOR COCINA

Prunes with Apples and Sherry

Pruimen en Appelen met Sherry

The author suggests that this dish should be accompanied by separate bowls of brown sugar and heavy cream.

	To serve 4	
½ lb.	prunes, soaked in water overnight and drained	¼ kg.
4	apples, peeled and cored	4
about 2 tbsp.	sugar	about 30 ml.
	the thinly pared peel of 1 lemon	
about 10	almonds, blanched and peeled	about 10
3 tbsp.	butter, cut into pieces	45 ml.
about ⅔ cup	dry sherry	about 150 ml.

In a nonreactive saucepan, simmer the prunes in a little water with some of the sugar and the lemon peel until the prunes are tender. Drain the prunes, let them cool, then cut them halfway through lengthwise so that you can remove the pits. Replace each pit with an almond.

Place the apples in a baking dish and put a piece of butter on top of each. Fill the spaces between the apples with the prunes. Pour enough dry sherry over the fruits so that the prunes are almost covered. Sprinkle a little sugar here and there. Bake the fruits in a preheated 400° F. [200° C.] oven until the apples are soft but not overcooked—approximately 20 minutes.

L. VAN PAREREN-BLES
ALLERHANDE RECEPTEN

Armagnac-and-Prune Ice Cream

Glace aux Pruneaux d'Agen

The technique of freezing ice cream in an ice-cream maker is demonstrated on pages 86-87.

	To make 1 quart [1 liter]	
1½ cups	prunes, pitted	375 ml.
⅓ cup	Armagnac	75 ml.
⅓ cup	medium to heavy sugar syrup (recipe, page 162), made with ¼ cup [50 ml.] each sugar and water	75 ml.
2 cups	milk	½ liter
⅔ cup	sugar	150 ml.
4	egg yolks	4

Place the Armagnac and sugar syrup in a nonreactive saucepan and bring to a boil; add the prunes, bring the liquid back to a boil, and remove the mixture from the heat. Cover the saucepan and leave the prunes to infuse in the liquid for one hour. Then pour the contents of the saucepan into an electric blender or food processor and blend until smooth. Pour the prune purée into a mixing bowl and reserve.

Place the milk and half of the sugar in a saucepan and bring to a boil. Once the milk boils, cover the pan, remove it from the heat and let the mixture cool for 10 minutes.

Beat the egg yolks and the remaining sugar until the mixture whitens and forms a ribbon. Bring the milk-and-sugar mixture back to a boil; pour a little into the egg-yolk mixture, whisking constantly. Remove the saucepan of milk from the heat and pour in the egg-yolk mixture, stirring this custard constantly with a wooden spoon or spatula.

Place the saucepan of custard over low heat and insert a candy thermometer. Stirring constantly, cook the custard for five to 10 minutes, or until it thickens enough to coat the spoon or spatula lightly; the thermometer will register 185° F. [85° C.]. Then remove the custard from the heat and continue stirring it for one to two minutes more.

Pour the custard a little at a time into the prune purée, stirring constantly. Whisk the mixture until it is smooth. Cool the mixture and freeze it.

GASTON LENÔTRE
LENÔTRE'S ICE CREAMS AND CANDIES

Armagnac-soaked Prune Bavarian Cream

Le Bavarois aux Pruneaux à l'Armagnac

Always have some good prunes soaking in young Armagnac in your cupboard. These should be pitted, but not previously cooked, and should not rise above the level of the Armagnac. Let them soak in the Armagnac for three weeks.

	To serve 6	
½ lb.	prunes, soaked in Armagnac	¼ kg.
½ cup	vanilla sugar	125 ml.
4	sheets leaf gelatin, soaked in cold water for 10 to 30 minutes and drained, or 1 tbsp. [15 ml.] unflavored powdered gelatin, softened in ¼ cup [50 ml.] cold water for 5 minutes	4
¾ cup	heavy cream, whipped	175 ml.

Purée half of the prunes with the vanilla sugar, and add the softened gelatin. Mix, and fold in the whipped cream before the gelatin begins to set. Pour into an oiled mold, then refrigerate. Just before serving, unmold the Bavarian cream onto a plate and decorate with the remaining prunes.

ANDRÉ DAGUIN
LE NOUVEAU CUISINIER GASCON

Chestnut Pudding

Legumina Kasztanowa

For a cold pudding, chill the chestnut purée in a serving bowl and serve it topped with sweetened whipped cream.

	To serve 4	
1 cup	mixed dried fruits (apricots, prunes, pears and apples), soaked in warm water for 15 minutes, drained, then halved or quartered	¼ liter
1 lb.	chestnuts, flat ends slit with 2 cuts in the form of a cross, parboiled for 15 minutes, shells and skins removed	½ kg.
3 to 4 cups	milk	¾ to 1 liter
2 to 3 tbsp.	vanilla sugar	30 to 45 ml.
2	egg whites, stiffly beaten with sugar to taste	2

Put the chestnuts in a saucepan, pour in enough milk to cover them, and simmer until they are very soft and have absorbed most of the milk—about 30 minutes. Strain the chestnuts, then mash them, add the sugar and press them through a sieve into a bowl. Arrange the purée in a mound in a buttered baking pan and garnish the purée with the dried fruits. Spread the beaten egg whites over the top and bake the pudding in a preheated 350° F. [180° C.] oven for 20 to 25 minutes, or until the meringue is well browned. Serve hot.

MARJA OCHOROWICZ-MONATOWA
POLISH COOKERY

Fried Fruit Puffs

Ruan Dza Go Jiu

	To make 30 to 40	
1 cup	pitted dried dates	¼ liter
½ cup	raisins	125 ml.
¼ cup	dried apricots	50 ml.
¼ cup	peanut butter	50 ml.
¼ tsp.	salt	1 ml.
1 tsp.	sugar	5 ml.
2 tsp.	sesame seeds	10 ml.
½ cup	cornstarch	125 ml.
2	egg whites	2
	red food coloring	
	vegetable oil for deep frying	

Chop or grind the dates, raisins and apricots. Then mix them with the peanut butter, salt, sugar and sesame seeds. Com-

bine the cornstarch, egg whites and a few drops of food coloring. Shape the fruit mixture into 30 to 40 balls, then roll the balls in the cornstarch mixture until they are evenly coated.

In a heavy pan, heat a 1-inch [2½-cm.] layer of vegetable oil to 375° F. [190° C.]. Deep fry the balls in small batches until they are delicately browned—about two minutes. Drain them on paper towels and serve them while still hot.

WONONA W. AND IRVING B. CHANG,
HELENE W. AND AUSTIN H. KUTSCHER
AN ENCYCLOPEDIA OF CHINESE FOOD AND COOKING

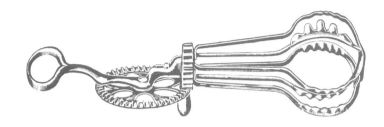

Fritters with Dried Fruits

Tiganites me Stafides

	To serve 8	
¼ cup	dried currants	50 ml.
¼ cup	seedless white raisins	50 ml.
1½ cups	flour	375 ml.
2 tsp.	baking powder	10 ml.
	salt	
4 tbsp.	granulated sugar	60 ml.
1	egg, beaten	1
	vanilla or lemon extract	
⅓ cup	milk	75 ml.
⅓ cup	water	75 ml.
	oil for deep frying	
	confectioners' sugar	
	ground cinnamon	

Sift the flour, baking powder and salt together into a bowl. Add the granulated sugar and dried fruits and mix well. Make a well in the middle of the mixture and stir in the beaten egg mixed with vanilla or lemon extract to taste. Mix the milk and water together and gradually pour the liquid into the fruit mixture. Beat for a few minutes. Heat the oil in a heavy skillet. Drop spoonfuls of the batter into almost-smoking hot oil and fry until they are golden brown on both sides. Drain the fritters on paper towels and sprinkle them with the confectioners' sugar and cinnamon.

MARO DUNCAN
COOKING THE GREEK WAY

Uncooked Fruitcake

*To make one 7½-by-3½-by-2½-inch
[19-by-9-by-6-cm.] loaf*

1 cup	pitted prunes	¼ liter
1 cup	seedless raisins	¼ liter
1 cup	dried apricots	¼ liter
1 cup	pitted dates	¼ liter
1 cup	mixed candied fruit peels and citron	¼ liter
1 cup	candied cherries	¼ liter
1½ cups	almonds, roasted in a 350° F. [180° C.] oven for 10 minutes, or until well browned	375 ml.
¼ tsp.	salt	1 ml.
1 cup	sweet sherry, port, Tokay or other dessert wine	¼ liter

Put the fruits, candied fruits and almonds through a food grinder using a medium disk. Combine them in a large bowl, sprinkle in the salt, add the wine and mix thoroughly. Pack the mixture into a 2-quart [2-liter] loaf pan. Cover with wax paper. Refrigerate the cake for two to three days to let the flavors develop before serving it directly from the loaf pan.

JEAN H. SHEPARD
THE FRESH FRUITS AND VEGETABLES COOKBOOK

Périgord Pudding

Flaugnarde

The technique of making Périgord pudding is demonstrated on pages 66-67. Instead of flavoring the milk with vanilla extract, you can place it in a pan with a vanilla bean and heat it very gently until bubbles appear around the edge of the pan; then remove the pan from the heat and let the vanilla bean infuse for 15 minutes before removing it from the milk.

	To serve 6	
½ cup	raisins	125 ml.
½ lb.	prunes	¼ kg.
¼ cup	Cognac or colorless prune brandy	50 ml.
½ cup	sugar	125 ml.
4	eggs	4
	salt	
½ cup	flour	125 ml.
1 cup	milk	¼ liter
½ tsp.	vanilla extract	2 ml.
2 tbsp.	butter	30 ml.

Cover the raisins with cold water, bring them just barely to a boil, remove from the heat, let them swell for 10 minutes and drain them in a sieve. Cut the prunes in half and remove the pits. Combine the prunes and the raisins in a glass jar with a tight-fitting lid, pour the brandy over them and screw the lid down tightly. Shake from time to time, turning the jar over. After six or seven hours, the liquid will have been absorbed—a few hours more or less will not matter.

Beat the sugar, eggs and a tiny pinch of salt together in a mixing bowl. Sift in the flour, a little at a time, stirring all the while with a whisk. Stir in the milk, the vanilla extract and the contents of the jar; the batter is meant to be very thin. Liberally butter a gratin dish, ladle in the bulk of the prune-and-raisin batter, then pour in the rest of the batter. Bake in a preheated 375° to 400° F. [190° to 200° C.] oven for 20 minutes, or until browned and risen.

RICHARD OLNEY
THE FRENCH MENU COOKBOOK

Mixed Fruits

Fruit and Pumpernickel Dessert

Götterspeise

The author suggests that the fresh fruit might be wild or garden strawberries, red currants, raspberries, blackberries or sour cherries—or a mixture of two or more of these fruits.

	To serve 4	
1 lb.	fresh fruit	½ kg.
¼ cup	granulated sugar	50 ml.
2 or 3	slices pumpernickel, lightly toasted and grated	2 or 3
2 oz.	semisweet chocolate, grated	60 g.
1 tsp.	vanilla sugar	5 ml.
1 cup	heavy cream, whipped and sweetened with 1 tbsp. [15 ml.] sugar	¼ liter

Sprinkle the fresh fruit with the granulated sugar. Put the fruit in a serving dish. Mix the pumpernickel with the chocolate and the vanilla sugar, and spread the mixture over the fruit. Heap the whipped cream on top. Chill in the refrigerator for two hours before serving.

HERMINE KIEHNLE AND MARIA HÄDECKE
DAS NEVE KIEHNLE-KOCHBUCH

Fruit Salad

Salade de Fruits

Our fruit salad, enhanced with alcohol and sugar, is served as a dessert. The mixture of preserves, lemon juice and sugar adds a certain acidity and preserves the color of the fruits.

To serve 6 to 8

⅓ cup	fresh lemon juice	75 ml.
3 tbsp.	apricot preserves, strained	45 ml.
2 tbsp.	kirsch or pear brandy	30 ml.
¼ cup	sugar	50 ml.
4	small plums, halved, pitted and cut into wedges	4
2	peaches, halved, pitted and cut into wedges	2
1	apple, peeled, cored and sliced	1
1	pear, peeled, cored and sliced	1
1	banana, peeled and sliced	1
1 cup	Thompson Seedless grapes	¼ liter
1 cup	Ribier or Emperor grapes	¼ liter

Mix the lemon juice, apricot preserves, kirsch and sugar in a stainless-steel or glass bowl until they are well combined. Cut the fruits directly into the bowl. Mix all of the fruits in the marinade and let them sit for at least one hour before serving. Serve the fruit salad in glasses or on dessert plates.

JACQUES PÉPIN
LA METHODE

Spiced Wine Fruit Salad

To serve 4

1½ pints	small strawberries, hulled	¾ liter
¾ cup	seedless grapes	175 ml.
2	peaches, blanched, peeled, halved, pitted and sliced	2
⅔ cup	red currants	150 ml.
⅔ cup	black currants	150 ml.
¼ to ½ tsp.	ground cinnamon	1 to 2 ml.
¼ to ½ cup	superfine sugar	50 to 125 ml.
⅓ cup	brandy or 3 tbsp. [45 ml.] liqueur	75 ml.

Place all of the fruits in a glass dish. Sprinkle with cinnamon, and add sugar according to your taste and the sweetness of the fruits. Pour over the brandy or liqueur and allow to stand for at least two hours. Stir well and serve chilled.

AUDREY ELLIS
WINE LOVERS COOKBOOK

Polynesian Fruit Bowl with Whipped Rum

To serve 6

3	papayas, peeled, halved and seeded	3
1 pint	strawberries, hulled and halved	½ liter
1	small pineapple, peeled, cored and cut into chunks	1
2 cups	sugar	½ liter
2 cups	water	½ liter
½ cup	fresh lemon juice	125 ml.
½ cup	dark rum	125 ml.
6	egg yolks	6

In a nonreactive saucepan, bring the sugar and water to a boil, stirring until the sugar dissolves. Without stirring, simmer this syrup for 15 minutes. Pour the syrup into a bowl and let it cool. Add the lemon juice and rum, then stir in the strawberries and pineapple chunks. Cover the bowl and allow the fruits to marinate in the refrigerator for several hours or overnight.

Drain off ⅔ cup [150 ml.] of the marinade from the fruits and set aside. In the top of a double boiler, beat the egg yolks until pale. Gradually beat in the reserved marinade. Set the yolk mixture over simmering water and, stirring occasionally, cook until this sauce is thick enough to coat a spoon—about 30 minutes. Remove the sauce from the heat and let it cool to room temperature.

Spoon the strawberries and pineapple chunks into the papaya halves and top with the sauce.

MAGGIE WALDRON
STRAWBERRIES

Fruit Salad with Yogurt

Froutosalata me yaourti

To serve 4

2	bananas, peeled and sliced	2
2	oranges, peeled, segmented and cut into small pieces	2
1	apple, peeled, cored and cut into small pieces	1
2 tbsp.	brandy	30 ml.
1 cup	yogurt	¼ liter
½ cup	superfine sugar	125 ml.

Combine the fruits in a bowl, stir in the brandy and mix well. Refrigerate for at least one hour. Beat the yogurt together with the sugar and lightly stir the mixture into the fruits. Serve immediately.

MARO DUNCAN
COOKING THE GREEK WAY

Cheese Cones with Fruit

Tvorog s Frouktami

	To serve 4	
1 lb.	fruit—strawberries, cherries, apricots or oranges—prepared for eating and cut into pieces if necessary	½ kg.
1 lb.	farmer cheese or ricotta, placed in a cloth-lined colander, covered with a heavy weight, set on a tray and drained in the refrigerator overnight	½ kg.
¼ cup	sugar	50 ml.
¼ cup	water	50 ml.
3 tbsp.	heavy cream	45 ml.

Make a syrup by boiling together the sugar and water, then set it aside to cool. Meanwhile press the cheese through a fine sieve or the fine disk of a food mill into a large bowl. Stir the cooled syrup into the cheese, then add the cream and beat everything together vigorously until the mixture is smooth.

Divide the cheese mixture into four equal portions and place each portion on an individual serving plate. With a wet table knife, mold each portion of cheese into a cone, rounding the top smoothly. Surround each cone with the fruit of your choice and serve.

DETSKOE PITANIE

Chinese Crackling Fruit

Every diner shares in cooking this dessert. To serve it, you will need a chafing dish with a container for water under the serving pan or a food warmer that will keep water simmering in the lower container of an improvised combination of nesting pots. From start to finish, handle the hot syrup with great care to prevent burns.

The author recommends using any desired combination of hulled strawberries, seedless grapes, seedless orange segments, and slices of bananas, peaches, plums, pears, nectarines and papayas.

	To serve 6	
3 to 4 cups	assorted fruits, prepared for eating and cut into pieces, if necessary	¾ to 1 liter
½ cup	light corn syrup	125 ml.
¾ cup	water	175 ml.
2 cups	sugar	½ liter

Combine the corn syrup, water and sugar in a 2½-quart [2½-liter] saucepan. Cook over high heat, stirring until the sugar has dissolved. Boil the syrup without stirring until it

reaches a temperature of 300° F. [150° C.] on a candy thermometer. Pour the syrup quickly into a chafing dish over a simmering water bath. Set individual bowls filled with cracked ice and water beside the chafing dish.

To cook each piece of fruit, spear it on a bamboo skewer, dip it into the syrup and then quickly dip it into a bowl of ice water to harden the syrup.

MAGGIE WALDRON
STRAWBERRIES

Dessert Tempura

Rice polish, the outer covering of rice grains obtained from polishing, is available at health-food stores.

	To serve 1	
1-inch	piece pineapple	2½-cm.
1	slice apple	1
½	dried apricot	½
1	strawberry	1
2-inch	slice pumpkin, ¼ inch [6 mm.] thick	5-cm.
2 tbsp.	whole-wheat flour	30 ml.
	oil for deep frying	
	Demerara or turbinado sugar	

Tempura batter		
2 tbsp.	whole-wheat flour	30 ml.
2 tbsp.	rice polish	30 ml.
¼ cup	ice water	50 ml.
1½ tbsp.	lightly beaten egg	22 ml.

To make the tempura batter, beat together the flour, rice polish, water and egg.

Shake the pieces of fruit in a bag with the flour to make sure the batter will cover them completely. Dip the fruit pieces in the cold batter and drop them into 3 inches [8 cm.] of oil heated to 350° F. [180° C.]. Fry the pieces until golden—about one minute. Drain, then sprinkle the fruits with a few grains of the sugar and serve them immediately.

YVONNE YOUNG TARR
THE NEW YORK TIMES NATURAL FOODS DIETING BOOK

Fruit Curry with Chocolate and Condiments

The author recommends using a combination of any of the following fruits: pineapples, mangoes, papayas, peaches, bananas, pears, apples, kiwi fruits, strawberries, cherries or passion fruits. Do not use citrus fruits for this recipe.

	To serve 4	
5 or 6	varied fruits	5 or 6
	fresh lemon juice	
	Condiments	
	bittersweet chocolate, grated	
	almonds, blanched, peeled, sliced and lightly toasted	
	dried currants or seedless white raisins	
	candied mint leaves	
	chopped candied ginger	
	large chocolate wafers	
	Curry sauce	
2 tbsp.	unsalted butter	30 ml.
1 tbsp.	granulated sugar	15 ml.
1 tbsp.	brown sugar	15 ml.
1 tbsp.	fresh lemon juice	15 ml.
¼ tsp.	ground cinnamon	1 ml.
½ tsp.	ground ginger	2 ml.
	freshly grated nutmeg	
3 tbsp.	dark rum	45 ml.

Have the condiments arranged in bowls on a tray. Pile the wafers in a small basket. Peel, seed, pit or core, and cut the fruits (except the banana and passion fruit) into large, bite-sized pieces. Place anything that might discolor in a bowl of water with lemon juice.

To make the curry sauce, place the butter, sugars, lemon juice, cinnamon, ginger and a few gratings of nutmeg in a 10-inch [25-cm.] skillet. Place the skillet over high heat and melt the butter and sugar, stirring all the time. Add the rum and any firm fruits (pears, pineapple, peach-colored fruits). Let the fruits sauté briefly as the syrup becomes thick and glossy.

Peel and slice the banana. Remove the pan from the heat, add the remaining fruits including the banana, and shake the pan to warm them. If you are using passion fruit, halve it, scoop out its seeds and juice, and add the flesh at this time. Serve the warm fruits at once, with the condiments.

JUDITH OLNEY
THE JOY OF CHOCOLATE

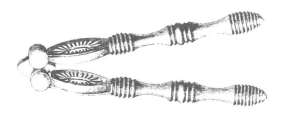

Baked Puréed Tropical Fruits

Poe

To make the coconut milk called for in this recipe, pour about 1 cup [¼ liter] of boiling water over ½ cup [125 ml.] of freshly grated coconut. After five minutes, strain through a cloth, pressing to extract all of the milk.

	To serve 12	
1	large pineapple (about 4 lb. [2 kg.]), peeled, quartered, cored and coarsely chopped	1
1	large mango (about 2 lb. [1 kg.]), peeled, pitted and coarsely chopped	1
2	medium-sized papayas (about 1 lb. [½ kg.] each), peeled, halved lengthwise, seeded and coarsely chopped	2
4	large bananas (about 1½ lb. [¾ kg.]), peeled and coarsely chopped	4
½ cup	arrowroot	125 ml.
1 cup	firmly packed light brown sugar	¼ liter
1 tsp.	vanilla extract	5 ml.
1 cup	coconut milk, chilled	¼ liter

Put the pineapple, mango, papaya and bananas through the coarsest disk of a food grinder. Transfer the fruit pulp and its liquid to a sieve set over a deep bowl, and stir until all the liquid has drained through. Measure 1 cup [¼ liter] of juice and combine it with the arrowroot in another bowl. Mix thoroughly. Then stir the arrowroot mixture into the fruit purée and add the remaining liquid, the brown sugar and vanilla extract.

Transfer the fruit mixture to a buttered baking dish that measures 14 by 8 by 2 inches [35 by 20 by 5 cm.]. Spread the mixture evenly with a spatula. Bake in the middle of a preheated 375° F. [190° C.] oven for one hour, or until the top is golden brown. Cool the mixture to room temperature, cover with plastic wrap and refrigerate until thoroughly chilled—at least four hours.

Serve the *poe* directly from the baking dish and present the coconut milk separately in a bowl.

FOODS OF THE WORLD
PACIFIC AND SOUTHEAST ASIAN COOKING

Fresh-Fruit Soufflé

You can use any selection of seasonal fruits for this soufflé.

	To serve 4	
2	peaches, blanched, peeled, halved, pitted and cut into small pieces	2
½	pineapple, peeled, quartered, cored and cut into small pieces	½
½ cup	strawberries, hulled and halved	125 ml.
2 tbsp.	kirsch	30 ml.
about ¼ cup	confectioners' sugar	about 50 ml.
4	egg yolks	4
1 tbsp.	superfine sugar	15 ml.
2 tbsp.	heavy cream, lightly whipped	30 ml.
5	egg whites, stiffly beaten	5

Lightly butter a large 7-inch [17½-cm.] soufflé dish. Tie a band of parchment paper around the rim of the dish. Pour the kirsch over the fruits and sprinkle them lightly with some of the confectioners' sugar. Toss the fruits together and place this mixture in the bottom of the soufflé dish—it will form a layer about 1 inch [2½ cm.] deep.

Beat the egg yolks well with the superfine sugar. Fold in the whipped cream. Add a spoonful of the beaten whites to the yolk mixture, then cut and fold in the remaining whites. Turn this into the soufflé dish, dust with a little confectioners' sugar and bake in the center of a preheated 375° F. [190° C.] oven for 15 to 20 minutes.

When the soufflé is well risen and brown, dredge the top quickly with more confectioners' sugar and put the soufflé back in the oven briefly to caramelize the sugar. Remove the paper band and serve the soufflé at once.

ROSEMARY HUME AND MURIEL DOWNES
CORDON BLEU DESSERTS AND PUDDINGS

Fruit Kebabs

Use this recipe as a guideline. The fruits listed below can generally be bought the year round, but there is no reason that a few strawberries, cherries, tangerines, pears, grapes or even watermelon chunks cannot be used as well. Softer-fleshed fruit should be a little firm; otherwise the pieces will fall apart during the broiling.

	To serve 6	
½	grapefruit, segments removed from shell, juice reserved	½
1	tart, medium-large apple, cored and cut into 12 chunks	1
1	large banana, peeled and cut into 12 pieces	1
½ cup	pineapple chunks	125 ml.
1	orange, peeled and segmented	1
Rum marinade		
¼ cup	dark rum	50 ml.
1 tbsp.	honey	15 ml.
3 tbsp.	fresh lemon juice	45 ml.
¼ tsp.	grated nutmeg	1 ml.
¼ tsp.	ground ginger	1 ml.

To make the marinade, heat the rum to the boiling point in a small pot and spoon the honey into a shallow dish. Stir the hot rum into the honey and add the lemon juice, nutmeg and ginger. Squeeze the juice from the grapefruit shell into the marinade.

Add the grapefruit segments, apple chunks, banana pieces, pineapple chunks and orange segments to the marinade, and spoon some of the marinade over the pieces. Cover the dish and let it stand for one hour, basting occasionally.

String the fruits onto six 6-inch [15-cm.] skewers, alternating the varieties, but beginning and finishing with apple chunks. Put the completed skewers on a baking dish and baste the fruits liberally with the marinade. Place under a preheated 550° F. [290° C.] broiler, about 6 inches [15 cm.] from the heat source. Baste the fruits with the remaining marinade several times during the broiling. The kebabs should be finished in about 10 minutes. For the last two or three minutes, raise the dish to within 3 inches [8 cm.] of the heat to partially brown the fruits. Serve the kebabs at once, spooning the basting liquid from the dish over each of them.

CAROL CUTLER
THE WOMAN'S DAY LOW-CALORIE DESSERT COOKBOOK

Sweet Tutti-Frutti Roll

Rotolo Dolce Tutti-Frutti

The dough for the roll is better if prepared the day before.

	To serve 8	
1 cup	raisins, soaked in warm water for 1 hour and drained	¼ liter
6	prunes, pitted and chopped	6
6	dried figs, chopped	6
½ cup	mixed candied fruit, chopped	125 ml.
½ cup	walnuts, chopped	125 ml.
½ cup	almonds, chopped	125 ml.
1 cup	fresh bread crumbs	¼ liter
½ cup	Marsala	125 ml.
2 tsp.	grated lemon peel	10 ml.
	ground cinnamon	
	grated nutmeg	

Sweet pastry dough

2½ cups	flour	625 ml.
	salt	
8 tbsp.	butter, cut into pieces and softened	125 ml.
½ cup	sugar	125 ml.
2	eggs, 1 yolk separated from the white	2
2 tbsp.	Marsala	30 ml.

To make the dough, sift the flour and a pinch of salt onto a work surface, form a well in the center, and put the butter, sugar, egg, egg yolk and Marsala into the well. Work the mixture quickly with your finger tips, form it into a ball, wrap the ball in a piece of aluminum foil or wax paper, and let it rest in the refrigerator for at least 30 minutes.

For the filling, soak the bread crumbs in the Marsala. Mix together the raisins, prunes, figs, candied fruit, walnuts, almonds and lemon peel. Squeeze the bread crumbs and add them to the fruits and nuts with a pinch each of cinnamon and nutmeg.

Go back to the dough, and work it a little if it is too cold. On a floured surface, or better still between two pieces of waxed paper, roll the dough out thin to form a rectangle about 10 inches [25 cm.] wide and 16 inches [40 cm.] long. Leaving a 1-inch [2½-cm.] border all around, cover the center of the dough with the filling, spreading this out with the back of a wet spoon to prevent the dough from tearing. Fold the dough at the sides onto the filling, and then—starting at one long edge—gently roll the dough over the filling. Bend the roll to form a ring shape and carefully transfer the ring to

a buttered baking sheet. Coat the top of the ring with the egg white. Bake in a preheated 350° F. [180° C.] oven for 55 minutes. Serve cold.

LYDIA B. SALVETTI
100 RICETTE DEL FUTURO

Curried Fruit Bake

	To serve 6 to 8	
4	peaches, blanched, peeled, halved and pitted	4
4	pears, peeled, halved and cored	4
½	pineapple, peeled, quartered, cored and cut into cubes	½
6 tbsp.	butter	90 ml.
2 tsp.	curry powder	10 ml.
⅓ cup	honey	75 ml.

Arrange the fruits in layers in a buttered 9- to 10-inch [23- to 25-cm.] round baking dish. Melt the butter; add the curry and honey, and spoon the mixture over the fruits. Bake in a preheated 325° F. [160° C.] oven, uncovered, for about one hour. Serve warm.

FAYE MARTIN
NATURALLY DELICIOUS DESSERTS AND SNACKS

Spiced Fruit Mishmash

	To serve 8	
½	pineapple, peeled, quartered, cored and cut into chunks	½
1½ lb.	apricots, blanched, peeled, halved and pitted	¾ kg.
1½ lb.	peaches, blanched, peeled, halved and pitted	¾ kg.
5 tbsp.	butter, melted	75 ml.
⅔ cup	firmly packed brown sugar	150 ml.
¼ tsp.	ground cloves	1 ml.
¼ tsp.	ground cinnamon	1 ml.
1 tbsp.	curry powder	15 ml.
	vanilla ice cream (recipe, page 167)	

Arrange the pineapple chunks and apricot and peach halves in layers in a shallow casserole. Combine the butter, brown sugar, cloves, cinnamon and curry powder, and sprinkle over the fruits. Bake in a preheated 350° F. [180° C.] oven for 45 minutes. Serve warm with homemade ice cream.

JEAN HEWITT
THE NEW YORK TIMES NATURAL FOODS COOKBOOK

Fruit Snowball

To serve 4

1 cup	strawberries, hulled	¼ liter
1	banana, peeled	1
¼ cup	fresh orange juice or other fruit juice	50 ml.

Place the strawberries in a plastic bag or box. Cut the banana into 1-inch [2½-cm.] chunks and immediately roll them tightly in plastic film. Place the fruits in the freezer to freeze solid—for about two hours.

Attach the metal blade to a food processor. Place the frozen fruits in the container of the processor, pour in the fruit juice and blend the ingredients together until the fruits are amalgamated into a creamy pink mass. Serve at once.

CAROL CUTLER
THE WOMAN'S DAY LOW-CALORIE DESSERT COOKBOOK

Fresh Fruit Salad in Jelly

La Macédoine de Fruits Frais à la Gelée

Suitable fruits for use in this recipe include strawberries, raspberries, peaches, apricots and oranges.

To serve 10 to 12

1 lb.	fresh fruits of 4 or 5 kinds, prepared for eating and cut up if necessary	½ liter
½ cup	brandy	125 ml.
½ cup	sugar	125 ml.

Kirsch jelly

⅔ cup	sugar	150 ml.
4 cups	water	1 liter
10	sheets leaf gelatin, soaked in cold water for 10 to 30 minutes and drained, or 2½ tbsp. [37 ml.] unflavored powdered gelatin, softened in ¾ cup [175 ml.] water for 5 minutes	10
1 cup	kirsch	¼ liter

Soak the mixed fruits in the brandy and sugar for one hour.

Meanwhile, prepare the jelly. Make a syrup by bringing the sugar and water to a boil together. Add the softened gelatin, and stir over low heat until it dissolves. Let the jelly cool, then add the kirsch.

Put a 6-cup [1½-liter] charlotte mold on ice and pour in about 1 cup [¼ liter] of the jelly. Leave the jelly on the ice or refrigerate it until nearly set—about 30 minutes. Drain the fruits and arrange a quarter of them on the jelly. Cover the fruits with more jelly and allow to set as before. Continue these layers until the mold is full. Leave the mold on ice or in the refrigerator for two hours to set. Unmold the jelly just before serving.

ARISTIDE QUILLET
LA CUISINE MODERNE

Standard Preparations

Sugar Syrup

This recipe produces a light syrup—most suitable for poaching or as a sweetener for uncooked fruits. For a medium sugar syrup, suitable for sweetening water ices and parfaits, mix ⅔ cup [150 ml.] of sugar with 1 cup [¼ liter] of water. For a medium to heavy syrup, mix 1 cup of sugar with 1 cup of water. And for a heavy syrup, mix 1 cup of sugar with ½ cup [125 ml.] of water.

To make 1 cup [¼ liter] syrup

½ cup	sugar	125 ml.
1 cup	water	¼ liter

Place the sugar and water in a saucepan. Over medium heat, stir the mixture constantly until all of the sugar dissolves. Then bring the syrup briefly to a boil. The syrup may be used immediately or cooled for later use.

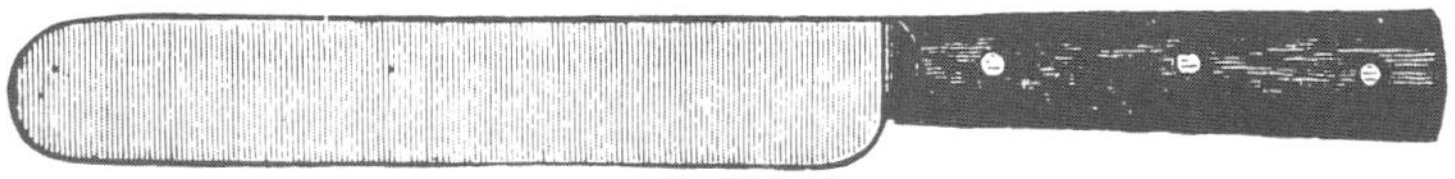

Tart Cream

For this recipe, an American version of France's *crème fraîche*, pasteurized—not ultrapasteurized—heavy cream should be used.

To make about 2 cups [½ liter] tart cream

2 cups	heavy cream	½ liter
1 tbsp.	buttermilk	15 ml.

In a small, heavy, enameled saucepan, stir the cream and buttermilk together until well blended. Set the pan over low heat and insert a meat-and-yeast thermometer into the cream mixture. Stirring gently but constantly, warm the mixture until the thermometer registers 85° F. [30° C.].

Immediately remove the pan from the heat and pour the cream mixture into a 1-quart [1-liter] jar. Loosely cover the jar with foil or wax paper. Set the cream mixture aside at a room temperature of 60° to 85° F. [15° to 30° C.] for eight to 24 hours, or until it reaches the consistency of lightly beaten cream. The heavy cream has now become *crème fraîche*.

Tightly cover the jar and refrigerate the cream until you are ready to use it. It will keep refrigerated for about a week.

Wine Custard

Sabayon

To make about 6 cups [1 ½ liters] custard

5	egg yolks	5
1 cup	superfine sugar	¼ liter
1 ¼ cups	dry white wine, port, Sauternes, Champagne, Marsala or sherry	300 ml.
6	strips lemon peel, cut into tiny julienne (optional)	6

In a sabayon pan or a broad 2-quart [2-liter] saucepan, heat together the egg yolks and sugar until the mixture is thick and creamy, and forms a slowly dissolving ribbon when it is dribbled back into the pan from the lifted whisk. This will take about seven to 10 minutes.

Set the pan over a larger pan partly filled with water heated to just below the boiling point. Whisking constantly, slowly pour in the wine of your choice and, if desired, add the lemon-peel julienne. Continue to whisk until the mixture froths to almost triple its original volume and is pale yellow in color. Remove the pan from the water bath and continue whisking for a minute or so.

The wine custard may be used hot or cold. For a cold sauce, chill the custard quickly by setting the pan in a bowl of ice cubes and whisking the custard until it is cold. Whipped cream may be added to the cold sauce, if desired.

Pouring Custard

Crème Anglaise

To make about 2 ½ cups [625 ml.] custard

6	egg yolks	6
½ cup	superfine sugar	125 ml.
2 ½ cups	milk, scalded and slightly cooled	625 ml.

In a mixing bowl, beat the eggs and sugar together with a wire whisk until the mixture is thick and pale, and forms a slowly dissolving ribbon when dribbled from the whisk. Whisking gently all the time, slowly add the scalded milk.

Transfer this custard mixture to a heavy saucepan and set it over very low heat, or put the pan on a trivet in a larger pan partly filled with simmering water. Cook the custard, stirring it constantly in a figure-8 pattern with a wooden spoon. Do not let it boil. When the custard coats the spoon, immediately remove the pan from the heat; in order to arrest the cooking and prevent the custard from curdling, stand the pan in a bowl filled with ice cubes and a little water. To ensure a smooth texture, continue to stir the custard for five minutes until it cools a little. To remove any lumps, strain the custard into a bowl.

For a warm custard, set the bowl in a pan partly filled with hot water and stir the custard occasionally. For a cold custard, set the bowl over ice cubes and stir until the custard is sufficiently chilled.

Vanilla custard. Place a vanilla bean in the pan of scalded milk, cover the pan and let the milk infuse for 20 minutes before removing the bean. (The bean can be rinsed and used one more time.)

Coffee custard. Place ⅓ cup [75 ml.] of fresh coffee beans in the pan of scalding hot milk; cover the pan and let the milk infuse for 20 minutes. Strain the milk through a fine sieve before using it.

Caramel custard. In a heavy pan, caramelize ⅓ cup of sugar with 1 tablespoon [15 ml.] of water. Remove the pan from the heat and immediately pour the scalded milk onto the caramel. Return the pan to low heat and stir until the caramel dissolves into the milk.

Rum custard. Stir about 1 tablespoon of rum into the prepared custard.

Pastry Cream

To make chocolate pastry cream stir 4 ounces [125 g.] of melted and cooled semisweet chocolate into the finished pastry cream. You may also substitute 3 tablespoons [45 ml.] of rum, brandy or liqueur for the vanilla bean; stir these ingredients into the pastry cream after you remove it from the heat. To flavor the finished cream with coffee, add 2 tablespoons [30 ml.] of instant-coffee crystals that have been dissolved in 2 tablespoons of hot water.

To make about 2 cups [½ liter] pastry cream

½ cup	sugar	125 ml.
5 or 6	egg yolks	5 or 6
⅓ cup	flour	75 ml.
	salt	
2 cups	milk	½ liter
2-inch	piece vanilla bean	5-cm.

Mix the sugar and egg yolks together with a spoon, beating until the mixture is thick and cream-colored. Gradually work in the flour, and season with a pinch of salt.

Heat the milk with the vanilla bean to the boiling point. Stirring constantly, pour the hot milk into the egg mixture in a thin stream. Turn the pastry-cream mixture into a saucepan and, stirring vigorously, cook over medium heat until the mixture comes to the boiling point. Boil for about two minutes. Strain the pastry cream and let it cool, stirring occasionally to prevent a skin from forming. The cream may be stored, covered, in the refrigerator for two days.

Bavarian Cream

To make about 6 cups [1 ½ liters] cream

8	egg yolks	8
1 cup	sugar	¼ liter
2 cups	milk, scalded, infused with a vanilla bean for 20 minutes, then strained	½ liter
¼ cup	cold water	50 ml.
2 tbsp.	unflavored powdered gelatin	30 ml.
1 cup	heavy cream	¼ liter

In a mixing bowl, beat the eggs and sugar together with a wire whisk until the mixture is thick and pale, and forms a slowly dissolving ribbon when dribbled from the whisk. Whisking vigorously, slowly add the scalded milk. Transfer this custard mixture to a heavy saucepan and set it over very low heat, or put the pan on a trivet in a larger pan partly filled with simmering water. Cook the custard, stirring it constantly in a figure-8 pattern with a wooden spoon. Do not let it boil. When the custard coats the spoon, remove the pan from the heat and strain the custard into a large bowl. Set it aside, stirring the custard from time to time.

Put the cold water into a small bowl and sprinkle the powdered gelatin onto the water. When the gelatin has absorbed the water and become spongy in texture—in about five minutes—stir it into the hot custard.

Continue stirring until the gelatin has dissolved, then set the bowl over a large bowl of ice and water. Stir frequently. Whip the cream until it forms soft peaks. When the custard mixture has jelled to the consistency of lightly whipped cream, remove it from the ice and fold in the whipped cream, blending it thoroughly with the custard. Pour into a lightly oiled 7-cup [1¾-liter] mold and refrigerate for four hours or until set. Unmold the cream onto a serving dish.

Rich Short-Crust Dough

To make 2 pounds [1 kg.] dough

4 cups	flour	1 liter
2 tbsp.	superfine or confectioners' sugar	30 ml.
2 tsp.	salt	10 ml.
1 ½ cups	unsalted butter, softened	375 ml.
2	eggs	2
	water (optional)	

Sift the dry ingredients together onto a marble slab or pastry board. Make a well in the center of the dry ingredients, and put in the butter and eggs. Using the fingers of one hand, pinch the butter and eggs together until they are lightly blended. With a spatula, gradually cut the dry ingredients into the butter-egg mixture, chopping and blending until the dough is crumbly. If necessary, add a little water, drop by drop, to make the dough cling together. Form the dough into a ball, pressing it together with your hands, and wrap it in plastic wrap or foil. Chill the dough in the refrigerator for at least two hours before rolling it out. Tightly covered, the dough can be safely kept in the refrigerator for two to three days, in the freezer for two to three months. If frozen, the dough should be defrosted overnight in the refrigerator before it is used.

Shortcake Biscuits

This recipe can also be used to provide a topping for a fruit cobbler made in a pan up to about 9 inches [23 cm.] wide and 13 inches [32 cm.] long. For the topping, roll the dough out to a thickness of ¼ inch [6 mm.] and cut it with a biscuit cutter or a shaped cookie cutter.

To make six 3-inch [8-cm.] biscuits

2 cups	sifted flour	½ liter
3 tbsp.	sugar	45 ml.
1 tbsp.	baking powder	15 ml.
	salt	
6 tbsp.	butter, cut into pieces and chilled	90 ml.
1	egg, the yolk separated from the white, and the white lightly beaten, plus 1 additional yolk	1
⅓ cup	half-and-half cream	75 ml.

Sift the flour, sugar, baking powder and a pinch of salt into a large bowl. Add the pieces of butter and quickly work them into the sifted ingredients using a pastry blender, two knives or your finger tips. The mixture should develop a coarse, mealy texture.

Beat the egg yolks with the cream. Add them to the bowl, and stir the mixture with a fork until the dry ingredients are thoroughly moistened. Gather the dough together; if the dough does not cohere, add a little more cream. When the mixture holds together, gather it into a ball with your hands. In the bowl, knead the dough briefly until it is smooth.

On a lightly floured board, pat the dough out to a thickness of 1 inch [2½ cm.]. Using a 3-inch [8-cm.] biscuit cutter, cut the dough into rounds; cut straight down into the dough without twisting the cutter and make your cuts as close together as possible. Any leftover dough can be pressed together gently and cut. Line a baking pan with parchment paper, place the rounds on the paper and brush the tops with the beaten egg white. Bake the biscuits in a preheated 450° F. [230° C.] oven for eight to 10 minutes, until nicely browned.

Crepes

To make about fifteen 6- to 7-inch [15- to 18-cm.] crepes

1 cup	flour	¼ liter
	salt	
2	eggs	2
1 to 1¼ cups	milk	250 to 300 ml.
2 tbsp.	melted butter	30 ml.
1 tbsp.	brandy or Grand Marnier (optional)	15 ml.

Sift the flour with a pinch of salt into a mixing bowl. Make a well in the center of the flour and break the eggs into the well. Gradually whisk the eggs into the flour, working from the center outward and adding 1 cup [¼ liter] of milk at the same time. Whisk only until smooth, then stir in the melted butter and the brandy or Grand Marnier if desired. The crepe batter should have the consistency of light cream; if necessary, add more milk to achieve the right consistency.

Heat a lightly buttered 6- to 7-inch [15- to 18-cm.] crepe pan. Pour in about 3 tablespoons [45 ml.] of crepe batter and quickly spread it by tilting the pan back and forth until the base is covered with a film of batter; pour the excess batter back into the bowl. Cook the crepe for about 10 seconds until it slides easily back and forth when you shake the pan. Slide a round-tipped knife or spatula under the crepe and turn it, then cook the other side for eight to 10 seconds until it is pale gold. Slide the crepe onto a warmed dish. Cook the rest of the crepe batter similarly, but do not butter the pan again unless the crepes stick: The butter in the batter should keep the pan greased.

Cream-Cheese Crepes

To make eight 7-inch [18-cm.] crepes

½ lb.	cream cheese, softened	¼ kg.
1 tbsp.	sugar	15 ml.
¼ tsp.	salt	1 ml.
1 tbsp.	heavy cream	15 ml.
3	eggs, beaten	3
3½ tbsp.	flour	52 ml.
1 tbsp.	brandy	15 ml.
¼ tsp.	vanilla extract	1 ml.

Beat the cream until it is smooth and fluffy. Beat in the sugar and salt, and blend well. Add the cream and, when it has been thoroughly incorporated, add the eggs—a little at a time—beating well after each addition. Stir in the flour, brandy and vanilla, and beat well. Let the batter rest for one hour before making the crepes.

Heat a lightly buttered 7-inch [18-cm.] crepe pan. Pour in about 3 tablespoons [45 ml.] of the batter and tilt the pan back and forth to coat the base with the batter. Pour any excess batter back into the bowl. Cook the crepe for about 30 seconds, then turn it and cook the other side for about 20 seconds, until lightly browned. Transfer the crepe to a warmed plate and cook the remaining crepes similarly, buttering the pan between crepes.

Souffléed Apricot Fritters

Beignets Soufflés aux Abricots

These fritters may also be made with other moist, firm-textured fruits, such as apples, pears, peaches, pineapples and strawberries.

To make 32 fritters

5	apricots, blanched, peeled, halved, pitted, diced and sprinkled with granulated sugar and lemon juice	5
1 cup	flour	¼ liter
1 tsp.	salt	5 ml.
1 cup	water	¼ liter
8 tbsp.	unsalted butter, cut into pieces	125 ml.
4	eggs	4
	oil for deep frying	
	confectioners' sugar	

Sift the flour and salt onto parchment or waxed paper, and set them aside. Put the water in a heavy saucepan and place it over low heat. Add the butter.

Stirring frequently, heat the liquid until the butter has melted. Increase the heat to bring the liquid to a boil. Turn off the heat and slide all of the flour off the paper into the hot liquid. Stir the mixture until the ingredients are thoroughly combined; then stir over medium heat until the mixture forms a solid mass that comes away cleanly from the sides of the pan. Reduce the heat to low and stir constantly for three minutes to dry the dough slightly. Remove the pan from the heat and cool the mixture for a few minutes.

Break one egg into a bowl and add it to the contents of the pan, beating with a spoon to incorporate the egg thoroughly. Repeat with the remaining eggs. Continue beating until the ingredients are smoothly blended.

Drain any liquid from the diced apricots and fold them into the dough, scraping the sides of the bowl to make sure all of the dough is incorporated.

In a heavy pan, heat the oil to 375° F. [190° C.]. Using two teaspoons, drop four or five pieces of the dough at a time into the hot oil; cook the fritters for five to seven minutes, until they are very rough-textured and puffy. Drain the fritters on paper towels and sprinkle them with confectioners' sugar.

Spongecake

To make one 8- or 9-inch [20- or 23-cm.] layer, 3 inches [8 cm.] deep

3	eggs	3
½ cup	sugar	125 ml.
½ cup	flour, sifted 3 times	125 ml.
3 tbsp.	butter, melted and cooled	45 ml.

In a heatproof bowl, beat the eggs and sugar lightly together. Place the bowl over a pan of simmering water; the bowl should fit snugly but not touch the water. Over low heat, beat the eggs and sugar with a whisk or electric mixer until the mixture is a thick, pale, creamy mass—five to 10 minutes. Take the pan from the heat and, without removing the bowl, continue to beat the mixture until it triples in bulk and falls from the whisk or mixer in a thick ribbon—10 to 20 minutes. Remove the bowl from the hot water. Using a metal spoon, fold the flour into the egg mixture in two or three stages, adding it alternately with the melted butter. Continue to fold the batter until the ingredients are well blended.

Pour the batter into a deep cake pan that has been buttered, floured and lined with parchment paper. Bake in a preheated 350° F. [180° C.] oven for 25 to 30 minutes. The cake is done when the top is springy and the edges have begun to shrink from the sides of the pan. Cool the pan on a wire rack for five minutes, then unmold the cake onto the rack, peel off the paper and let the cake cool completely.

Almond Tulip Wafers

To make 6 tulip wafers

4	large egg whites	4
½ cup	sugar	125 ml.
¾ cup	almonds, blanched, peeled and ground	175 ml.
3 tbsp.	sifted cake flour	45 ml.
4 tbsp.	butter, clarified	60 ml.

Whisk the egg whites until frothy, and then whisk in the sugar. Add the ground almonds. Stir in the flour and, when it has been thoroughly incorporated, add the butter. Stir until all of the ingredients are well blended. Let the batter rest for 20 minutes.

Butter and lightly flour a baking sheet. Drop the batter onto the prepared baking sheet by the heaping spoonful to form four mounds spaced well apart. Spread the batter with the back of the spoon to shape the mounds into wafers about 5 inches [13 cm.] across. Bake the wafers in a preheated 425° F. [220° C.] oven until lightly browned—approximately seven minutes.

To make the tulips, remove the wafers from the oven as soon as they are done and loosen them from the baking sheet with a metal spatula. Slightly overlap two of them and invert them onto a bowl that has been turned upside down. Using another bowl of the same dimensions, press down lightly on the wafers for about five seconds to mold them into a tulip. Remove the tulip wafer and repeat the molding process with the remaining pair of wafers. If they have become too brittle to mold, return them to the hot oven for a moment to soften them. Form, bake and mold the remaining batter into four additional tulip wafers.

Orange Jelly

The technique of assembling a layered jelly incorporating fruit is shown on pages 74-75. If you wish to flavor jelly with wine instead of orange, substitute 2½ cups [625 ml.] of wine for the orange juice and follow the instructions given below. If red wine is used, the jelly it produces will be opaque.

To make about 3 cups [¾ liter] jelly

3¼ cups	fresh orange juice, left to stand for 30 minutes	800 ml.
8	sheets leaf gelatin, soaked in cold water for 10 to 30 minutes and drained, or 2 tbsp. [30 ml.] powdered gelatin, softened in 3 tbsp. [45 ml.] cold water in a heatproof bowl	8
⅔ cup	warm medium sugar syrup (recipe, page 162)	150 ml.

Put the softened gelatin leaves into a small, heavy pan and pour on just enough water to cover them. Place the pan over low heat for five minutes, or until the gelatin has dissolved and the liquid in the pan is clear, then remove it from the heat. If using powdered gelatin, stand the bowl of softened gelatin in a pan of hot water over low heat until the liquid is clear—about three minutes—then remove it from the heat. Stir the dissolved gelatin into the sugar syrup.

Strain the orange juice through a sieve lined with a double layer of dampened cheesecloth or muslin and set over a large bowl. Discard the pulp. Stir the warm gelatin mixture into the strained orange juice.

Stand the bowl containing this orange jelly in a larger bowl containing ice. Stir the jelly constantly until it becomes syrupy and begins to thicken, then ladle the jelly into a chilled mold and refrigerate it for at least four hours. To ensure that the jelly has set, remove the mold from the refrigerator and tilt it—if the jelly stays firm, it is ready to be unmolded.

To unmold the jelly, run a knife tip round the rim of the mold, then dip the entire mold in warm water. Invert a chilled plate over the mold. Hold the mold firmly against the plate and turn both over together quickly. Lift the mold away from the jelly; if the jelly does not slip out, give the mold and the plate a strong shake—you should feel the pressure in the mold change as the jelly loosens. Chill the jelly briefly before serving so that the surface is firmly set.

Water Ice

Water ices can be made from any kind of fruit; for maximum flavor, use the ripest fruit available. Both light and medium sugar syrup will yield a satisfactory ice; the choice depends on the sweetness of the fruit and on your own taste. The techniques of producing fruit purées and juices are demonstrated on pages 20-21.

The more often the ice is stirred or processed, the smoother it will be. For a velvet-smooth ice, churn the mixture in an ice-cream maker.

To make about 1 quart [1 liter] water ice

2 cups	fruit purée or juice, chilled	½ liter
2 cups	light or medium sugar syrup (recipe, page 162), chilled	½ liter
	fresh lemon juice (optional)	

In a large bowl, combine the fruit purée or juice with the sugar syrup. If you like, add lemon juice to taste. Pour the mixture into metal ice trays or shallow baking pans and place them in the freezer.

To finish the ice by hand: Freeze the fruit mixture until crystals form around the edges of the trays or pans—about 30 minutes. Remove the ice from the freezer, stir the frozen edges of the mixture into the center, breaking up any large crystals. Replace the ice in the freezer and repeat the stirring process every hour for three or four hours, until the ice has reached the desired texture. Scrape the mixture into a chilled bowl and whisk it until smooth.

To finish the ice in a blender or food processor: Freeze the fruit mixture until it is hard—three to four hours. Remove the trays or pans from the freezer, place the ice in the container of a blender or food processor, and blend until smooth. Spoon the ice back into the trays or pans and refreeze it. Repeat this process until the water ice reaches the consistency that you desire.

Basic Ice Cream

The technique of using an ice-cream maker is demonstrated on pages 86-87.

To make about 4 quarts [4 liters] ice cream

2½ quarts	heavy cream	2½ liters
2 cups	sugar	½ liter
1	vanilla bean	1
¼ tsp.	salt	1 ml.

In a heavy saucepan, mix 1 quart [1 liter] of the cream with the sugar, vanilla bean and salt. Stir over medium heat until the sugar dissolves and the mixture is scalded, but not boiling. Remove the pan from the heat, cover it and let the cream cool to room temperature. Take out the vanilla bean, and wash and dry it to reserve it for another use. Stir the remaining 1½ quarts [1½ liters] of cream into the mixture. Cover the pan and refrigerate the mixture for one hour, or until well chilled. Pour the mixture into the canister of an ice-cream maker and freeze it.

Philadelphia vanilla ice cream. As soon as the cream mixture is removed from the heat, take out the vanilla bean and split it lengthwise. Scrape the vanilla-bean seeds into the pan and discard the pod.

Chocolate ice cream. Melt 4 ounces [125 g.] of semisweet chocolate in 1 cup [¼ liter] of the cream and stir it into the sweetened mixture after removing the vanilla bean.

Chocolate-chip ice cream. Grate 14 ounces [420 g.] of semisweet chocolate and stir it into the frozen ice cream while it is still soft.

Fruit ice cream. While the frozen ice cream is still soft, stir in 3 cups [¾ liter] of peeled, pitted, and crushed or sliced peaches; 3 cups of crushed or sliced strawberries; 3 cups of crushed raspberries; or 12 mashed and sieved bananas.

Nut ice cream. Stir 1 cup [¼ liter] of chopped or coarsely ground pecans or walnuts plus 1½ tablespoons [22 ml.] of vanilla extract into the mixture while or after churning.

Basic Custard Ice Cream

All of the flavorings for basic ice cream *(recipe, above)* can be added in the same way to this custard-based mixture. To ensure an especially smooth ice cream, the heavy cream called for can be whipped before it is added to the custard; in this case the custard should be chilled alone and the cream added just before the mixture is frozen. The technique of using an ice-cream maker is demonstrated on pages 86-87.

To make about 1 gallon [4 liters] ice cream

4 cups	milk	1 liter
1	vanilla bean	1
12	egg yolks	12
2 cups	sugar	½ liter
4 cups	heavy cream	1 liter

In a large, heavy saucepan, warm the milk over medium heat until bubbles appear around the rim of the pan. Remove the pan from the heat, add the vanilla bean, cover the pan and let the milk infuse for 20 minutes. Remove the bean.

Meanwhile, with a whisk, beat the egg yolks and sugar together in a bowl until the mixture is thick and pale, and forms a slowly dissolving ribbon when it is dribbled from the whisk. Gradually add the warm milk, stirring constantly. Pour the mixture into the saucepan and set over very low heat—or place the pan on a trivet in a larger pan partly filled with hot water. Stir and cook the custard mixture, without allowing it to boil, until it coats the spoon. Strain the custard into a bowl and stir occasionally as it cools. Stir in the cream, cover the bowl and refrigerate for about one hour. Then pour the mixture into the canister of an ice-cream maker and freeze it.

Recipe Index

All recipes in the index that follows are listed by the English title except in cases where a dish of foreign origin, such as coeur à la crème, is widely recognized by its source name. Entries are organized in separate categories by major ingredients specified in the recipe titles. Foreign recipes are listed under the country or region of origin. Recipe credits appear on pages 174-176.

Tart cream, 162
Tempura:
  batter, 158
  dessert, 158
Thai recipe: candied sesame
  bananas, 142
Tipsy black apple fool, 93
Topping, sugar, 108
Turnovers, apple, 93
Tutti-frutti, sweet, roll, 161

Uncooked fruitcake, 156
Upside-down orange cake, 137

Vanilla:
  custard, 163
  Philadelphia, ice cream, 167
Vinegar: strawberries with, 119

Wafers, almond tulip, 166
Water ice, 167

Watermelon snow, 128
West Indian recipe: bananitos, 143
Wine:
  cherries with red, 110
  custard, 163
  melon and red currants in, 127
  peaches in white, 101
  prunes in white, 152
  sauce, 98
  spiced, fruit salad, 157

Yogurt:
  fruit salad with, 157
  grape-nectarine, salad, 125
  orange, 133
  and strawberry jelly, 123
Yugoslavian recipes:
  baked stuffed peaches, 102
  chestnut and banana roll, 142
  poached quinces filled with cream,
    100

General Index/ Glossary

Included in this index to the cooking demonstrations are definitions, in italics, of special culinary terms not explained elsewhere in this volume. The Recipe Index begins on page 168.

Acidulated water: preventing fruit discoloration, 7
Almonds: blanching, 85; mixing and shaping tulip wafers, 84-85
Anjou pear, 6, 7
Apples, 6, 7; availability, 7; baking, 60; cheese to accompany, 34; coring, 7; dried, in a steamed pudding, 48; filling with butter, sugar and cinnamon and baking in pastry, 62-63; history of, 5; obtaining juice from, 21; poaching, 40; preventing discoloration, 7; in a pudding, 66; puréed, in a mousse, 78-79; puréeing cooked, 20; sautéed and caramelized, 53; selecting, 7; storing, 7; varieties, 6
Apricots, 8, 9; buying, 9; dried, in pudding, 66; dried, in a steamed pudding, 48; in filled dumplings, 44; in fruit compote, 42; mixing with chou paste and deep frying (souffléed fritters), 56-57; pitting, 9; puréeing for a sauce, 78, 79
Baked Alaska: fruits for, 86; homemade ice cream, 86-87; made with cherry ice cream and spongecake, 86-88; making and piping meringue, 86, 88; poaching cherries, 86; spongecake, 87

Baking fruit, 59, 60-69; apples wrapped in pastry, 62-63; bananas baked with dates and nuts, 60-61; basting fruit, 60; blueberry soufflé, 68-69; cobbler of mixed fruits, 64-65; cooking liquid, 60; filling fruit, 60; fruit for, 60; orange soufflés, 68-69; pears filled with nut mixture, 60-61; Périgord pudding, 66-67; preparing fruit, 60; rhubarb crisp, 64-65
Bananas, 16, 17; availability, 16; baking with dates and nuts, 60-61; buying, 16; coating with batter and deep frying, 54-55; sieving, 20; storing, 17; varieties, 16
Bartlett pear, 6, 7; poaching in wine, 40-41
Batter: based on water-chestnut powder, 54-55; coating fruit for frying, 54; for Périgord pudding, 66-67
Bavarian cream, 78; custard base, 22
Beignets soufflés, 56-57
Berries, 10-11; availability, 10; blending with cheese, 34; brushing with egg white and dipping in sugar, 26; buying, 10; crushing and straining, 21; in fruit fools, 32-33; in a mousse, 78; preparing, 10; puréeing through a sieve, 20; steeping, 40; storing, 10; tossing with flour, 64; varieties, 10, 11
Bing cherries, 8, 9
Biscuits: baking-powder, for strawberry shortcake, 36-37
Blackberries, 10; buying, 10; cultivated, 10; garnishing pineapple slices, 27; puréeing, for fruit fool, 32-33; in water ice, 82; wild, 10
Blood orange, 14; mixing juice in honeycomb pudding, 76-77

Blueberries, 10; baking with peaches in a cobbler, 64-65; buying, 10; cultivated, 10; poaching for compote, 42, 43; puréeing, as soufflé base, 68-69; stewed, filling crepes with, 46-47; wild, 10
Bosc pear, 6, 7; baking in pastry, 62; serving with cheese, 34
Brandy: flavoring crepe batter, 46; macerating fruit in, 66; sauce for sautéed peaches, 52
Broiling fruit, 59; gratin of mixed fruit and sabayon, 70-71; raspberries topped with sour cream, 70-71
Butter: baking fruit in, 60; clarifying, 52; in dumpling dough, 44; in rich short-crust dough, 62; sautéing fruit in, 52
Calimyrna fig, 16; cooking in a steamed pudding, 48-49
Cantaloupes, 12, 13; buying, 12; cutting to serve, 12; making melon balls, 12; in melon salad, 30-31
Carambola, 16, 17; availability, 16; selecting ripe, 16; serving, 17; storing, 17; in watermelon salad, 30-31
Caramel: coating fritters with, 54-55
Casaba melon, 12, 13; in melon salad, 30-31; selecting ripe, 12
Charleston Gray watermelon, 12, 13
Cheese: blending with fruit, 34; farmer, in *coeur à la crème,* 34-35; selecting appropriate, 34; serving with fresh fruit, 34
Cherimoya (custard apple), 16, 17; availability, 16; preparing for serving, 17; puréeing through strainer, 20; selecting ripe, 16; storing, 17
Cherries, 8, 9; in baked Alaska, 86-88; brushing with egg white and

dipping in sugar, 26; buying, 9; in filled dumplings, 44; in a mousse, 78; pitting, 9; poaching for compote, 42, 43; poaching in kirsch-flavored syrup, 86; in a pudding, 66; storing, 9; varieties, 9
Chou paste: flavoring with liqueur, 56; mixing apricots with and deep frying (souffléed fritters), 56-57; preparing, 56-57
Christmas pudding, 48
Citrus fruits, 14-15; availability, 14; obtaining juice from, 21; peel, avoiding dye in, 14; peeling, 15; preparing to serve, 14, 15; ripeness of, 14; in *rosace,* 80-81; salad of oranges and grapefruits, 28-29; serving orange soufflés in shells, 68-69; steeping, 40; storing, 14; using peel, 14; using shells as containers, 14; varieties, 14-15; zest, 15
Clarified butter: *butter with its easily burned milk solids removed. To make, melt butter over low heat, spoon off the foam, and let stand off the heat until the milk solids settle. Then decant the clear yellow liquid on top, discarding the milk solids;* 52, 53
Cobbler: combining peaches and blueberries, 64-65; fruits for, 64; mixing dough for a topping, 64
Coconut: baking with bananas and dates, 60-61; grating, 29; opening, 29
Coeur à la crème, 34-35; garnishing with strawberries, 35; lining molds, 34; molds for, 34; thickening cream with gelatin, 34; unmolding, 35
Comice pear, 6, 7; baking in pastry, 62
Compote: fruits for, 42; of mixed

Recipe Credits

The sources for the recipes in this volume are shown below. Page references in parentheses indicate where the recipes appear in the anthology.

Ackart, Robert, *Fruits in Cooking.* Copyright © 1974 by Robert Ackart. By permission of Macmillan Publishing Co., Inc., New York(112, 133, 145, 147).

Adams, Charlotte, and Doris McFerran Townsend, *The Family Cookbook: Desserts.* Copyright 1972 by the Ridge Press, Inc., and Holt, Rinehart and Winston, New York. By permission of Crown Publishers, Inc., New York(105, 124).

Alexander, Agnes B., *How to Use Hawaiian Fruit.* Copyright 1974 by The Petroglyph Press, Ltd. Published by The Petroglyph Press, Ltd., Hilo, Hawaii. By permission of The Petroglyph Press, Ltd.(144).

Allen, Ida Bailey, *Best Loved Recipes of the American People.* Copyright © 1973 by Ruth Allen Castelli. Reprinted by permission of Doubleday & Company, Inc., New York(92, 93).

Bayley, Monica, *Black Africa Cook Book.* Copyright © 1977 by Determined Productions, Inc., San Francisco. By permission of the publisher, Determined Productions, Inc.(106).

Beard, James, *The James Beard Cookbook.* Copyright © 1959 by James Beard. Reprinted by permission of Dell Publishing Co., Inc., New York(109, 113, 117).

Beeton, Mrs., *Mrs. Beeton's All about Cookery.* © Ward Lock Limited, 1961. Published by Ward Lock Limited, London. By permission of Ward Lock Limited(151).

Bergeron, Victor J., *Trader Vic's Rum Cookery and Drinkery.* Copyright © 1974 by Victor J. Bergeron. Published by Doubleday & Company, Inc., New York. By permission of Harold Matson Co., Inc. (author's agent)(149).

Bertholle, Louisette, *Une Grande Cuisine pour Tous.* © Opera Mundi, Paris. Published by Éditions Albin Michel, Paris. Translated by permission of Éditions Albin Michel(104).

Berto, Hazel, *Cooking with Honey.* Copyright © 1972 by Hazel Berto. Published by Gramercy Publishing Company, New York. By permission of Crown Publishers, Inc., New York(114).

Bettónica, Luís (Editor), *Cocina Regional Española.* © 1981 Ediciones Hymsa (Barcelona) y Arnoldo Mondadori Editore S.p.A. (Milan). Published by Ediciones Hymsa. Translated by permission of Arnoldo Mondadori Editore S.p.A.(152).

Bize-Leroy, Lalou, *Le Nouveau Guide Gault Millau, Connaissance des Voyages.* September 1981 (magazine). Copyright by Agence Presse-Loisirs. Published by Jour-Azur S.A., Paris. Translated by permission of Jour-Azur S.A.(102).

Bouillard, Paul, *La Cuisine au Coin du Feu.* Copyright 1928 by Albin Michel. Published by Éditions Albin Michel, Paris. Translated by permission of Éditions Albin Michel(143).

Boulestin, X. Marcel, *Recipes of Boulestin.* © The Estate of X. M. Boulestin, 1971. Published by William Heinemann Ltd., London. By permission of William Heinemann Ltd.(119).

Brennan, Jennifer, *The Original Thai Cookbook.* Copyright © 1981 by Jennifer Brennan. By permission of the publisher, Richard Marek Publisher, Inc., a division of the Putnam Publishing Group, New York(142).

Brown, Dorothy (Editor), *Symposium Fare.* © Aileen Hall, 1981. Published by Prospect Books, London. By permission of Prospect Books(96).

Burros, Marian Fox, and Lois Levine, *The Elegant but Easy Cookbook.* Copyright © 1960, 1963, 1967 by Marian Burros and Lois Levine. By permission of Macmillan Publishing Co., Inc., New York(108).

Buszek, Beatrice Ross, *The Blueberry Connection.* © 1979, 1980 by Beatrice Ross Buszek. Published by The Stephen Greene Press, Brattleboro, Vermont. By permission of the publisher(113). *The Cranberry Connection.* © 1977, 1978 by Beatrice Ross Buszek. Published by The Stephen Greene Press, Brattleboro, Vermont. By permission of the publisher(115, 116).

Cabané, Juan, and Alejandro Doménech, *Nuestra Mejor Cocina.* © Juan Cabané y Alejandro Doménech—1969. Published by Editorial Bruguera, S.A., Barcelona. Translated by permission of Editorial Bruguera, S.A.(153).

Carcione, Joe, *The Greengrocer Cookbook.* Copyright © 1975 by Joe Carcione. Published by Celestial Arts, Millbrae, California. By permission of Celestial Arts(106).

Carlton, Jan McBride, *The Old Fashioned Cookbook.* Copyright © 1975 by Jan McBride Carlton. By permission of Holt, Rinehart and Winston, Publishers, New York(103, 141).

Chandonnet, Ann, *The Complete Fruit Cookbook.* Copyright 1972 by Ann Chandonnet. By permission of the publisher, 101 Productions, San Francisco(122, 128, 138).

Chang, Wonona W. and Irving B. and Helene W. and Austin H. Kutscher, *An Encyclopedia of Chinese Food and Cooking.* Copyright © 1970 by Wonona W. Chang and Austin H. Kutscher. Published by Crown Publishers, Inc., New York. By permission of the publisher(155).

Colchie, Elizabeth Schneider, *Ready When You Are.* Copyright © 1982 by Elizabeth Schneider Colchie. Published by Crown Publishers, Inc., New York. By permission of the publisher(105, 150).

Conway, Tess, *Seychelles Delights.* By permission of the Women's Corona Society, Seychelles Branch, Mahe, Republic of Seychelles(131).

Corrado, Vincenzo, *Il Cuoco Galante.* Published in Naples, 1820(91).

Costa, Margaret, *Margaret Costa's Four Seasons Cookery Book.* Copyright © Margaret Costa. Published by Sphere Books Limited, London, 1976. By permission of the author, London(119).

Cùnsolo, Felice, *La Cucina Lombarda.* Copyright © by Novedit Milano. Published by Novedit Milano, 1963(101).

Cutler, Carol, *The Woman's Day Low-Calorie Dessert Cookbook.* Copyright © 1980 by CBS Consumer Publications, a division of CBS, Inc. Reprinted by permission of Houghton Mifflin Company, Boston(122, 135, 160, 162).

Czerny, Zofia, *Polish Cookbook.* Copyright © 1961, 1975, Panstwowe Wydawnictwo Edonomiczne. Published by Panstwowe Wydawnictwo Edonomiczne, Warsaw. By permission of Agencja Autorska, Warsaw, for the author(116).

Czerny, Zofia, and Maria Strasburger, *Zywienie Rodziny.* Copyright by Zofia Czerny and Maria Strasburger. Published by Czytelnik Spóldzielnia Wydawnicza, 1948. Translated by permission of Agencja Autorska, Warsaw, for the heiress to the authors(123).

Daguin, André, *Le Nouveau Cuisinier Gascon.* © 1981, Éditions Stock. Published by Éditions Stock, Paris. Translated by permission of Éditions Stock(154).

Dannenbaum, Julie, *Menus for All Occasions.* © Copyright 1974 by Julie Dannenbaum. Published by Saturday Review Press/E. P. Dutton & Co., Inc., New York. By permission of Edward Acton, Inc., New York(96).

David, Elizabeth, *French Country Cooking.* © Elizabeth David, 1950, 1951, 1955, 1958, 1965, 1980. Published in 1980 under the title *Elizabeth David Classics,* comprising *A Book of Mediterranean Food, French Country Cooking* and *Summer Cooking,* by Jill Norman Ltd., London. By permission of Jill Norman & Hobhouse Ltd.(108). *French Provincial Cooking.* Copyright © Elizabeth David, 1960, 1962, 1967, 1970. Published by Penguin Books Ltd., London, in association with Michael Joseph Ltd., London. By permission of the author(92, 101).

David, Josephine, *Every-Day Cookery for Families of Moderate Income.* Published by Frederick Warne and Co. Ltd., London. By permission of Frederick Warne and Co. Ltd.(117).

De Gouy, L. P., *Ice Cream and Ice Cream Desserts.* Copyright 1938 by Louis P. de Gouy. Copyright renewed 1966 by Mrs. Louis P. de Gouy. Reprinted by Dover Publications, Inc., New York. By permission of Jacqueline S. Dooner(93).

Delgado, Carlos (Editor), *Cien Recetas Magistrales.* © de la seleccion y el prologo: Carlos Delgado. © Alianza Editorial, S.A., Madrid, 1981. Published by Alianza Editorial, S.A. Translated by permission of Alianza Editorial, S.A.(99).

Detsko Pitanie. Published by Gostorgizdat, Moscow, 1958. Translated by permission of VAAP—The Copyright Agency of the U.S.S.R., Moscow(158).

Dixon, Pamela, *New Ways with Fresh Fruit and Vegetables.* Copyright © 1973 by Pamela Dixon. Published by Faber and Faber, Ltd., London. By permission of the author(130, 144).

Duncan, Maro, *Cooking the Greek Way.* © Paul Hamlyn Limited, 1964. Published by Spring Books, London. By permission of the Hamlyn Publishing Group Limited, Feltham, Middlesex, England(125, 155, 157).

Ellis, Audrey, *Wine Lovers Cookbook.* © Audrey Ellis, 1975. Published by Hutchinson & Co. (Publishers) Ltd., London. By permission of The Hutchinson Publishing Group Limited(157).

English, Sandal, *Fruits of the Desert.* Copyright 1982 by the Arizona Daily Star, Tucson, Arizona. By permission of the publisher, The Arizona Daily Star(125, 139, 140, 148).

Field, Michael, *Cooking Adventures with Michael Field.* © 1972 by Frances Field and Nelson Doubleday, Inc. Copyright © 1978 by the Estate of Frances Field. Reprinted by permission of Holt, Rinehart and Winston, Publishers(111).

Florida Fruit and Vegetable Recipes. Distributed by the Florida Department of Agriculture, Tallahassee(107, 147).

Foods of the World, *American Cooking: New England.* Copyright © 1970 Time Inc. Published by Time-Life Books, Alexandria, Virginia(115). *The Cooking of the Caribbean Islands.* Copyright © 1970 Time Inc. Published by Time-Life Books, Alexandria, Virginia (107). *The Cooking of China.* Copyright © 1968 Time Inc. Published by Time-Life Books, Alexandria, Virginia(134). *Pacific and Southeast Asian Cooking.* Copyright © 1970 Time Inc. Published by Time-Life Books, Alexandria, Virginia(129, 147, 159). *A Quintet of Cuisines.* Copyright © 1970 Time Inc. Published by Time-Life Books, Alexandria, Virginia(134).

Gili, Elizabeth, *Apple Recipes from A to Z.* Copyright © Elizabeth Gili, 1975. Published by Kaye & Ward Ltd., London. By permission of Kaye & Ward Ltd.(91, 93).

Giusti-Lanham, Hedy, and Andrea Dodi, *The Cuisine of Venice and Surrounding Northern Regions.* Copyright © 1978 by Barron's Educational Series, Inc., Woodbury, New York. Reprinted by permission of Barron's(119).

Gordon, Jean, *Orange Recipes.* Copyright © 1962 by Jean Gordon. Published by Red Rose Publications, Woodstock, Vermont. By permission of the author(136).

Gorman, Marion, and Felipe P. de Alba, *The Dione Lucas Book of Natural French Cooking.* Copyright © 1977 by Marion Gorman and Felipe P. de Alba. Published by E. P. Dutton. Reprinted by permission of Hawthorn Properties (Elsevier-Dutton Publishing Co., Inc.)(129).

Graves, Eleanor, *Great Dinners from Life.* Copyright © 1969 Time Inc. Published by Time-Life Books, Alexandria, Virginia(133).

The Great Cooks Cookbook. Copyright © 1974 by the Good Cooking School, Inc. By permission of the publisher, J. G. Ferguson Publishing Company, Chicago(148, 150).

Greene, Bert, *Bert Greene's Kitchen Bouquets.* © 1979 by Bert Greene. Published by Contemporary Books, Inc., Chicago. By permission of the publisher(99, 122).

Grigson, Jane, *Good Things.* Copyright © 1971 by Jane Grigson. By permission of Harold Ober Associates Inc., New York(132). *Jane Grigson's Fruit Book.* Copyright © 1982 by Jane Grigson (New York: Atheneum 1982). Reprinted with the permission of Atheneum Publishers(120, 125, 140).

Guillot, André, *La Vraie Cuisine Légère.* © 1981 Flammarion. Published by Flammarion, Paris. Translated by permission of Librairie Ernest Flammarion(103).

Hazelton, Nika Standen, *The Swiss Cookbook.* Copyright © 1967 by Nika Standen Hazelton. By permission of Atheneum Publishers, Inc., New York(110).

Hemker, Coen, and Jacques Zeguers, *De*

Verstandige Keuken. © 1978 Uitgeverij Luitingh B.V., Laren N.H. Published by Uitgeverij Luitingh B.V. Translated by permission of Uitgeverij Luitingh B.V.(153).
Hewitt, Jean, *The New York Times Weekend Cookbook.* Copyright © 1975 by Jean Hewitt. By permission of Times Books, The New York Times Book Co., Inc., New York(131). *The New York Times Natural Foods Cookbook.* Copyright © 1971 by Jean Hewitt. By permission of Times Books, The New York Times Book Co., Inc., New York(148, 161).
Hom, Ken, *Chinese Technique.* Copyright © 1981 by Ken Hom and Harvey Steiman. By permission of the publisher, Simon & Schuster, a division of Gulf & Western Corporation, New York(91).
Horvath, Maria, *Balkan-Küche.* Copyright © 1963 by Wilhelm Heyne Verlag, Munich. Published by Wilhelm Heyne Verlag. Translated by permission of Wilhelm Heyne Verlag(105).
Hume, Rosemary, and Muriel Downes, *Cordon Bleu Desserts and Puddings.* Copyright © Rosemary Hume and Muriel Downes, 1975. Published by Penguin Books Ltd., London. By permission of Penguin Books Ltd.(118, 160).
Jans, Hugh, *Vrij Nederland.* November 1974, June 1978 (magazine). Translated by permission of Hugh Jans(120, 127, 138). *Vrij Nederlands Kookboek.* © 1975 Unieboek B.V., Bussum, Holland. Published by Unieboek B.V. Translated by permission of Unieboek B.V.(132).
Kamman, Madeleine, *Dinner against the Clock.* Copyright © 1973 by Madeleine Kamman (New York: Atheneum, 1973). Reprinted with the permission of Atheneum Publishers(137). *The Making of a Cook.* Copyright © 1971 by Madeleine Kamman (New York: Atheneum, 1971). Reprinted with the permission of Atheneum Publishers(151).
Katz, Carol, *The Berry Cookbook.* © 1980 by Butterick Publishing, New York. By permission of New Century Publishers, Inc., Piscataway, New Jersey(115, 116, 121).
Kiehnle, Hermine, and Maria Hadecke, *Das Neue Kiehnle Kochbuch.* © Walter Hadecke Verlag (Vorm Suddeutsches Verlagshaus). Published by Walter Hadecke Verlag. Translated by permission of Walter Hadecke Verlag(156).
Leith, Prudence, and Caroline Waldegrave, *Leith's Cookery Course.* Copyright © Leith's Farm Ltd. 1979. Published by André Deutsch and Fontana Paperbacks, London, 1980. By permission of Fontana Paperbacks, London(118).
Lemnis, Maria, and Henryk Vitry, *Old Polish Traditions in the Kitchen and at the Table.* © Interpress Publishers, Warsaw, 1979. Published by Interpress Publishers, Warsaw. By permission of Agencja Autorska, Warsaw, for the authors(114, 153).
Lenôtre, Gaston, *Lenôtre's Desserts and Pastries.* © 1977, Barron's Educational Series, Inc. Published by Barron's Educational Series, Inc., New York. By permission of Barron's Educational Series, Inc.(137). *Lenôtre's Ice Creams and Candies.* © 1979, Barron's Educational Series, Inc. Published by Barron's Educational Series. By permission of the publisher(154).
Levy, Faye, *La Varenne Tour Book.* © 1979 La Varenne U.S.A., Inc. Published by Peanut Butter Publishing, Seattle. By permission of Latoque International Limited, Gladwyne(135).
Macnicol, Fred, *Hungarian Cookery.* Copyright © Fred Macnicol, 1978. Published by Penguin Books Ltd., London. By permission of Penguin Books Ltd.(94).
Mann, Gertrude, *Berry Cooking.* Published by André Deutsch Limited, London, 1954. By permission of the publisher(113).
Marković, Spasenija-Pata (Editor), *Veliki Narodni Kuvar.* Copyright by the author. First Edition "Politika," Belgrade, 1938. Published by Narodna Knjiiga, Belgrade, 1979. Translated by permission of Jugoslovenska Autorska Agencija, Belgrade, for the heir to the author(100, 103, 142).
Martin, Faye, *Rodale's Naturally Delicious Desserts and Snacks.* © 1978 by Rodale Press, Inc., Emmaus, Pennsylvania. By permission of the publisher, Rodale Press, Inc.(131, 133, 161).
Masson, Madeleine, *The International Wine and Food Society's Guide to Jewish Cookery.* © Madeleine Masson, 1971. Published by David & Charles, Newton Abbot. By permission of David & Charles(152).
Mathiot, Ginette, *Je Sais Faire la Pâtisserie.* Published by Éditions Albin Michel. Translated by permission of Éditions Albin Michel(96).
Mendes, Helen, *The African Heritage Cookbook.* Copyright © 1970 by Helen Mendes. Published by the Macmillan Company, New York. By permission of the Sterling Lord Agency, New York(90).
Meyers, Perla, *The Seasonal Kitchen.* Copyright © 1973 by Perla Meyers. By permission of Holt, Rinehart and Winston, Publishers, New York(97, 98)
Montagné, Prosper, *The New Larousse Gastronomique.* © Copyright English text The Hamlyn Publishing Group Limited 1977. Published by Crown Publishers, Inc., New York. By permission of The Hamlyn Publishing Group Limited and Crown Publishers, Inc.(92).
Munks, Bertha, *Florida's Favorite Foods.* Reprinted by permission of the State of Florida, Department of Agriculture, Tallahassee(149).
Nakken-Rövekamp, E., *Exotische Groenten en Vruchten.* © 1979 Elsevier Nederland B.V., Amsterdam/Brussels. Published by Elsevier Nederland B.V. Translated by permission of Elsevier Nederland B.V., Amsterdam(146).
Nilson, Bee, *The Penguin Cookery Book.* Copyright © Bee Nilson, 1952, 1959, 1972. Published by Penguin Books Ltd., London. By permission of Penguin Books Ltd.(92, 129).
Nyaho, E. Chapman, E. Amarteifio, and J. Asare, *Ghana Recipe Book.* Copyright © 1970 by E. Chapman Nyaho, E. Amarteifio, and J. Asare. Published by Ghana Publishing Corporation, Tema, Ghana. By permission of the publisher(139).
Ochorowicz Monatowa, Marja, *Polish Cookery.* Translated by Jean Karsavina. © 1958 by Crown Publishers, Inc. Published by Crown Publishers, Inc., New York. By permission of Crown Publishers, Inc.(155).
Olney, Judith, *The Joy of Chocolate.* Copyright © 1982 by Barron's Educational Series, Inc. Woodbury, New York. Published by Barron's Educational Series. By permission of the publisher(109, 159). *Summer Food.* Copyright © 1978 by Judith Olney. Published by Atheneum Publishers, New York. By permission of Atheneum Publishers(101).
Olney, Richard, *French Menu Cookbook.* © 1975 Richard Olney. Published by William Collins Sons & Co. Ltd., Glasgow and London. By permission of the author, Sollies-Pont(95, 145, 146, 156).
Ortega, Simone, *Mil Ochenta Recetas de Cocina.* © Simone K. de Ortega, 1972. © Alianza Editorial, S.A., Madrid, 1972, 1974, 1975, 1977, 1978, 1979, 1980. Published by Alianza Editorial, S.A. Translated by permission of Alianza Editorial, S.A.(94).
Ortiz, Elisabeth Lambert, *The Complete Book of Caribbean Cooking.* Copyright © 1973, 1983, by Elisabeth Lambert Ortiz. By permission of the publisher, M. Evans and Co., Inc., New York(144).
Oxfordshire Federation of Women's Institutes, *500 Jolly Good Things.* By permission of the Oxfordshire Federation of Women's Institutes, Summertown, Oxford, England(132).
Parenti, Giovanni Righi, *La Grande Cucina Toscana.* Copyright © by SugarCo Edizioni S.r.l., Milan. Published by SugarCo Edizioni. Translated by permission of SugarCo Edizioni(91).
Pareren-Bles, L. Van (Editor), *Allerhande Recepten.* Published by Meijer Pers n.v., Wormerveer, 1967. Translated by permission of Meijer Pers n.v., Amsterdam(97, 154).
Payne, Selma and W.J.A., *Cooking with Exotic Fruit.* © 1979 by Selma and W.J.A. Payne. Published by B. T. Batsford, Ltd., London. By permission of the publisher(139).
Pellaprat, Henri Paul, *The Great Book of French Cuisine.* Copyright © 1966 by Rene Kramer, Publisher, Castagnola/Lugano, Switzerland. By permission of Harper & Row, Publishers, Inc., New York(126).
Pépin, Jacques, *A French Chef Cooks at Home.* © 1975 by Jacques Pépin. By permission of the publisher, Simon & Schuster, a division of Gulf & Western Corporation, New York(121, 123). *La Methode.* Copyright © 1979 by Jacques
Pépin. By permission of Times Books, The New York Times Book Co., Inc., New York(157).
Plucińska, Ida, *Ksiazka Kucharska.* Copyright by the author. Poznan, 1945. Translated by permission of Agencja Autorska, Warsaw, for the author(107).
Polushkin, Maria, *The Dumpling Cookbook.* Copyright © 1977 by Maria Polushkin. By permission of the publisher, Workman Publishing Company, Inc., New York(108, 110, 112, 130).
Poole, Mrs. Hester M., *Fruits, and How to Use Them.* Copyright 1889 Fowler & Wells Company, New York. Published by Fowler & Wells Company(102, 109).
Portinari, Laura Gras, *Cucina e Vini del Piemonte e della Valle d'Aosta.* © Copyright 1971 Ugo Mursia Editore, Milan. Published by Ugo Mursia Editore S.p.A., Milan. Translated by permission of Ugo Mursia Editore(110).
Puck, Wolfgang, *Wolfgang Puck's Modern French Cooking for the American Kitchen.* Copyright © 1981 by Wolfgang Puck. Published by Houghton Mifflin Company, Boston. By permission of Houghton Mifflin Company(126).
Puga y Parga, Manuel M. (Picadillo), *La Cocina Práctica.* Copyright by Libreria-Editorial Gali. Published by Libreria-Editorial "Gali," Santiago, 1966. Translated by permission of Libreria-Editorial "Gali"(102).
Quillet, Aristide, *La Cuisine Moderne.* Copyright Libraire Aristide Quillet, 1946. Published by Libraire Aristide Quillet. Translated by permission of Libraire Aristide Quillet(162).
Rare Fruit Council, *Tropical Fruit Recipes: Rare and Exotic Fruits.* Copyright 1981 by Rare Fruit Council International, Inc., Miami. By permission of Banyan Books, Inc., Miami(106, 146, 147, 149).
Reese, Ralph H., *The Flavor of Pittsburgh.* Copyright © 1976 by Pittsburgh Diners Guild, Inc., Pittsburgh. By permission of Pittsburgh Diners Guild, Inc.(121).
Roden, Claudia, *Picnic: The Complete Guide to Outdoor Food.* Copyright © Claudia Roden, 1981. Published by Jill Norman & Hobhouse Ltd., London. By permission of Jill Norman & Hobhouse Ltd.(97).
Romagnoli, Margaret and G. Franco, *The New Italian Cooking.* © 1980 by Margaret and G. Franco Romagnoli. By permission of Little, Brown & Co. in association with the Atlantic Monthly Press(99, 130).
Salvetti, Lydia B., *Cento Ricette Spendendo Meno.* Copyright © by G. C. Sansoni S.p.A., Florence. Published by G. C. Sansoni Editore Nuova S.p.A. Translated by permission of G. C. Sansoni Editore Nuova S.p.A.(100). *100 Ricette del Futuro.* Copyright © by G. C. Sansoni S.p.A., Florence. Published by G. C. Sansoni Editore Nuova S.p.A., 1973. Translated by permission of G. C. Sansoni Editore Nuova S.p.A.(161).
Samuelson, M. K., *Sussex Recipe Book.* First published 1937 by Country Life Limited, London. By permission of The Hamlyn Publishing Group Limited, Feltham, Middlesex, England(148).
Schindler, Roana and Gene, *Hawaiian Cookbook.* Copyright © 1970 by Roana and Gene Schindler. Published by Dover Publications, Inc., New York. By permission of Andiron Press Inc., Tamarac, Florida(143).
Senderens, Alain and Eventhia, *La Cuisine Réussie.* © 1981, Éditions Jean-Claude Lattès. Published by Éditions Jean-Claude Lattès, Paris. Translated by permission of Éditions Jean-Claude Lattès(98, 127).
Shepard, Jean H., *The Fresh Fruits and Vegetables Cookbook.* Copyright © 1975 by Jean H. Shepard. Published by Little, Brown and Company, Boston. By permission of the author(104, 128, 156).
Sokolov, Raymond A., *Great Recipes from The New York Times.* Copyright © 1973 by Raymond A. Sokolov. By permission of Times Books, The New York Times Book Co., Inc., New York(110).
Standard, Stella, *The Art of Fruit Cookery.* Copyright © 1964 by Stella Standard. Published by Doubleday & Company, Inc., Garden City, New York. By permission of Curtis Brown, Ltd., New York(111, 124, 149).
Tarr, Yvonne Young, *The New York Times Natural Foods Dieting Book.* Copyright © 1972 by Quadrangle Books, Inc. By permission of Times Books, The New

York Times Book Co., Inc., New York(158).
Tascon, Jose Gutierrez, *La Cocina Leonesa.* © Editorial Everest, S.A., Leon-Espana. Published by Editorial Everest, S.A. Translated by permission of Editorial Everest, S.A.(126).
Thurber, Carol Collver (The Mad Hatter), *The Calypso Cookbook.* Copyright © 1974 by Carol Collver Thurber. By permission of the publisher, Ashley Books, Inc., Port Washington, New York(143).
Topper, Suzanne, *The Fruit Cookbook.* Copyright © 1973 by Suzanne Topper. Published by Avon Books, Flare edition, New York. By permission of the author(128, 137, 138).
Tsolova, M., V. Stoilova, and Sn. Ekimova, *Izpol-zouvane na Zelenchoutsite i Plodovete v Domakinstvoto.* © by the authors. Published by Zemizdat, Sofia, 1978. Translated by permission of Jusautor Copyright Agency, Sofia(112).
Van Zuylen, Guirne, *Gourmet Cooking for Everyone.* Copyright © 1969 by Guirne Van Zuylen. Published by

Faber and Faber, Ltd., London. By permission of the author(117).
Vergé, Roger, *Roger Vergé's Cuisine of the South of France.* Copyright © 1979 by Éditions Robert Laffont, S.A. Originally published in French under the title, *Ma Cuisine du Soleil.* English translation © 1980 by William Morrow and Company, Inc. By permission of the publisher(127, 128, 141).
Waldron, Maggie, *Strawberries.* Copyright 1977 by Maggie Waldron. By permission of the publishers, 101 Productions, San Francisco(119, 157, 158).
Westbury, Lord, and Donald Downes, *With Gusto and Relish.* © Lord Westbury and Donald Downes, 1957. Published by Andre Deutsch Limited, London. By permission of Andre Deutsch Limited(100, 150).
Westland, Pamela, *A Taste of the Country.* Copyright © Pamela Westland, 1974. Published by Penguin Books Ltd., London, 1976. By permission of Hamish Hamilton Ltd., London(90, 117, 121).
Willan, Anne, *La Varenne's Paris Kitchen.* Copyright ©

1981 by La Varenne U.S.A. Inc. By permission of the publisher, William Morrow & Company, New York(136). *French Regional Cooking.* Copyright © 1981 by Anne Willan & l'École de Cuisine La Varenne. Published by William Morrow and Company, Inc., New York. By permission of the publisher(152).
Wolfert, Paula, *Mediterranean Cooking.* Copyright © 1977 by Paula Wolfert. By permission of Times Books, The New York Times Book Co., Inc., New York(124, 134, 140).
Worstman, Gail L., *The Natural Fruit Cookbook.* Copyright 1982 by Gail L. Worstman. By permission of the publisher, Pacific Search Press, Seattle(140).
Yockelson, Lisa, *The Efficient Epicure.* Copyright © 1982 by Lisa Yockelson. Reprinted by permission of Harper & Row, Publishers, Inc., New York(113).
Zawistowska, Zofia, *Surówki i Salatki.* Published by Wydawnictwo "Watra," Warsaw, 1979. Translated by permission of Agencja Autorska, Warsaw, for the author(143).

Acknowledgments

The indexes for this book were prepared by Louise W. Hedberg.

The editors are particularly indebted to Gail Duff, Kent, England; Dr. Julia Morton, Morton Collectanea, University of Miami, Coral Gables, Florida; Ann O'Sullivan, Majorca, Spain; Anna Maria Perez, Barcelona; Chris B. Rollins, Preston B. Bird and Mary Heinlein, Fruit and Spice Park, Metro Dade County, Florida; Deborah A. Stapell, United Fresh Fruit and Vegetable Association, Alexandria, Virginia; Elisabeth Williams, London.

The editors also wish to thank: Leroy Archer, Melvin Barnes, Georgetown Safeway, Produce Department, Washington, D.C.; Alison Attenborough, Essex, England;

Mrs. J. Baum, London; Bell Farms, Boonville, Missouri; Margaret Beutel, Anna Maria Coccia, The Lipton Kitchens, Thomas J. Lipton, Inc., Englewood Cliffs, New Jersey; Nicola Blount, London; Mike Brown, London; California Apricot Advisory Board, Walnut Creek; California Date Administrative Committee, Indio; California Fig Institute, Fresno; California Prune Board, San Francisco; California Rare Fruit Growers, Inc., Fullerton; Frieda Caplan, Carol Bowman-Williams, Frieda's Finest, Los Angeles; Nora Carey, Paris; Josephine Christian, Somerset, England; Crafton Clift, Rare Fruit Council International, Miami; Lesley Coates, Essex, England; Emma Codrington, Surrey, England; June Dowding, Essex, England; Empire Fruit & Produce, Brooklyn, New York; Mimi Errington, Nottinghamshire, England; Sarah Jane Evans, London; Terry M. Freed, Bountiful Ridge Nurseries, Inc., Princess Anne, Maryland; Neyla Freeman, London; The Fresh Fruit & Vegetable Information Bureau, London; Georgia Peach Commission, Atlanta; Dr. William Grierson, University of Florida, Lake Alfred; Mary Harron, London; Maggi Heinz,

London; Hilary Hockman, London; Christopher Howell, Hollywood, Florida; International Apple Institute, McLean, Virginia; Maria Johnson, Kent, England; Lotte Keeble, Middlesex, England; Wanda Kemp-Welch, Nottingham, England; Margot Levy, London; Katie Lloyd, London; Alan Lothian, London; Philippa Millard, London; Wendy Morris, London; National Peach Council, Martinsburg, West Virginia; Rosemary Oates, London; Winona O'Connor, Essex, England; Judith Olney, Durham Hills, North Carolina; Neil Philip, Oxford, England; Sylvia Robertson, Surrey, England; Vicki Robinson, London; Safeway Stores, Produce Merchandising, Landover, Maryland; Nicole Segre, London; Straight from the Crate, Alexandria, Virginia; Sunkist Growers Inc., Van Nuys, California; Stephanie Thompson, London; Fiona Tillett, London; Tropical Products Institute, London; J. M. Turnell & Co., New Covent Garden Market, London; Tina Walker, London; Rita Walters, Essex, England; Steve White, Cal Flavor, Escondido, California; Robyn Wilk, California Tree Fruit Agreement, Sacramento.

Picture Credits

The sources for the pictures in this book are listed below. Credits for each of the photographers and illustrators are listed by page number in sequence with successive pages indicated by hyphens; where necessary, the locations of pictures within pages are also indicated—separated from page numbers by dashes.

Photographs by Aldo Tutino: 7—except bottom right, 9—bottom left, 11—bottom left, 15—top, 17—top right and bottom left, 19—center left and bottom, 20—except bottom right, 21, 22—bottom, 26—top, 28—top, 29—except bottom left, 34—bottom, 36-37, 40-41, 43—top, 46-47, 50, 52-57, 60-61, 64-65—top, 69—bottom

right, 70-71—top, 76-77, 82-83—bottom, 84-88. Other photographs (alphabetically): Tom Belshaw, 42, 43—bottom. John Cook, 22-23—top, 58, 62-63, 78-79. Alan Duns, 11—bottom center, 19—center right, 20—bottom right, 24. John Elliott, 23—bottom left, 32-33—bottom, 44-45, 80—top, 81—top left and bottom left. Clara Griffin, 31—bottom. Fil Hunter, 7—bottom right, 9—except bottom left, 11—bottom right, 12, 17—top left, 19—top, 26—bottom, 27, 30, 31—top, 38, 64-65—bottom, 68-69—top, 70-71—bottom. Louis Klein, 2. Bob Komar, cover, 4, 17—bottom right, 23—bottom center and right, 28—bottom, 29—bottom left, 32-33—top, 34—top, 35, 48-49, 66-67, 68—bottom, 69—bottom left and center, 72-75, 80—bottom, 81—except top left and bottom left, 82-83—top.

Illustrations: Rick Lovell, 6, 8, 10-11—top, 13, 14-15—bottom, 16-17—top, 18. From the Mary Evans Picture Library and private sources and *Food & Drink: A Pictorial Archive from Nineteenth Century Sources* by Jim Harter, published by Dover Publications, Inc., 1979, 90-164.

Library of Congress Cataloguing in Publication Data
Main entry under title:
Fruits.
    (The Good cook, techniques & recipes)
    Includes index.
    1. Cookery (Fruit) I. Time-Life Books. II. Series.
TX811.F77 1983   641.6'4   83-627
ISBN 0-8094-2984-5 (retail ed.)
ISBN 0-8094-2985-3 (lib. bdg.)